GIVING
COUNSEL

Also by Donald Capps
published by Chalice Press:

*Fragile Connections: Memoirs of Mental Illness
for Pastoral Care Professionals*

Jesus: A Psychological Biography

Social Phobia: Alleviating Anxiety in an Age of Self-promotion

*The Pastoral Care Case:
Learning about Care in Congregations*
with Gene Fowler

Edited by Donald Capps
published by Chalice Press:

Re-Calling Ministry, by James E. Dittes

GIVING COUNSEL

A Minister's Guidebook

Donald Capps

CHALICE
PRESS
ST. LOUIS, MISSOURI

Cover design: Bob Currie
Interior design: Connie Wang
Art direction: Michael Domínguez

Visit Chalice Press on the World Wide Web at
www.chalicepress.com

10 9 8 7 6 5 4   06 07 08 09 10 11

Library of Congress Cataloging–in–Publication Data

Capps, Donald.
    Giving counsel : a minister's guidebook / Donald Capps.
        p.   cm.
    Includes bibliographical references and index.
    ISBN-13: 978-0-827212-47-3
    ISBN-10: 0-827212-47-X (alk. paper)
1. Pastoral counseling.   I. Title.
    BV4012.2 .C263   2001
253.5--dc21
                                                          2001002421

Printed in the United States of America

In dedication to
Robert Dykstra and Antoinette Goodwin
"A word in season, how good it is!"
(Proverbs 15:23)

Acknowledgments

A conversation over lunch with Jon Berquist, Academic Editor at Chalice Press, played a crucial role in the inspiration and conceptualization of this book. Given the approach I have taken here, it seems especially appropriate that the book was conceived during a conversation between friends in a very informal setting. I am also grateful to the whole staff at Chalice Press for their efficiency and good will. I want especially to express my appreciation to Joan Blyth for typing the manuscript. Her work, and the way in which she goes about it, have become invaluable to me over the years that she has been a faculty secretary at Princeton Theological Seminary.

This book is dedicated to Robert Dykstra and Antoinette Goodwin. As ministers who give counsel, they exemplify the spirit and values that I have sought, however imperfectly, to convey here.

Contents

Introduction

Most if not all seminaries in North America offer courses in pastoral care and counseling. Among these course offerings, one or more are usually designated as introductory or basic. Professors who teach these courses typically consider what they believe future ministers will need to know in order to function with reasonable effectiveness in their ministry of care and counseling. They are aware that a single introductory course is rudimentary at best, but many seminaries require only a single course in pastoral care and counseling, so the professor—and students—need to make much out of little.

Most of us who teach in the field have in our minds the perfect textbook for the introductory courses we teach. Each of us, however, has a different notion of what would be a perfect textbook. A book that approximates the ideal of one professor may hold little attraction for another. This may explain why quite a number of persons have written introductions to the field of pastoral care, pastoral counseling, or both, over the past couple of decades (for example, Arnold, 1982; Taylor, 1991; Gerkin, 1997; Dittes, 1999a). One of these textbooks, Howard Clinebell's *Basic Types of Pastoral Care and Counseling* (1984) is an expanded version

1

of an earlier work, *Basic Types of Pastoral Counseling* (1966). This textbook, which is currently undergoing another revision, has had great influence in the field of pastoral care and counseling and is undoubtedly the best known textbook in the field. It has made a great contribution toward shaping and defining the field itself.

I have no such aspirations for the book you now hold in your hands. I leave the shaping and defining of the field of pastoral care and counseling to others. Instead, what I have tried to do here is to write a book that, if read all the way through, would enable the student to say, "I think I now know enough to be able to counsel someone without either making a fool of myself or a mess of things." This may not seem like much to those who are experienced in the field, but I would have liked to have a book that made a similar claim—and disclaimer—some thirty years ago. I will not be so presumptuous as to say that if you only read one book on pastoral counseling while a student in seminary, *this* is the book you should read. This *is*, however, the assumption on which I wrote this book.

In the introductions to several previous books, I made the disclaimer that they were not "how-to books." It wasn't that I looked down on how-to books, but simply that the books I had written did not qualify. In the writing of this book, I decided it was high time that I at least attempted to write a how-to book. I soon discovered, however, that there are different ways to go about formulating a how-to book. Some how-to books begin at a very simple, some might say simplistic, level. A book on carpentry, for example, might have a drawing of a hammer and explain that it is used to drive nails through boards and to extract nails from boards. Since most of us learned to use a hammer of sorts—a wooden mallet to pound round and square pegs into round and square holes—well before we learned to read, we usually skip over the pages that explain the uses of a hammer. On the other hand, there are how-to books that are so complex that the reader could understand what is being said only if he already knew how to do it in the first place. When my wife first took up knitting, she claimed that many "how-to knit" books are of this kind.

I have tried to find some middle ground. I assume that if the reader is a seminary student, she already knows a few things about what is involved in a minister's giving some counsel to another person as she has already assumed this role with a college friend, a friend at work, or a son or daughter. It would be patronizing, therefore, for me to pitch this book at the "this is what a hammer looks like" level. By the same token, I do not assume that the reader already knows her way about in the world of *pastoral* counseling, which has similarities to these other experiences of offering counsel, but differences as well. This means beginning at the beginning. Many seminary students already know how to create a good listening environment; others believe that they do, but need confirmation of this belief; others are certain that they do *not* know how to do this; and still others are skeptical that creating a good listening environment matters all that much. Given this diversity, I devote a whole chapter to this seemingly minor and, for some, elementary issue.

Because this is an *introductory* how-to book, I do not claim that it is exhaustive in any sense of the word. "How-to knit" books are pitched at various levels from beginner to intermediate to expert. As I have indicated, this book is for the beginner. While I believe that I have managed to cover many of the most important how-to issues, I fully anticipate that my colleagues in the field will suggest other issues that they deem more important—even at the introductory level—than the ones I have discussed here. And, of course, the ones I have chosen to discuss reflect my own view of what is involved in being a minister who gives counsel. To anticipate one such criticism, some would argue that a book that claims to be a how-to book should focus on, or at least include extensive discussions of, the "basic types" of pastoral counseling. In his first book, Clinebell (1966) identified these as marriage, family, supportive, crisis, referral, educative, group, confrontational, counseling on religious-existential problems, and depth pastoral counseling. While he modifies the language somewhat in his later book, the types remain essentially the same with the addition of bereavement counseling. I took the "types" approach in one of my first books, *Biblical Approaches to Pastoral Counseling* (1982), in which I focused on three types of pastoral counseling—grief, premarital, marital—and correlated these with three biblical literary forms—psalms (of lament), proverbs, and parables (I called these "the three p's of pastoral counseling"). I do not now disown this typological approach to pastoral counseling, but over the years I have become increasingly sold on a kind of "problem-resolving" approach to pastoral counseling (which was itself prefigured in two other early books: Capps, 1979 and 1980), and this has resulted in my tendency to see pastoral counseling in this light, whatever the specific type might happen to be. While it might seem odd to say that giving counsel to someone who is in a state of bereavement is "problem-centered"—is *death* the problem in this case?—it was actually when I was writing about grief counseling in light of the psalms of lament that I realized *all* pastoral counseling is problem-oriented, for every griever experiences problems associated with irretrievable loss. If the minister does not recognize this fact, he is likely not to provide the support and comfort that is needed. For the grieving, emotional catharsis is rarely enough and is rarely an end in itself. As the psalm writers understood, the griever is faced with difficult problems following the death of a loved one and, whether overtly or not, is "petitioning" for help in relation to these problems.

As will become abundantly clear, this is also a book that reflects my own judgment—and practice—that pastoral counseling should, for various reasons, consist of a very few sessions or meetings. These reasons are spelled out in detail in the following chapters. At the same time, unlike those who have assumed that because it is very short-term, pastoral counseling is also of rather modest value, I believe that much can be accomplished in a small number of meetings if the minister does not minimize their value and knows how to make maximum use of these meetings. To make the most out of the limited time available is a challenge that we face on a daily basis in many areas of our lives, and the minister's role as counselor is no exception.

Throughout this book, I have tried to avoid the term "pastoral counseling" as much as possible. Instead, I have used the phrase "the minister who provides counsel." My primary reason for this seemingly wordier verbal construction is that I want to emphasize the fact that ministers, whatever may be their professional setting, are often asked to provide counsel and are often considered to be persons who, by virtue of their calling and training, are capable of doing so. This does not necessarily mean that the one who is asking for the minister's counsel is requesting "pastoral counseling." While the distinction between "providing counsel" and "pastoral counseling" may appear to be the sort of verbal nicety that only a seminary professor would get paid for, it is actually a very important one. If, for example, a parishioner asks her minister what he thinks of the campus religious group that her daughter joined when she went off to the University and what, if anything, she should do about it, she is asking for the minister's counsel. However, she is not asking for what is commonly known as "pastoral counseling," that is, several meetings in which she comes to the pastor's office at a predetermined time to talk. The minister in this case might suspect that the issue of the campus religious group hides a deeper issue or problem, such as the mother's sense of loss over her daughter's absence or her desire to maintain control over her daughter, but the question she has asked is a very legitimate question to ask her minister. Ministers, after all, are considered by most parishioners to have knowledge about these groups that the average parishioner does not have, and they are assumed to have insights about these groups that a parishioner may find helpful or valuable.

Many books would simply refer to this episode as an example of "pastoral care," thus invoking the distinction between "pastoral care" and "pastoral counseling" to cover a situation of this nature. In my view, however, the minister, in responding to the mother's question, *is* assuming the role of counselor. We therefore unnecessarily limit the word "counselor" when we associate it only with what, over the past several decades, has come to be known as "pastoral counseling." What I hope my use of this more unwieldy verbal construction will accomplish is greater recognition of the fact that ministers do much more "counseling" than the more formal definition of "pastoral counseling" would lead us to believe.

I have also chosen to use the word *minister* rather than the word *pastor* throughout this book. One reason for doing so is that *pastor* is more closely identified with certain denominations than others, whereas *minister* applies more broadly (and is inclusive of pastors). Another is that the word minister applies equally well to clergy who are not pastors of congregations. Some of us are teachers or administrators in educational settings (schools, colleges, universities, seminaries), campus ministers, chaplains (hospital, military, prison, state and national legislative bodies), workers in social service agencies or pastoral counseling centers, and many other contexts. Ministers serving in these various contexts are frequently called on to offer counsel. While the majority of students in an introductory or basic course in pastoral care and counseling are likely to be headed toward congregational ministry, a substantial minority are contemplating careers in other forms of ministry. My use of the word *minister* is intended to convey the more inclusive perspective of this book. This has the added benefit for me personally that I have been able to draw from my own personal experiences in my role as a counselor to students.

Most books in the pastoral care and counseling field have what is often called a "theological dimension." Sometimes this theological dimension is presented in the final chapter of the book; other times discussions of "theological implications" are scattered throughout the text. I have written such books myself. In the design and writing of this book, however, it seemed to me that a brief or even more sustained theological discussion was inappropriate for the purposes of this book.

This is not because I consider theology to be expendable. Rather, I want this book to be one that professors representing a very broad theological spectrum would be comfortable in adopting in their courses. The Clinebell textbook is instructive in this regard. This book has an early chapter (chap. 2) in which he advocates "a holistic liberation-growth model of pastoral care and counseling" and a later chapter (chap. 5) that is about "facilitating spiritual wholeness: the heart of pastoral care and counseling." While I have used this book in my courses, I have not assigned these particular chapters because I did not want students to think that the course itself was based on this theological perspective. I recognize that the failure to make one's theology explicit means that it will remain implicit in the text one has written, but I believe that this is the lesser of two evils. What I have written here about creating a listening environment, making conversation, and so forth, could have been written by a theological conservative, moderate, or liberal. Some nuances might have been different, and some additions or substitutions would undoubtedly have been made, but, to the extent possible, I have tried to make this a "generic" book, one that the vast majority of my colleagues in the field would not be embarrassed—for theological reasons—to assign, or be placed on the defensive by students for having assigned, in their classes.

A second reason for my decision not to include a theological discussion in this book is that I do not view it as the single assigned text in a course on pastoral care and counseling. For one thing, it is a book that focuses exclusively on the minister's role as counselor. Other ministerial roles also come under the heading of pastoral care. Moreover, pastoral care is commonly assumed to be present in preaching, worship, teaching, and administration. Various other books address these topics (for example, Dittes, 1999a). In addition, many books in recent decades have been written for the expressed purpose of expanding the field to include gender, race, sexual orientation, sociopolitical, multicultural, and ecological issues and concerns. A book designed as a "how-to" cannot pretend to cover this range of issues, and, conversely, the fact that excellent books on these subjects are now available has allowed me to employ a rather circumscribed definition of the minister as counselor, to give emphasis, for example, to a conversation between a minister and one other person, and to leave to one side how gender, race, sexual orientation, and other factors are likely to influence the conversation. Of course, this does not mean that a conversation between two persons of one ethnic or racial group will not differ significantly from one involving persons of another group, even as a conversation between two women will differ from one between two men, or between one man and one woman, or between two gay or two lesbian individuals. My concern here, however, has been to present a framework for ensuring that such conversations between a minister and another person (or persons) will be valuable and not harmful to the persons involved. From this, professors and their students can move to readings and discussions of these gender, racial, socioeconomic and cultural differences, thereby greatly expanding the framework presented here.

It would be misleading for me to claim that I have written a book that reflects no personal commitments, values, or biases whatsoever. I am especially aware of two of these. One is largely theoretical, but it has practical implications. This is my belief that, during the latter half of the twentieth century, the most useful models for ministry via counseling have been the systemic and the psychodynamic approaches. The systemic approach takes the view that a problem manifesting itself in one member of the family is largely due to the relationships and interactions of the family (or group) as a whole. It should not therefore be viewed or treated in isolation from the "system" of which this individual is part. The psychodynamic approach centers on the mental and emotional processes underlying human behavior and its motivation, especially as these processes have developed unconsciously in response to environmental influences. Over the past several decades, advocates of the one approach have been critical of the other approach. Since the psychodynamic approach came first, much of the criticism has come from advocates of the systemic approach who have claimed, for example, that the psychodynamic approach is too individualistic. Advocates of the psychodynamic approach have fought back, noting, for example, that the systemic model does not take the workings of the individual mind into sufficient account. There is increasing evidence, however, of a rapprochement between these two approaches; and the view that they can not only live peaceably together but that they can be mutually supportive and energizing is the position that I take in this book. A key text for me in this regard is Michael P. Nichols' *The Self in the System* (1987). The systemic/psychodynamic approach that he advocates is reflected throughout my book.

The second bias is one that is shared by the overwhelming majority of my colleagues in the field, though occasional violations have occurred. This is my conviction that ministers should hold themselves to the very highest professional standards of conduct. This being the case, it has been a matter of considerable professional embarrassment and personal pain that the counseling ministry has been the locus or occasion for the great majority of violations of these professional standards. I am aware of arguments that these standards are the product of a conformist society, which is itself morally corrupt, and I am also aware of the fact that Christianity is based not on law and prohibition, but an ethic of love. I believe, however, that such an ethic of love requires that ministers uphold rather than suspend these professional standards. I also believe that living according to these standards is not constricting, but freeing.

A heterosexual male minister's conversation with a heterosexual woman can be more spontaneous and alive when he knows that he will *not* violate these professional standards (for example, make sexual advances). In addition, he will be able to think more freely and spontaneously, thus participating more fully and actively in the goal of resolving her problem.

When I was a doctoral student at the University of Chicago in the late 1960s, I was walking across the quadrangle with a psychology professor who had written books on Freud's Jewishness and the book of Job. As we passed by a group of students wearing the military garb and hippie–"flower children"–attire that were so popular during the Vietnam War era, he commented, "I wear conventional clothes so that I can think unconventional thoughts." As I looked at his rather drab, ill-fitting suit and tie, it struck me that this professor was more "liberated" than the students who were wearing very unconventional attire. The point is not that behind every Brooks Brothers suit there is a radical or anarchist mind at work. However, the minister who is scrupulously professional in his or her relations with parishioners, students, patients, or clients has not less, but greater freedom to engage in lively and spirited conversation, and to talk easily about problems and concerns that another minister who is professionally or morally compromised–or in danger of becoming so–will find disconcerting or troubling to pursue. This particular bias, which is most evident in the chapter on how to manage boundaries, is neither a judgmental nor a self-righteous one. As I contend in that chapter, the moral difficulties of ministers have systemic as well as psychodynamic causes. This being the case, not one of us has the right to stand in judgment or contempt of one of our minister colleagues, nor, as I will show, do we have any right to fall back on the cliché that a systemic/psychodynamic analysis discredits, that "there are a few bad apples in every bushel." I know personally several such "offenders," and they are not "bad apples." They have, however, been "spoiled" by the system (systemic analysis) and their inability to sublimate their sexual desire (psychodynamic analysis).

In order to make this book optimally useful in a course on pastoral care and counseling, I have limited the number of chapters to five, thereby allowing a fuller discussion of each topic than would be possible if there were a chapter for each week of a quarter- or semester-long course. Because this book is an introduction to the counseling role only, I do not envision that it would be a text that would be read and discussed throughout the whole quarter or semester. It *is*, however, designed to be read (together with supplementary articles, book chapters, etc.) over several weeks. I assume that the book would lend itself to a five-week format, or roughly half of a quarter-long course and somewhat more than a third of a semester-long course. It seems appropriate to me that consideration of the minister as counselor would compose at least a third of an introductory course on pastoral care and counseling, especially in light of most students' expectation that such a course will "teach me how to be a counselor." Although it is certainly a professor's prerogative to challenge this very expectation in hopes that students will have a broader, less utilitarian view of the course, I have learned from experience that it is much better to work with this expectation than to give elaborate and lofty explanations for why one intends to frustrate it.

I have not included practice exercises or study questions, a fairly common practice with introductory texts. My primary reason for this is that the book is intended for use in courses where there is not only significant opportunity for students to ask questions but also some form of practice activity (for example, the writing of their own pastoral care cases) already built in. Nor have I included suggestions for further reading. The expanding lists of publications in pastoral care and counseling, together with the countervailing tendency of publishers to withdraw these books before potential readers have even heard of them, limit the usefulness of such suggestions.

Finally, when I wrote *Living Stories: Pastoral Counseling in Congregational Context* (1998), I assumed that I had written my "final word" on the subject of pastoral counseling. However, my subsequent work with Gene Fowler on our coauthored book *The Pastoral Care Case* (2001), prompted me to feel that another book on the subject would be justified if it were not as "advanced" as *Living Stories* has been perceived to be. (Despite its emphasis on the congregational context, ministers who specialize in pastoral counseling have found it especially useful.) This book, then, is the result of an imaginative leap—envisioning myself as a student enrolled in her first and perhaps only course in pastoral care and counseling—an attempt, insofar as possible, to reexperience the feelings and thoughts of such a student as if for the first time. Philosopher Ludwig Wittgenstein once wrote: "A problem has the form: 'I don't know my way about'" (1958, p. 123). For a student confronted with the daunting prospect of assuming the role of counselor, this sense of not knowing one's way about is bound to loom especially large. This is the problem that this book addresses. My hope is that the student who reads this book all the way through will be able to say at the end, "While I may not yet be comfortable in the role of counselor, I think I know my way about in this role." This would be rather like a traveler on a first visit to a city taking a three-hour ride on a tour bus. At the end of the tour, the guide might say, "There is so much to know about this city—its history, its people, its buildings. But I hope that you now have a feel for the place and that you can now get about on your own." The author of an introductory text on the minister as counselor is in much the same position as the tour guide; and, in this respect, is also like the minister whose hope is that the other, as a result of their conversation together, will be able to get about on his own. He may not return to say that this is what the minister has enabled him to do, but ministry is not about keeping score. It is about being faithful to one's calling.

1

How to Create a
Listening Environment

In *The Art of Pastoral Conversation* (1981), Gaylord Noyce points out: "listening is hard work. It is far easier to translate a foreign language that we know into our own tongue than to translate our own into the foreign speech. Likewise, it is far easier to direct a conversation along the lines of our own thinking than to respond along the lines of thought and feeling and in accord with the assumptions of others. Sensitive, thoughtful listening makes it more possible" (p. 31).

"Preaching courses teach seminary students how to speak, while pastoral counseling courses teach them how to listen." I have heard this said, and there is much truth in it. As this chapter unfolds, however, it will become clear that there is one very important similarity between preaching and pastoral counseling, and this is that both involve communication. The problem is that the communication skills developed for preaching do not work very well in counseling, which may help to explain the widely held perception (even if it exaggerates the point a bit) that the best preachers are often the worst counselors, and that the best counselors are often ineffective preachers.

This chapter will focus on the important role that listening plays in any situation in which a minister assumes the role of counselor. Some readers may feel that they do not need to read a chapter on "how to create a listening environment" because they are "natural listeners." If there is a phenomenon known as the "natural reader"–the child of three or four years old who takes to reading with relative ease–surely there is also a category of persons who are "natural listeners." This ability, in fact, may be an important reason why they were drawn to ministry as a profession, and why they are especially attracted to counseling. At the same time, I believe that reading about listening will, at the very least, help these "natural listeners" to identify what they are already doing that makes them effective listeners. It may also help them to see how their listening ability fits within the larger framework of a helping process.

Others are convinced that they will never become good listeners. To read about listening will merely make them feel more inadequate. While it may be risky to say this (as there are always exceptions), my experience has been that students who truly wanted to become better listeners have in fact become so. With rare exceptions, any student whose listening capacity has not improved as a result of taking a course in pastoral care and counseling was not really interested in becoming a good listener. Listening is a skill that can be taught, but not to an unreceptive learner. A sort of circularity, perhaps even a paradox, in this regard is that to become a listener, one must be able to listen to suggestions or advice about listening from someone else. Reading about listening is itself a form of listening. The reader can "talk back"– challenge or question what has been said–but such "talking back" will have much greater force if the reader has first listened to what the author has to say.

Of course, reading about effective listening and actually engaging in it as a counselor are two different things. What seems simple enough as we read about it may prove more difficult in practice. This gap between reading about effective listening and actually doing it should not be minimized. On the other hand, effective listening is something one can practice outside the counseling role. Since we communicate with many persons throughout the course of a normal day, we can practice effective listening in many natural contexts. When I was first introduced to the "client-centered" approach to counseling–an approach that places great emphasis on listening and reflecting what one hears– I tried it out at parties and other social gatherings. As I was driving home, my frequent reflection on the fact that I had learned a great deal about quite a number of persons—and had said virtually nothing about myself—confirmed the value of this approach. (I later discovered that persons who suffer from social phobia or anxiety often use this very "method" because they dislike being the center of attention; see Capps, 1998). Readers of this chapter may want to put its claims to a test. They might, for example, use the ideas presented here in talking with one friend and deliberately not use them—or even violate them—in a conversation with another friend, and then assess the two conversations. When engaging in the counseling role itself, one is not as free to experiment in this way.

I suggest, then, that reading about listening can benefit any reader except one who is simply not interested in becoming a better listener. (I have in mind here a lack of interest and not resistance, which, as James E. Dittes points out, is typically "a sign of vitality"; Dittes, 1967, p. 136ff.) Because this is a book on the minister as counselor, the listening that concerns us here is listening that occurs within the context or framework of *a helping process.* When we hear the term *helping process,* we are likely to think of a situation in which the minister is talking with a parishioner in her office about a personal problem. Most of the situations I will discuss in this book will be of this kind. The term also applies, however, to situations in which the minister is helping the budget committee decide between two options, or assisting the education committee in addressing the problem of a shortage of teachers, or counseling the chairperson of the music committee concerning his efforts to resolve a dispute between the organist and the choir director. It may also apply to a seminary professor who is counseling a doctoral student on how to get her dissertation proposal accepted by the faculty committee that reviews such proposals. The same listening skills that are effective in counseling an individual or couple on a personal matter are likely to be effective with these other situations. This is why Carl R. Rogers, one of the therapists who developed the listening methods that are so widely used by psychotherapists and counselors today, was often asked to speak to educators and managers and was even involved in an experiment with Catholic and Protestant youth of Northern Ireland who were brought together in a neutral site for mutual conversation.

In this chapter, I will be concerned with what we might view as an adult learning problem, the problem of how to learn to listen. My approach to this problem will not be instructional, much less didactic. I will not set forth a step-by-step model for learning to listen. Instead, I will address this adult learning problem through indirection, that is, by focusing on ways to create a listening environment, an environment conducive to listening. In taking this more indirect approach, I show, in effect, that I myself have been listening to educators who say that it is very difficult to teach if the environment is not conducive to learning. Similarly, it is difficult to become a good, effective listener if a listening environment has not been created. Once the environment is in place, the difficulty of listening is greatly reduced.

Of course, the word "environment" is a notoriously slippery term, and our politicians have taken full advantage of this fact when they have claimed to be "for the environment" or represented themselves as "the environmental candidate." This slipperiness is reflected in the dictionary definition of environment as "all the conditions, circumstances, and influences surrounding, and affecting the development of, an organism or group of organisms." The key word here, however, is "surrounding," or that which encircles or encloses the organism in question. What are the conditions, circumstances, and influences that "surround" the act or process of listening? What are the conditions that inhibit listening from taking place? And what are the conditions that facilitate its occurrence? I will be concerned in this chapter with these surrounding factors. Then, in chapter 2, I will focus more narrowly on the communication process—the give-and-take between the person who provides a listening ear and the person (or persons) who have asked or expect to be listened to.

How Anxiety Inhibits Listening

What is listening? The dictionary defines it as "to make a conscious effort to hear; attend closely, so as to hear; to pay close attention." This definition emphasizes that it is a *conscious* effort and that it involves being *attentive*. *Conscious* in this case means being *intentional*, or purposeful, while *attention* means the act of keeping one's mind closely on something. Thus, listening has an *intentional* and an *attentional* aspect, and both are needed for true listening to occur. One might be very intentional—"I will make every effort to listen"—and yet be unable to attend to what is being said or communicated.

A person might not be able to attend to what is being said for many reasons. He may be so conscious of his intention to listen that he is unable to attend to what the other person is trying to communicate. We might call this the paradox of intentional listening. The more intentional one is, the greater the danger that one will not be attentional. Other reasons, however, have more to do with the anxieties that are evoked in oneself by what the other person is saying.

Erik H. Erikson (1963) makes a useful contrast between anxieties and fears. Fears, he says, "are states of apprehension which focus on isolated and recognizable dangers so that they may be judiciously appraised and realistically countered," whereas anxieties "are diffuse states of tension which magnify and even cause the illusion of an outer danger, without pointing to appropriate avenues of defense or mastery" (pp. 406–7).

For someone who has not previously needed to be intentional about listening, the first few experiences of doing this may inherently produce anxiety. One of the goals of this book is that the reader will find intentional listening less inherently anxiety-producing because he has a good idea of what such listening entails. But anxieties are also evoked or created by the things another person says to us. The things that are said or communicated can make us anxious, producing a "diffuse state of tension" that magnifies or causes a sense of endangerment from which we are unable, at the moment at least, to defend ourselves. An obvious example is when we are verbally condemned, as when a parishioner says that she "completely disagrees" with the sermon, or when the senior minister calls the associate minister into his office and begins to list the "complaints" he has heard from a few church members about how she has been handling her youth ministry assignments. Even if the senior minister minimizes these complaints, stressing that the vast majority of the members are enthusiastic about the associate's work with the youth, his use of the word "complaints" is likely to evoke anxiety, and the associate may have difficulty listening to the senior minister's description of the complaints and his assurances that they represent the views of only a few members.

Or when a parishioner comes to the minister and says that he has learned something about the minister's past that the minister had hoped her congregation would never learn about, she is very likely to have an initial response of anxiety, as she is faced with what appears to be a danger for which she has no appropriate defense. If she subsequently calms herself and says to her accuser, "This is something that happened a long time ago for which I have asked and received God's forgiveness," what appeared to be an experience of endangerment has become an opportunity to witness to the efficacy of the Christian faith. Initially, though, she feels anxious because she experiences an inability to defend herself.

Things said to a counselor can make the counselor anxious for various other reasons. They may be categorized as follows:

1. *The subject matter itself produces anxiety.* Certain topics that arise in the course of a conversation may make the minister feel uneasy, threatened, or endangered. Talk about death, marital conflicts, conflicts between siblings, or sexual topics may be threatening because they open up wounds from childhood or adolescence. A male parishioner describing a sexual relationship with another male may produce anxiety in a male minister who had an unwanted sexual encounter with a man when he was a teenager. Or a parishioner who says she is thinking seriously about committing suicide may produce anxiety in the minister because his mother committed suicide when he was a boy and he continues to feel that he was partly to blame even though he knows he was not. When anyone brings up the subject of suicide, this minister's anxiety is raised, and he finds that he is unable to hear what is being said from that point on. All he can think about for the next several minutes is his experience of looking at his dead mother's face as she lay in the casket and of asking her why she didn't want to live anymore.

2. *The subject matter produces anxiety when this particular person talks about it.* Topics that may not ordinarily result in anxiety for the minister, but do so when a particular individual brings them up. For example, a male minister may not become anxious when other persons talk about sexual matters, but when a particular woman does so, he becomes anxious, perhaps because he finds her talking about it to be sexually arousing. Or a minister may ordinarily be able to listen to other persons' expressions of anger, but finds herself anxious when a particular person talks in an angry voice because his way of expressing anger is very similar to how her father spoke angrily toward her when she was a child. Thus, even though the man being listened to is expressing anger toward someone else, she feels personally threatened, and reexperiences her inability to defend herself against a threat.

3. *A particular person produces anxiety whatever the subject matter is.* Some individuals make a minister feel anxious by their physical presence alone. The reasons for this may be self-evident. For example, whenever this person comes to a committee meeting, he can be counted on to insult another person, causing the other person to break out in tears, or leave the meeting altogether. Thus, the very appearance of this person raises the minister's anxiety level, as she feels relatively defenseless, not knowing when the insults will occur, who they will be directed against, and what their repercussions will be. Other times, the reasons are less self-evident. The minister may not be aware, for example, that a particular person produces feelings in him that were evoked by his mother

when he felt that she was trying to control him. When this person enters the room, the minister feels unaccountably trapped, like an animal, and looks about for some means of escape. When she speaks, he doesn't hear much of what she has to say.

4. *The anxiety is due to anticipatory dread.* A minister may have difficulty listening to what the other person is saying because he is thinking about what he will need to do later in the conversation. For example, he may be aware that this parishioner will expect him to say a prayer at the end of the conversation, and he may be anxious about what he is going to say. Or a minister in the teaching profession may be dreading the fact that she will need to tell the student that his course work is quite poor. Knowing that he expects that she will have nothing but praise for his work makes this task especially difficult. Or a minister may be anxious about what her next move should be. Will she suggest another conversation together? Will she refer the other person to another professional, and, if so, to whom? Or he may be thinking about something else that he needs to do later in the day, such as a funeral he is dreading because he knows it will be an especially difficult one for the family involved. Or she may be thinking about the fact that her husband is going to undergo medical tests later in the day. If the previous cause of anxiety was more likely to be due to its associations with the past, this one has more to do with dread related to the future, causing one to be less than fully attentive to what is being said right now.

5. *The anxiety is due to an inability to understand what the other person is saying.* Here, the anxiety does not concern the subject matter or the person who is speaking, but the difficulty the hearer is having in understanding what is being said. The reason for the difficulty may be that the minister does not know much, if anything, about the topic of discussion or about how the person who is speaking about the topic appears to be viewing it. For example, the topic may have to do with a person's feeling she is getting the runaround at a social agency. If the minister does not know anything about this agency or its procedures, he may feel that the conversation is simply beyond his ability to follow, and this absence of understanding may cause him to become anxious because his ignorance is self-evident to him, and will no doubt become obvious to the other person as well. Or a parishioner may be telling the minister about a situation involving her extended family and the minister may find that she cannot keep all the names and relations straight. She becomes anxious, afraid her effort to respond will be met with, "Oh, no, no, no, it wasn't Ruthie who had the baby out of wedlock;

it was Amy. Ruthie was the one who ran off with that sailor boy we all despised." Or the other person may be discussing a medical procedure that he is about to undergo, and the minister realizes that if she knew more about the procedure, she would be able to understand much better the nature and degree of the other person's anxiety. Although the minister is aware of the fact that one is not expected to know everything, this awareness may be ineffectual in combating the anxiety that her lack of understanding will be discovered and that she may be judged incompetent or even become the object of contempt.

Subjects in which one's understanding may be challenged can be those involving technological developments about which one is uninformed or sociocultural experiences that are very different from one's own. An older minister may simply not understand the slang or jargon of a younger person, while a younger minister may find an older person's stories or anecdotes hard to understand because their sociocultural reference points no longer exist. Ways of speaking that are difficult to understand may be due to age, racial, regional, occupational, or sociocultural differences, so that listening to the other requires heightened attentiveness, which can be fatiguing or exhausting. When I was in Sweden some years ago, I was talking with the wife of a professor friend of mine. As our conversation continued, I became aware that talking with me was physically exhausting for her in that she was having to listen and talk in English. I suddenly realized that this conversation was far more demanding on her than it was on me even though I was doing more of the talking. It isn't especially flattering to discover that one is hard for another to listen to, but it was an excellent illustration of Noyce's point that listening is hard work.

6. *The anxiety is due to one's awareness of differing points of view.* Here, the anxiety is not due to one's difficulty in understanding what the other person is talking about, but to the fact that one understands only too well. How does one listen attentively when what is being said seems altogether wrongheaded, if not perverse? And how does one remain faithful to one's own beliefs while listening to another person who is espousing opposing beliefs? The minister may feel threatened even though the other person is not saying anything negative about the minister. An especially threatening conversation is one in which the other person assumes—perhaps because the minister *is* a minister—that his viewpoint is shared by the minister. The other person may be attacking the views of someone else, assuming that the minister shares her distaste for these ideas, while in point of fact the minister is in agreement with

the one being criticized. Should the minister say that he disagrees with the speaker, thus jeopardizing the helping process itself, or should he express his disagreement on the grounds that the process cannot really be helpful if he is not straightforward and honest? Topics that are most likely to engender anxiety are ones that concern theological and moral issues. Largely because of their seminary education, many ministers do not have the same theological views as many—perhaps most—of the persons they work with (parishioners, patients, etc.). This is often true of their views on moral issues as well. If these were merely "theoretical" differences, they might not be cause for anxiety, but many of these issues have practical consequences and are therefore integral to the helping process itself. A minister's anxiety in such a case can range from not wanting her personal views to be found out to concern that she is not being faithful to her calling if she "goes along with" the other person's beliefs and seemingly endorses their practical consequences.

7. *The anxiety is due to the minister's current emotional or psychological health.* A minister may be suffering from depression, apathy, or chronic fatigue, and the very thought of needing to listen to the problems or complaints of another person is a threatening prospect. She does not know if she is even capable of being attentive. Even if she is able to hear the words, she is unable to respond to their felt meanings. She wants to care about the other person's concerns or worries but is having difficulty marshaling this caring, and this very difficulty creates further anxiety. Another minister may not be feeling depressed, apathetic, or fatigued, but he may be feeling the normal burdens of his work and responsibilities. Unlike the full-time pastoral counselor, who anticipates a relatively full day of counseling, the minister in other settings may feel that the role of counselor is a distraction from other, more pressing obligations. Or the fact that it is more occasional—while his role as worship leader is a more definite, routine responsibility—makes it seem somehow more burdensome. His emotional state of resentment at having to talk with this person about her worries—which may seem overblown anyway—may create anxieties, especially if he is aware of his emotional state: "I worry that my hidden resentment will become evident in the way I listen to her."

The minister who is aware of her troubled emotional or psychological state may make an intentional decision to avoid situations where she is placed in the counselor role, but she may then become anxious that the congregation will wonder why she is doing this and that her own problem will come out in the open, with undesired consequences. If she does not make this decision, however, she may fear that the counsel she gives to others will be colored by her own emotional state and may therefore be harmful to the other person. Either way, she feels defenseless, and the state of diffuse tension that accompanies this feeling inhibits her ability to listen.

These seven categories may not exhaust all the possible reasons that a minister may become anxious in his role as counselor, but they make my point that anxiety is the most likely reason that a minister may be having difficulty attending to what the other person is saying in spite of the intention to listen carefully. As Freud pointed out nearly a century ago, anxiety is likely to be paralyzing (Freud, 1959). In the context that concerns us here, it paralyzes the minister's capacity to listen—to attend fully—to what the other person is saying. Freud also noted, however, that the very symptoms that we develop in order to ward off the anxiety tell us a great deal about the basis for our anxiety, and about how we characteristically respond to anxiety-producing situations. If, for example, the parishioner's threat to tell others in the congregation what he knows about the minister's past were to prompt her to go home that evening and draft a letter of resignation, this very action would reveal that behind her anxiety is the fear of exposure, and that her characteristic response to such exposure is to punish herself. A similar fear of exposure may, however, be present in the case of the minister who is made anxious by the fact that he does not understand what the parishioner is talking about, though *his* response to such exposure may be to change the subject to a topic that he does know something about, whether or not this is useful to the parishioner in working through her problem. Thus, his characteristic defense against exposure is to introduce a distraction. I know a professor who can be counted on to tell a joke when the conversation moves into an area where his lack of knowledge about it will be evident to the others. The joke is a defensive strategy. It says to his conversation partners, "The topic isn't worth taking seriously."

Usually a fear is hidden behind one's anxieties, and identifying what this fear is can be helpful in dealing with the anxiety itself. The first minister did not in fact go home and write her resignation letter. Instead, after a brief pause during which she collected herself, she informed her accuser that she did not fear exposure, for she had already exposed her shame and guilt to God, and God had granted her forgiveness. The minister who feared the exposure of his lack of understanding took the risk of not changing the subject—his usual defense—and said to the person to whom he was offering counsel, "Perhaps I should know about the medical procedure you are talking about, but I'm afraid I've never heard of it. Could you describe it for me?" Instead of ridiculing him for his ignorance, she chuckled and said, "Oh my, I hope I can describe it. It took me several days even to be able to say the word for it." Thus, he discovered that his lack of understanding was actually shared by the other person, and in this shared experience his anxiety disappeared.

Erikson identifies several of the fears that lie behind our anxieties, including the fear of sudden or unexpected change, of being attacked from behind, of losing autonomy, of being impoverished, of being exposed, of being closed up, of losing one's boundaries, of being immobilized, of being manipulated, of being abandoned, and of not being guided (1963, pp. 408–11). He suggests that these fears can usually be traced to childhood and that at least some of these fears survive into adulthood, and persist as a "sense of smallness" substratum in our otherwise adult minds. Our triumphs are measured against this smallness, and our defeats substantiate it. In an adult, however, they come to expression in diffuse states of anxious tension, and we may not be able to discern the fear or fears behind our anxieties unless and until we make an effort to identify the connection between our anxiety and the fear that first produced it.

The reader may wish to look over this list of fears in order to determine which one—or ones—are most likely to be activated in a situation where she finds herself in the role of counselor. (Other situations may evoke other, different fears.) For example, she may discern or discover that her anxiety is most likely to be evoked when the other person suddenly begins to speak in a vehement tone, when the other person makes a cutting remark that seems to come out of nowhere, when the other person begins making demands that make it difficult for her to relax in the other's company, when she feels that the other person fails to give her due credit for what they have accomplished together, when she feels that her weaknesses may be in danger of being revealed, when she feels that she is being pushed around against her will, when she feels that the other person has failed her, when she feels that she has been thrown into the counselor role without proper training—"sink or swim." Alternatively, Erikson's list of fears may prompt the reader to identify another one that is more likely to be at the root of his anxiety in this situation.

If anxiety is a diffuse state of tension in which one feels endangered but has no appropriate avenue of defense or mastery, identifying the fear behind the anxiety enables one to focus on the danger involved and to develop a judicious and realistic counter-defense. The minister who was able to identify the fear behind her anxiety–the fear of exposure–was able to present an adequate counterdefense to her threatening parishioner. She said, in effect, "If you think that I am worried about your threat of exposure, I need to tell you–for your own benefit, not mine–that I am not worried about it. I have already exposed myself to the One whose judgment and condemnation I most feared, and I have been fully forgiven. Expose me to other members of the congregation if you wish, but my response will be the same to them as it has been to you." The message here is that she intends to be evaluated by her current behavior and performance, and will, as it were, let the dead bury the dead.

From this exploration into the anxieties that may inhibit our listening to another (or others), I conclude that if a minister has the *intention* to listen, and if she is relatively free of anxiety so that she is able to give *attention* to what is being communicated (to be, in other words, a nonanxious presence), she is well on her way toward being a good and effective listener. This is not to say, however, that the minister is expected always to be able to be without anxiety. In *On Becoming a Person* (1961), Carl R. Rogers discusses the importance of "congruence" in the counselor's interaction with his client. By this he means that whatever feeling or attitude the counselor is experiencing is matched by the counselor's awareness of this attitude. A closely related issue is whether the counselor is also able to communicate this feeling or attitude unambiguously (pp. 50–51). I will discuss Rogers' views on congruence more fully in the following chapter, focusing on the counseled person's congruence. In the context of our discussion of anxiety, however, it suggests that the critical issue is whether the minister is aware of her anxiety and, if so, if she is able to communicate this anxiety unambiguously to the other person. Such communications often have the effect of reducing anxiety, as I've discovered from confessing being anxious in speaking before an audience. The audience nods understandingly, and I begin to feel their support and encouragement as I begin to talk about the topic at hand. In a similar way, revelations of our anxiety in our role as counselors typically put the other person at ease–"I'm a little nervous myself"–and leads the other to pay more, not less, attention to what we have to say.

Attitudes That Assist Good Listening

I have discussed anxiety as the major impediment to listening and have suggested the various situational factors and kinds of fear that may cause one to become anxious. Now I want to focus on the more "productive" side of listening, centering on the *attitudes* and *conditions* that help to establish a listening environment. As we will see, this distinction between attitudes and conditions is somewhat arbitrary, for the conditions that help to create a good listening environment are a reflection of the attitudes of the listener, and vice versa. Still, the distinction is a useful one, because attitudes have more to do with the disposition of the listener, while conditions relate more directly to the situation, which in this case is the listening process itself. In other words, attitudes have more to do with the listener's internal desire to be a good listener, while conditions relate more directly to one's awareness that listening is a communicative act.

In *The Lost Art of Listening* (1995), Michael P. Nichols suggests that good listening requires the following: *Attention, appreciation,* and *affirmation* (pp. 109–19). In emphasizing *attention,* he wants to make the point that better listening does not begin with techniques. Instead, it starts with making a sincere effort to pay attention to what is going on in the conversation partner's private world of experience. Some invitational comments may help to open another person up: "Tough day?" "Are you worried about something?" "Is something bothering you?" This is not, however, technique, but simply saying something that indicates a willingness to listen.

As for *appreciation,* Nichols advises showing genuine appreciation for the other's point of view. One should assume, until proven otherwise, that the other person has a valid and valuable perspective on the problem or concern being discussed. The hardest situation in which to be genuinely appreciative is when the other's point of view is critical of oneself. Nichols notes, however, that one should take this to heart: If you listen without defensiveness, you earn the right to have such nondefensive listening reciprocated. The other person owes you this much. Appreciative listening is often *silent* but never *passive.* It means focusing on the other and on what the other is saying. It often means asking questions for *clarification* and *elaboration.* As Nichols puts it: "Real listening means imagining yourself into the other's experience: concentrating, asking questions. Understanding is furthered not by knowing ('I understand') but by investigating–asking for elaboration, inquiring into the concrete particularity of the speaker's experience" (p. 113).

Such inquiries should not be perfunctory: "So then what happened?" followed by "So what happened next?" Perfunctory responses will come across to the speaker as mechanical and perhaps as evidence of a lack of interest. She may respond, "I'm boring you, aren't I?" or "It's really a stupid little story, isn't it?" Instead, one might respond, "so down came the vase–flowers, water and all." Technically speaking, this merely repeats what has already been said, but it communicates interest and encouragement to continue. Also, these inquiries should not focus on getting the other person to say more about what someone else was thinking, as though she is a mind reader, but about her own thoughts and emotions. The listener does not say, "Why do you suppose he said that?" or "Don't you wonder what possessed her to behave this way?" (eliciting responses ranging from "Oh, it's just her way" to "Oh, it's the devil in her"). Rather, one says, "And this made you feel…" or "And you were thinking…" This way, it is not the speaker's clairvoyance– her capacity to read the mind of another–but her own world of experience that the minister is appreciating, seeing it as valid and valuable in its own right. Requests for clarification and elaboration are primarily intended to enable the person being counseled to present her own experiential world as accurately as possible. This *is* something to which she *can* attest, whereas the experiential world of another–the person she is talking about–is accessible to her only by inference.

On the other hand, if the speaker has expressed her view that the other person "acted out of spite" or "said it because he knew it would hurt me," the minister shows appreciation for the speaker by refraining from saying that she could be mistaken about the other person's motives or, even worse, supplying another possible motive: "But maybe he just wasn't thinking when he said that" or "Could it be that he was just teasing you?" If the issue is worth pursuing at all, the minister might suggest that the speaker try a little experiment such as the one that Patricia O'Hanlon Hudson proposed to a couple whose fights usually began in the kitchen. When she asked how the fights began, the husband said that his wife gave him her "get-out-of-my-kitchen" look. Hudson suggested that he check out his impression by asking her, each time she had this look, what she was actually thinking. When they returned the following week, they had found that about half the time she had "that look" she was not even thinking about her husband but was eavesdropping on the children arguing in the other room or thinking about some ingredient she had forgotten to buy for the dinner preparation (Hudson and O'Hanlon, 1991, pp. 17–18). At best, the husband was half-right about what his wife was thinking.

To the extent possible, showing appreciation for the other's point of view means setting aside one's own prejudgments and listening to what the other has to say. As Nichols puts it, one should assume, until proven otherwise, that the other person has a valid point of view. To illustrate, Philip W. Cook in *Abused Men: The Hidden Side of Domestic Violence* (1997) relates that men who are being physically abused by their wives find it difficult to get anyone to appreciate their stories, to take them seriously. Because they are afraid of being personally shamed and ridiculed, when they try to get useful advice for how to handle problem, they often represent the problem as one that a male relative or a work associate is having. One man called up a woman's shelter to find out what they advised abused women to do, but the person who answered the phone suspected that he was a batterer himself and was trying to find out how to sabotage the protection process, so he was refused the advice that he desperately needed. If this man had come to a minister for help, would his point of view have been appreciated? Would the minister have assumed, until proven otherwise, that he had a valid perspective on the matter? Or would the minister have immediately doubted the veracity of his claim? Would he have thought, "He is playing me for a sucker. How gullible does he think I am?" To show genuine appreciation for another's point of view means suspending our preconceived convictions and prejudgments—at least initially—in order to hear what the other person has to say and wants to be able to communicate.

Finally, the *affirmation* Nichols writes about is essentially an affirmation of one's understanding of what one has heard. Silence, he notes, is ambiguous, so it is necessary that we communicate—with words—what we have understood the other person to be saying to us. If we do not do this, the other person may imagine that we do not think that what he is saying makes sense, or that it is even worth talking about. He may begin to have doubts, feeling that he made a mistake in making an appointment to see the minister. As Nichols points out, "Ordinarily, we take turns talking: The roles of speaker and listener alternate so naturally that it may be artificial to call what one person says 'the listener's response.' Responding turns listeners into speakers. But listening well is a two-step process: First we take in what the speaker says, then we let him or her know it. A failed response is like an unanswered letter; you never know if you got through" (1995, p. 114).

There are individuals, some of whom are intending to become ministers, who simply do not have much to say, especially when it comes to "small talk." Men are often this way, viewing themselves as the "strong, silent type." It may seem paradoxical—and it is—that these quiet ones are likely to be experienced as "ineffective listeners," not because they are unable to allow the other person to say what is on her mind, but because they had little to say by way of response. These individuals may need to force themselves to talk in ways they have never talked before. Otherwise, they may be experienced as aloof, even arrogant.

Nichols offers the following examples of responses that affirm the listener's understanding: "So you're saying that you don't think Kevin should join Little League because it will put a lot of unnecessary competitive pressure on him and because you'll be the one who gets stuck driving him to all the games?" Or, "OK, I want to make sure I understand. You're saying we should hire Gloria but that we should make it very clear to her what we expect, and we should be very serious about the probationary period, and if she doesn't do the job, we should let her go at the end of six months. Have I got that right?" (pp. 114–15).

The statement in response to Kevin's mother affirms the listener's understanding that she has two reasons for her objection to his joining Little League. She is then free to indicate to the listener that he has understood her ("Yes, that's what I'm saying") or to indicate that he has understood some but not all of what she is saying ("Plus the fact that Little League keeps us confined to home through the whole summer") or to add some further remarks to what the listener has said ("I wonder if my resentment over being the one who will have to drive him to games is causing me to magnify the competitive pressure on Kevin himself" or "You know, it's really the competitive pressure on Kevin that bothers me. If it weren't for that, I wouldn't really mind driving him to the games."). Would she have come to these subsequent clarifications if the listener had not affirmed his understanding at this particular interval in the conversation? Perhaps so. More likely, though, his response enabled her to take the next step in identifying which of the two objections was uppermost in her mind.

In the statement about the hiring of Gloria, the speaker indicates that she understands the importance to the selection committee of the conditions on which they are willing to offer Gloria the position. Her beginning and concluding sentences are quite explicit about her desire to affirm what she believes she has heard, and they communicate her awareness that the committee is counting on her to ensure that its conditions are honored. As with the listener's response to Kevin's mother, this affirmation of understanding gives the others the opportunity to say that she has heard correctly, or to amend or add to what she has heard. Had she not verbalized this response, the committee members might have been left to wonder if she had actually heard the conditions of Gloria's hiring, or, if she heard them, whether or not she would support them. Silence, as Nichols puts it, is ambiguous.

Some readers may feel that the listener should not have to give such careful attention to understanding a small matter, such as a mother's objections to her son's joining Little League, while others may feel that such careful attention to the conditions for hiring Gloria is unwarranted. Still others may feel that neither situation warrants this concentrated effort to understand and communicate one's understanding to the speakers involved. To say that these readers are wrong, or to dismiss them with a formulaic response ("God is in the details") would be to violate the principle of appreciation, which assumes, until proven otherwise, that the other person has a valid perspective on the matter. I would want to listen without prejudice to why the reader thinks or feels this way, to be able to affirm what I understand to be the reader's reasons for this, and to not jump to a premature conclusion, such as, "If you think it is not worth your time and effort to try to express your understanding of Kevin's mother's thoughts and feelings about his participation in Little League, you will have a hard go of it in ministry, because, like it or not, this is the stuff you'll be confronted with day after day after day." This conclusion may ultimately be warranted, but at this initial stage, it forecloses the conversation and communicates an absence of appreciation for what the other is thinking, feeling, and saying. The speaker, for example, may not be saying that he deems it not worth his time and effort to try to express his understanding of Kevin's mother's thoughts and feelings about her son's participation in Little League, but may instead be wondering if the whole issue of Kevin's involvement in Little League is a smoke screen for something else that is bothering her, such as her anger at her husband for not giving Kevin the attention a teenage boy needs from his father. Were this the speaker's real point, I would find myself saying something to this effect: "You are probably on to something, though you may be getting a little ahead of the story, so hold that thought—don't let it go—but let's take it one step at a time."

While *attention, appreciation,* and *affirmation* can be artificially separated, together they reflect a listening attitude. This attitude may be distinguished from the listener's responses, but, as we have seen, this is also an artificial distinction, for the minister's listening attitude is communicated primarily through her verbal responses—mainly of understanding—to what she has heard.

The Conditions That Support Good Listening

Besides the three *attitudes* that Nichols identifies, there is a model presented by Robert R. Carkhuff in *Helping and Human Relations* (1969) that suggests seven fundamental *conditions* that facilitate positive change in a helping relationship. These conditions, which have been presented in several books on pastoral counseling and pastoral care (e.g., Switzer, 1974, pp. 72–77; Switzer, 1979, pp. 72–94), will be viewed here as the conditions that enable good listening to occur: accurate communication of *empathy,* communication of genuine *respect* for the other person in the helping relationship, a manner of communication that is *concrete,* one that is *genuine,* one that is *appropriately self-disclosive;* an ability to use *confrontation* when necessary, and a focus on the *immediate.* David Switzer (1979) has made the very interesting proposal that these are also the necessary conditions for effective preaching. As with Nichols' three attitudes, these seven conditions blur the lines between conditions and verbal communication. One demonstrates the conditions by saying things that reveal their presence, and what one says contributes to the realization of these conditions. Since we are all aware of the traditional model of the seven deadly sins, we might want to call these "the seven saving conditions" of effective listening.

Accurate communication of empathy. This condition is largely a matter of perception, though this perception may involve a rather complex mixture of thought and emotion. The minister perceives where the parishioner is at this moment and seeks to communicate this perception through tone of voice and body language. Empathy has been described variously in the psychotherapeutic literature in general and in pastoral counseling texts in particular, and it has been compared and contrasted with sympathy, which often connotes a feeling of pity or compassion. Carl R. Rogers, the psychotherapist who is generally credited with having introduced *empathy* into the psychotherapeutic lexicon, has described it as the listener's assumption of "the internal frame of reference" of the other. Thus, it means "to perceive the world as the client sees it, to perceive the client himself as he is seen by himself, to lay aside all perceptions from the external frame of reference while doing so, and to communicate something of this empathic understanding to the client" (Rogers, 1951, p. 29). In other words, the counselor "concentrates upon trying to understand the client *as the client seems to himself*" (p. 30). The objective is to enter, insofar as possible, into the other person's own world of experience, to know and feel it as though I were the one who is troubled, confused, upset, vulnerable, content, happy, overjoyed.

This, of course, is not an easy thing to do, and Rogers and his colleagues were aware that the effort to abandon the observer role and to absorb oneself in the attitudes, ideas, and emotions of the other requires a kind of self-abandonment that is relatively foreign to us. We have worked hard throughout our lives to differentiate ourselves from others, and now we are being asked, on a provisional basis, to do precisely the opposite. James E. Dittes has described this empathy as one in which the "things that we usually suppose make for personality and a sense of self-presence are absent—sociability, opinions and attitudes, feelings, and history." Watching Rogers on film, one senses that he is "so radically other-directed" that he becomes "totally abdicating of his distinctiveness" and is "so engrossed in the other" that he is "oblivious to the boundaries that constitute and define the self" (Dittes, 1999b, p. 179).

Approximating this empathic entry into the experiencing of the other is difficult enough, but communicating how the world looks from the other's point of view compounds the difficulty. We assume that the other person is able to give verbal expression to the world of her own experiencing, but this is not necessarily the case, and even if it were, she would not know that the listener had become a participant in her world of experience unless she finds a way to express what this world of the other's experience feels like to her. The listener may think that she has communicated her empathic involvement in the other's world by saying, "I feel what you are going through" or "I can imagine how difficult this is for you," but these are "I" words, words that are about the listener. Instead of communicating empathy, they actually communicate the listener's distance from the other's experience. A statement that gets closer to the experiencing of a person who, for example, is confused, is, "Things seem jumbled, muddled, sort of…" If this is said in an empathic tone of voice, one that cannot be mistaken as condemnatory or judgmental, the person who is confused will feel understood and this very understanding will encourage her to enter more deeply the experiential world, which, at this time, is mostly one of confusion. She might find the word "jumbled" to be an especially accurate description, as her confusion may seem to be a set of letters or words that are out of order, it being her task somehow to put them back where they belong. Or she may fix on the word "muddled" (with "muddy" and "puddle" hovering in the background) and note that she feels as though her experience is one of being in a mess from which she cannot seem to extricate herself. In either case, her confusion is part mental and part emotional, and this, no doubt, partly explains why it is, in fact, confusing: "My mind tells me one thing; my heart tells me another."

Michael Nichols tells a fascinating story about a therapist in training that illustrates what the accurate communication of empathy is *not.* A man in therapy was explaining his relationship with his living but distant father when he suddenly remembered the happy times they'd spent together playing with his electric trains. Caught up in the memory, the man grew increasingly excited as he recalled the joy and pride and sense of belonging he had felt in sharing this family tradition with his father. As the man's enthusiasm mounted, the therapist launched into a long narrative about *his* train set and how he had gotten the other neighborhood kids to bring their tracks and train cars to his house to build a huge neighborhood setup in his basement. After he had gone on at some length, the client could no longer contain his anger about being, as it were, derailed: "Why are you telling me about *your* trains?" he demanded. The therapist hesitated, then, "with that level, impersonal voice we reserve for confiding something intimate, he said lamely, 'I was just trying to be friendly'" (Nichols, 1995, p. 14).

Real empathy is rarely communicated by the minister's telling the other person a story that demonstrates that the minister has had a similar experience. If she were to tell the man who is experiencing a debilitating confusion about a time when she too was very confused, hoping thereby to communicate her empathy, the feelings evoked in him are likely to be similar to those of the man in Nichols' story. The only common element in the therapist's and client's experiences is their train sets. For the client, the story was told in the context of his exploration of his relationship to his father, whereas for the therapist, the story was about his role in getting the other kids to pool their train sets. These were very different experiences, and, even if they had not been, the fact that the therapist had a similar experience does not necessarily mean that he is therefore more capable of entering empathetically into the other's experience than if he had not had such an experience. For example, the minister who had an experience of debilitating confusion earlier in life may have found it so disconcerting that she cannot bring herself to enter the experiential world of the man who has come to her for help. Her account of her own experience of confusion some years ago may, in fact, have the intention (probably unconscious) of distancing herself from his present confusion.

Some readers may feel that the accurate communication of empathy is dangerous for ministers because they may enter the experiential world of the other so fully that they lose all sense of the boundaries between themselves and the other. Although I will discuss boundaries at greater length in chapter 5, it should be noted here that the self-abandonment that Rogers has in mind, or "the obliviousness to the boundaries that constitute and define the self" that Dittes is speaking about, is a provisional one, arranged or established for the time being, so that the minister can truly appreciate (Nichols' word) the perspective or point of view of the other. In other words, one temporarily suspends one's value judgments, resistance, and defenses, and sees the world from the perspective of a person who is confused about life. The minister may ordinarily have little tolerance for confusion or for persons who seem to "go around in a fog," and she may have spent the better part of her life avoiding situations in which she might be thrown into the kind of confusion she personally experienced years earlier. What she is being asked to do now is not to merge with the man she is providing counsel, but to cross the gulf that currently separates the clarity that exemplifies her life and the confusion that exemplifies the other's life. She enters the other's experiencing at the point of his confusion. It is not that her life merges with his, for, after all, her life of relative clarity and his present life of debilitating confusion have little, if any, common ground, much less basis for interpenetration or merging. What the minister *does* give herself away to is the confusion that the other person is experiencing. She walks in and around this world and takes its measure, feeling it as fully and profoundly as she is able to do, and out of this immersion she communicates her understanding of how it is with him. If, later in their conversation, his confusion begins to lift, in part because he *has* felt understood, the minister will be equally prepared to enter this brave new world of the other's experience, as reflected, for example, in his resolve to try a course of action that, if it works out, will enable him to leave his current muddle behind.

Communicating genuine respect. Our respect for the other is communicated by our treatment of the other as someone of worth who has the potential for growth (Switzer, 1979, p. 77). It is also expressed through our confidence in this person's ability eventually to make decisions in a responsible way. As Switzer points out, respect is not communication primarily, and certainly not exclusively, by the specific words, "I respect you; I value your worth as a person." Such a statement may actually feel condescending or patronizing: "So what qualifies you to say that *you* respect *me?*" Rather, it is communicated through our "persistent focused attention which enables us to communicate empathy with accuracy. Struggling to understand and coming to understand another person, and showing that understanding, is a powerful statement about our sense of his or her worth" (p. 78). Thus, the condition of respect is closely tied to the condition of empathy, as they are mutually reinforcing.

Switzer identifies several ways in which a preacher may show *disrespect* for the congregation. Two of these are especially relevant to the minister as counselor. First is a tendency to be *patronizing,* or treating the other as if he lacks the capacity to understand and/or the freedom and maturity to make his own judgments and decisions. This is perhaps most common when counseling a very young or very old person, but it is also a factor when a male minister is providing counsel to a female parishioner, or when a more educated minister is giving counsel to a less educated person. One can be patronizing toward another without adopting a haughty or supercilious tone of voice. It may occur, for example, when the minister makes an observation and then repeats it a couple more times as though it were too subtle for the other person to understand the first time it was said. A patronizing attitude or tone may also be communicated through questions designed to force the other to think about her problem or situation more systematically or more logically. One minister in pastoral counseling training, for example, conveyed through his questions his feeling that the counselee was not paying careful enough attention to what her husband was saying to her. When she would recount what her husband had said, he would ask her, "So what does that mean? What is he saying?" implying that to anyone who was capable of thinking, the answers should be obvious (Justes, 1985).

On the other hand, an example of respect involves a minister who had taken a troubled teenage boy to a local fast-food restaurant to have a conversation because the boy's mother was trying to dissuade him from his desire to transfer to another high school for its fine theater program (see Capps, 1990, chap. 5). Instead of doing what the boy's mother had asked him to do—reinforce her efforts to dissuade her son—the minister encouraged the boy to talk about his love for the theater, and he affirmed the boy's judgment that if his desire was to go into acting, the other high school would be much better able to help him prepare for this. He did not attempt to discourage the boy from his aspirations to become an actor, as his mother had done, on the grounds that it is a career in which few succeed, and he credited the boy's ability to think for himself by agreeing with him that the other high school would be better for him, given his aspirations. Because he communicated respect for the boy, it was possible for the boy to talk to him about his own misgivings about transferring from one high school to another and about a career in acting. These were misgivings and doubts that he could not express to his parents because they had placed him in the position of having to defend his ideas and desires.

The second form of disrespect is *manipulation.* Switzer (1979)describes this as a preacher's use of the sermon to manipulate a congregation into making a response that the preacher has already decided for them. It is one thing to preach passionately and persuasively, and another thing to be manipulative and controlling. A similar manipulation occurs in counseling when the minister knows in advance where she wants the conversation to end up, so anything that threatens to take the conversation in a different direction is blocked. Often, such manipulation may disguise itself as providing guidance, and it may be that, in some cases, the line between guidance and manipulation is difficult to draw. Guidance, however, implies that the person receiving counsel will experience the conversation as one in which various outcomes are possible, whereas manipulation suggests that there is only one possible outcome, and this outcome has been decided in advance. For example, the same counselor who suggested to his counselee that she was not paying careful enough attention to what her husband was saying to her was determined to impress upon her that her husband really was in love with her in spite of the fact that he was inattentive to her and did nothing to show that he really cared about her. In fact, she now doubted that he had *ever* loved her. Instead of crediting her experience, much less entering empathetically into her experience of feeling that her husband did not love her and never had, the counselor directed his efforts toward persuading her that her perceptions were wrong, that they couldn't possibly be warranted.

There are many other ways in which a minister may be disrespectful toward the other person, such as becoming *impatient* when it takes the other person a longer time than most people to verbalize what is on his mind. The minister, frustrated by the slow pace of the conversation, may begin supplying the words the parishioner is struggling for, and may also assume that slowness of speech is evidence that he does not think very well, which can result in a patronizing tone as well. *Impatience* may also be felt toward a person who appears to talk–and reflect–in circles, exhibiting little appreciation for the logical flow of thoughts. The minister may find himself trying to teach her to order her thoughts instead of recognizing that this is the way she thinks through an issue or problem.

Still another form of disrespect is being *too lax*, as when the minister allows the other person to miss appointments without prior notification or explanation. One may also be too lax in allowing a person to trivialize the occasion by engaging in superficial or flippant talk, or in some other way make a mockery of what the minister, as counselor, represents. This is different from genuine "resistance," where the person receiving counsel is struggling with the very issue of whether to discuss and explore the problem that prompted her to request this meeting, and who therefore avoids the issue by talking about the weather or her conversation with a friend about an unrelated matter, or suggests that the problem she had wanted to talk about has completely resolved itself (for an instance of the latter, see Dittes, 1999b, chap. 11). Instead, what I have reference to here is behavior comparable to a high school student who makes faces at the teacher and emits grunting sounds at regular intervals while the teacher is attempting to explain today's math lesson. If such behavior is a sign of disrespect for the counselor, so, too, is the counselor's laxness with the person who is being counseled. It suggests that the minister does not view the other as a person of worth or dignity, but instead takes his disrespectful behavior as a true reflection of who he is.

Concreteness. Switzer says that "our task in counseling is to assist the other person in being very specific and detailed about feelings and experiences and their meanings" (1979, pp. 82–83). For example, if a person says, "I have really been upset lately," the counselor encourages her to identify more precisely what "upset" suggests or means. This may involve finding a more precise word or phrase. Is she, Switzer asks, upset sad, upset mad, or upset fearful? It could also entail, however, asking her to provide an illustration of what "upset" means. A therapist who does not take for granted that he knows what a client is experiencing when she says, "I am depressed" asks her to describe times when she is "depressed" and then describe times when she is "not depressed" or when her "depression" has temporarily lifted (see Capps, 1998, pp. 139–141). The therapeutic goal then becomes to find ways to increase the times when she is "not depressed." The concreteness is in the two stories she tells about when she is "depressed" and "not depressed."

The same approach might be used, for example, when a husband proclaims that his wife is a "perfectionist" or a wife complains that her husband "lacks ambition." These words and their meanings may seem self-evident, but the minister perceives that they are laden with emotion, and he wants to find some point of entry into the experiential worlds that these words simultaneously reveal and disguise. Does "perfectionist" in this case mean that his wife criticizes his every move? Or does it mean that she holds herself to such a high standard of behavior and decorum that she cannot enjoy life, which both worries and saddens him? Does "lacks ambition" in this case mean that her husband puts very little effort into his work? Or does it mean that he is so devoted to the work he is currently doing that he refuses to consider opportunities for advancement? One way to find out is to encourage the speaker to say more about what "perfectionist" or "lacks ambition" means. Another is to ask the speaker to provide a "for instance."

Concreteness, however, also applies to the minister's own verbal expressions. To say to Mrs. Smith, "I am sure your father's death has been a great shock to you" may elicit the response, "No, I knew he was dying. If anything, it was a great relief to me" (see Hiltner, 1949, p. 37). Perhaps a natural death *should* be more "shocking" to us than it is, but "shock" usually applies to accidental death and unexpected suicide. The minister's misjudgment in this case was in his assumption that he knew— on the basis of past experience? or his intuitive powers?–how her father's death had affected her. Until one has entered the experiential world of the other, one cannot be sure of very much, and this is certainly true concerning the other person's emotions surrounding the death of a close relative.

A better use of words, more acutely in tune with the bereaved person's experiential world, was the minister's question of a parishioner who had lost her husband several weeks earlier, "How has it been with you since John's death?" (See Cryer and Vayhinger, 1962, p. 67). The "it" in his question, while seemingly vague, is, paradoxically perhaps, precise in its imprecision. He did not say, "How has life been treating you?" a far more diffuse way of putting it, and undoubtedly callous sounding as well. And the phrase "with you" is beautifully focused and concrete. We are not surprised that this simple, direct question elicited not only an account of how the woman had been getting along but also a full narrative of the day's events that led up to her husband's heart attack and his death that evening. In contrast, the minister who asked a woman whose father and husband had recently died, "How is everything today?" received a very noncommittal, "As well as can be expected, I guess" (p. 71). "Everything" is much too general and encompassing, and, for someone who may already be feeling overwhelmed, the question itself reinforces this sense of things. With the loss of her husband and father, "everything" has gone awry, but perhaps "something," if it can be identified and focused on, offers some promise and possible grounds for hope.

For persons who are seminary trained, one of the most difficult challenges that providing counsel for another person poses is that of learning–or relearning–to talk in concrete ways. Seminary education often encourages the use of abstractions–"humanity," "church," "sin," "mission," "Godself," "involvement," "commitment," "faith." These are important words, but they are not very descriptive. As I have argued in *The Poet's Gift* (1993a), one of the best ways to recover one's sensitivity to concrete language is by reading poetry, for in poetry each word is carefully chosen. Denise Levertov begins "The Blue Rim of Memory" with the line, "The way sorrow enters the bone is with stabs and hoverings" (Levertov, 1978, p. 93). There is no room in poetry for the rather facile "great shock" that the minister assumed Miss Smith was feeling on the occasion of her father's death. In a poem about his deceased father, Li-Young Lee confesses that he was "a remarkable disappointment to his father" (1990, p. 39). The word "remarkable" removes this comment from the world of cliché and places it within a richer, more nuanced experiential world. What does it mean to be not merely a garden-variety disappointment to one's now-deceased father, but one who disappointed his father *remarkably*? Is he saying that he disappointed his father in an unusual, perhaps even extraordinary way? But might he also be implying that, in some strange or even perverse way, he *exceeded* his father's expectations for him, that the disappointment was not so much in the fact that he fell short–though perhaps this was true in a sense–but that he fell completely outside his father's more narrow and circumscribed range of expectations?

Of course, poets have the luxury of being able to spend hours, days, and even weeks searching for the word that communicates precisely the experiential world they want to express in language. If a minister has some of this luxury in the writing of a sermon, she rarely has it in the course of talking with another person in a situation of counsel. It may also be the case that the other person does not feel any particular need to be precise or exacting in her own use of words. If the minister says, "Upset in what way?" she may respond, "Well, you know, just upset." She may even feel she is being interrogated and lash back, "Don't tell me you have never been upset."

Still, as we also learn from poets, concreteness is a verbal skill that can be learned with practice, and this may apply to both the minister and the person being counseled. We have all had the experience of discovering that, after several conversations with a friend during which we each came to know how the other thinks, the quality of our manner of communicating seemed to have improved. As we take our leave of each other, we find ourselves saying, "Now, that was a great conversation!" In a clinical practicum taught by one of Carl Rogers' associates, we listened to the audiotapes of a woman who was very inarticulate when she first entered therapy. By the end of therapy, however, she was not only speaking much more freely but had also acquired a whole new experiential vocabulary. The practicum instructor noted that while her marital problems had been more or less successfully addressed, a more lasting effect of therapy was that she was now able to verbalize what was occurring in her experiential world. Concreteness can be acquired or, for those who have gone through an extensive educational process that deals in abstractions, it can be reacquired.

Genuineness. In this context, genuineness and the communication that flows from it mean something different from not misrepresenting oneself and one's intentions. (This form of disingenuousness or insincerity is a boundary issue, and thus more relevant to our discussion in chapter 5.) Here, genuineness "refers to the degree to which we are in touch with our own feelings at any given time, our motivations for doing what we are doing" (Switzer, 1979, p. 85). Thus, genuineness is a measure of "the extent to which there is a correspondence or congruence between our own experience and our awareness of that experience" (p. 85). Switzer emphasizes the role played by defenses and distortions in keeping our own experiences from view, and he notes that anxiety is often at the root of these defenses and distortions. If, for example, we have strong anxieties about death, sexual matters, divorce, or the expression of anger, it is very difficult to keep our feelings—or defenses against these feelings—from inhibiting or distorting conversation with a person who is terminally ill, who wants to discuss a problem involving sexual behavior or feelings, who is considering divorce, or who expresses anger or stimulates anger in us.

In *The Abuse of Power* (1991), James N. Poling relates his counseling experiences with a man who was sexually abusing his five-year-old son (pp. 54–61). Because he *was* aware of his revulsion at what the man was doing, Poling was able to counsel him. On the other hand, a male seminarian who had befriended a single man at church experienced a debilitating anxiety when they went together to a restaurant after an evening service and the man confided that he enjoyed dressing in women's clothing. The seminarian was concerned that the other man had "misunderstood" his pastoral interest in him, but it also bothered him that a man who seemed so decorous in church should have such a "bizarre" private life. He found he could no longer "be himself" in the relationship, and he made an excuse the next time the man suggested going out for pie and coffee after an evening service.

Other types of anxiety leading to a relative absence of genuineness are anxiety regarding certain "kinds" or "types" of persons (such as a person of a much higher social or professional status) and anxiety about one's own lack of expertise or experience as one who counsels. Such anxieties often require a decision, either to keep them in the background–being aware of them but leaving them unspoken because talking about them will not contribute to the helping process–or openly acknowledging them, thus possibly risking that the other will be scared off. I would emphasize that the decision *not* to inform the other about one's anxieties is not, in itself, a lack of genuineness, for oftentimes it is better not to burden the other person with one's own anxieties when he already has anxieties of his own relating to the problem for which he seeks the minister's counsel.

Perhaps a useful analogy is the mother who has the awesome task of communicating to her first baby, through her demeanor, that she knows what she is doing, for her expression of confidence will provide her infant with the "calming structure" that he needs in order to feel secure (Kohut, 1984, p. 30). She needs, as it were, to create a credible, believable world for him. This is precisely the opposite of the TV character Sledge Hammer, a takeoff on Mickey Spillane's detective hero Mike Hammer, who says, "Trust me, I know what I'm doing," while making a total mess of a crime investigation. The minister who is too forthcoming about her anxieties may undermine the confidence the other needs in order to make optimum use of the helping process. The doctor who responds to the patient's declaration that this is the first time she has been in surgery with, "Well, that's a coincidence, as it's the first time I've performed surgery" may create in the patient an anxiety–bordering on panic–that has a negative influence on her recovery. A seminarian or minister just out of seminary may not "feel" like a counselor, but *is* one by virtue of professional calling, so it is not a lack of genuineness to act like one. The absence or lack of genuineness is an internal process, one where the minister is unaware of his anxiety–or any other emotion that may be inhibiting or distorting his ability to hear and respond to what the other person is communicating–and of the role that it is playing in the way he goes about providing counsel. The issue, as Switzer, following Rogers, expresses it, is the *congruence* between our own experience and our awareness of that experience. In the chapter on managing boundaries, I will discuss this "self-awareness" in more detail.

Appropriate self-disclosure. A related condition of effective listening is appropriate self- disclosure, which Switzer describes as one's willingness "to be known as a human being to the other person. Not only are we *aware* of who we are, including the feelings and motivations that we have at a particular time, but we have the ability to communicate ourselves in appropriate ways to the other person" (1979, pp. 86–87). In one sense, this bridge has already been crossed in the case of ministers, for in most cases they are already known as human beings to the other person. Unlike psychotherapists or specialized pastoral counselors, they have already been in contact with the other person, and it is likely that these very contacts are the reason why the other person has sought their counsel. The setting in which counseling occurs, however, frequently gives the other person a glimpse into a side of the minister that is inaccessible in any other setting. Because it is more private than the other settings in which the minister and other person have experienced each other, and because the other person is making self-disclosures, the opportunity, even the desire, to be self-disclosive in return can be very strong. For a person whose other roles are usually quite public–preaching, teaching, leading and participating in meetings, and so on–the longing to "let one's hair down" is something that virtually every minister will experience. The minister who does not have this experience probably isn't very human.

The key word here is therefore "appropriate." For Switzer, the most important reason for self-disclosure by the minister is to enable the other person to have "the feeling of being a part of an authentic human relationship" (p. 87). He emphasizes, however, the importance of timing, noting that "too much self-disclosure too soon can hinder rather than facilitate the other person's exploration," and he also stresses that it should be "linked in some helpful way to the other person's needs right at this moment...We must guard against the kind of disclosure that comes primarily out of the strength of our own need to disclose ourselves" (p. 87). Too much talk about oneself, especially if it occurs early in the process, can frighten the other person away. While one's self-disclosure may be intended as a way to express one's empathy, it can be misunderstood as an expression of one's own neediness. The other person may say to herself, "She needs me as much as I thought I needed her, and I'm in no position to help her. After all, if I didn't have troubles of my own, I wouldn't be here, talking like this." Self-disclosure can also be self-indulgent, and can make the other feel as though he, not the minister, is a captive listener. It may even cause the other person to censure her own thoughts and feelings because "a married woman who obviously loves her children as this person does couldn't possibly approve of my wanting to get a divorce and leave my children with my husband." In this case, the attempt to establish rapport on the grounds that "we are both young married women struggling to raise two young children" has not had the intended effect.

Switzer also mentions that self-disclosure may help the other feel more fully understood. In my own view, however, this is often better communicated through one's capacity to empathize and communicate this empathy than through the relating of a personal experience similar to the one that the other person is relating. To say, "I lost my mother when I was about your age" is normally not as helpful as using one's own loss as a means to enter the experiential world of the other. (Nichols' illustration of the client and therapist who had train sets when they were boys is illustrative in this regard.) Moreover, the minister's experience of losing her *mother* may be less comparable to what the other person is feeling than the loss of her *father* or her experience of greeting her dramatically altered brother on his return from military service overseas and realizing that she had "lost" the wonderful brother she had known before. The minister who discloses that she lost her mother "when I was your age" may also cause the other person to think or feel, "But for you the experience was long enough ago that you have come to terms with it. For me, it is still painful." Thus, what appears to be a common experience—loss of mother—is only superficially so.

Exceptions to this general rule are shared experiences that, when disclosed, are likely to create a special bond between the minister and the other person, such as their common loss of a child at a very early age, or the suicidal death of a son or daughter, or the fact that both have a gay son or lesbian daughter. There are some shared experiences that, if not disclosed, would prompt the other person to say, "I cannot believe that all the while that I was telling him about my experience he did not share his own experience. Why did he hold it in?" If she discovered from a third party that the minister had had the same experience as hers, she might, if it had not been disclosed, chastise herself: "How could I have been so stupid—or insensitive—to talk about my problem to a person who apparently hasn't come to terms with it in his own life." Here again, the key word is *appropriate* self-disclosure.

Another consideration is the need of the other person to experience the minister in this context as "the counselor." For some parishioners, their anxieties will be increased, not diminished, by the minister's self-disclosure. To illustrate, I had been going to the same medical doctor for several years and we had developed a good doctor-patient relationship, much of it centered around some good-natured joking about which of us was in better physical condition. One day, however, he told me, more or less in passing, that his wife had left him and was subsequently placed in a mental health facility, and that he was now faced with the gargantuan task of raising four children, all under the age of ten. When I asked him if there was any hope of a reconciliation once she was released, he said, "No, she's got her demons. Even if she wanted to come back, I couldn't handle her and the kids too." Suddenly, our roles were reversed, and I was the one who was asking him the kinds of questions he had routinely asked of me: "So, how have you been?" "Any problems or symptoms?"

I found this role reversal rather disorienting, and I left his office feeling that I wanted to do something for him, but what would this be? Our relationship was strictly that of doctor and patient, and it seemed inappropriate for me to ask him—a person with whom I had no contact outside his office—if he wanted to go to lunch where we could talk about his self-disclosure further. I realized, during these reflections, that I needed to see him as the "doctor" and not as a person who was going through a very difficult period in his life. I am glad that he told me about these difficulties, and was rather flattered that he felt our relationship was such that he *could* tell me about them, but the experience also strengthened my conviction that the minister should keep a rather tight rein on the need for self-disclosure, as this can become a burden for the other person and also undermine, to some degree at least, his need for the minister to be "the counselor." No doubt, too, certain persons are more open to hearing the self-disclosures of others, and this very fact—their own emotional availability to others—may well be a reason for seeking counsel, as they feel overburdened from carrying the cares and worries of others. (Other issues involved in "appropriate" self-disclosure are best reserved for our discussion in chapter 5 of managing boundaries.)

By issuing so many cautionary notes about self-disclosure, I hope that I have not implied that the minister needs to be tight-lipped and anal-retentive. Appropriate self-disclosure signals a willingness to be known as a human being to another person and the absence of a need to hide behind the facade of one's pastoral identity or the counselor role. Nothing can be more maddening than the minister who affects the tone and demeanor of the resident psychiatrist and responds to the other person's communications with a series of "hmms" and an occasional raised eyebrow. Appropriate self-disclosure can also be genuinely valuable to a person who is having to find her way through an experience she has never had before. Disclosing how one tried to navigate through similar uncharted waters can be a means of expressing understanding of what the other person is going through. It may also provide her some guidance, perhaps because it offers suggestions for how she might navigate these waters herself, but also, and perhaps more importantly, because there is a certain solidarity in the knowledge that she is not the first one—nor will she be the last one—to have this experience of not knowing where she is and where it may all come out. She will also be able to see the minister as one who appears to have survived a period of confusion and darkness and who seems to be relatively healthy, and this may, in and of itself, provide some encouragement. If such self-disclosure is appropriately understated (not "I had my dark times and, hey, I'm a better woman for it," but "I managed to muddle through somehow"), it adds an element of solidarity ("I'm in this thing with you") to the empathy that is already present.

Confrontation. Switzer points out that confrontation does not mean verbal shock treatment, accusations, harshness, or punishing types of statements (1979, p. 90). Instead, it is defined very precisely in terms of *discrepancies* that the minister perceives in the other person's communication. For example, there may be a discrepancy between what the other person says and how she says it, a discrepancy that the minister may gently point out: "You are talking about being angry with your son, and yet, at least in this moment, you seem more perplexed than angry." Or there is a discrepancy between what the other person identifies as his goals and the actions he is taking to realize them: "You are saying that you want to move up the corporate ladder, and yet you confess that you are not doing the very things you would need to do in order to achieve this. You refuse, for example, to 'suck up to' the guy who runs your division." Another type of discrepancy is the other person's perception of herself and her actual achievements: "You continue to talk about yourself as a failure as a parent, and yet your children are doing well in school, and they seem happy and well-adjusted." Or, "You tell me about how intelligent your son is, and yet he is having a very tough time with his college courses." These illustrations indicate that such confrontations are not designed to catch the other person in a logical inconsistency—it *is* possible to be very intelligent and *not* be doing well in college—but to encourage the other person to take a closer look at what appears to be a discrepancy to another person, but which may have a very good explanation: "That's just it. My children *are* doing well, and yet I can't seem to take any personal credit for this. Instead, I tell myself that they have turned out well in spite of the fact that they had me for a mother. Why do you suppose I feel this way?"

While Switzer emphasizes the noting of discrepancies as inherently confrontational, it may also be noted that the third condition for effective listening, *concreteness*, may also be experienced as confrontational. We tend to talk rather vaguely about ourselves and others, and when we are deprived of this vagueness in the interests of greater concreteness, we may feel as confronted as we would when a discrepancy is pointed out to us. The husband who says that his wife is a perfectionist may feel confronted when the minister indicates that he is uncertain what he means by this. He may look puzzled ("I thought everyone knew what 'perfectionist' means"), respond somewhat defensively ("I thought it was obvious to anyone who has spent time, as you have done, in her presence"), or even lash out in anger ("You don't believe me? Spend a day at our house and you'll see what I mean"). Similarly, the wife who says that her husband "lacks ambition" may feel confronted when the minister asks her to say what she means by this: "What do you want me to say? That my husband's a lazy, good-for-nothing bum?" Here, the minister's request for greater concreteness may seem to have failed, but not necessarily. The minister now knows what he did not know before, that "lacks ambition" means that he doesn't apply himself, *not* that he is satisfied to work in the company's machine shop at tasks he enjoys and forgoes opportunities to move into a managerial position. Even so, when we seek greater concreteness, we need to be aware that this can feel as confrontational as when we point out a discrepancy.

Switzer emphasizes that confrontation is an "expression of love" because it especially seeks to help others become in touch with the reality of their own beings (p. 92). Helping the woman to truly experience herself as a good mother may prove difficult, but the fact that the discrepancy between her children's success and her perception of herself as a failure is now out on the table is a good starting point. The minister's confrontation in this case was truly loving, as her intention was to help the other woman see that she was being too hard on herself. Also, to the extent that she communicates her low self-image as a mother to her children, she places them in the same position as she has placed the minister, that of having to provide her continual reassurances that she is not the failure she proclaims herself to be. If her children feel vulnerable to failure themselves, they may secretly resent providing their mother the reassurances she appears to need—or crave—besides carrying the additional burden of proving through their achievements that their mother *has* been a good parent to them. Thus, as Switzer also notes, as an expression of love, confrontation not only helps to bring persons into "greater harmony with themselves" but also with "the social realities"—in this case, the children—which they influence and are influenced by (p. 92).

In a similar way, Ralph L. Underwood notes in *Empathy and Confrontation in Pastoral Care* (1985) that the three conditions of respect, empathy, and confrontation go together. Thus, "Respect is a moral connection that discloses how empathy and certain ways of being confrontive go together. Respectful considerate confrontation goes hand in hand with empathy" and "for all their differences, there is no fundamental contradiction when ministers who are empathic are also confrontational, so long as there is respect" (p. 90). It is easy, of course, to justify being inappropriately confrontational by claiming to be "speaking the truth in love"—such "truth-sayers" rarely love the other—or prefacing a confrontational statement by saying, "With all due respect." The confrontation being described here—the noting of discrepancies— is unlikely to lead to such abuses, however, because it is expressed not as a challenge, but as a query: "I see a difference here between how you perceive yourself as a parent and how your children have actually turned out. Do you see it too?"

When I was in my first quarter of clinical pastoral education in a very large, multibuilding mental health facility, I was talking with a patient who informed me that she had been hospitalized for nine years. Later in the conversation she made reference to her children, a six-year-old boy and a three-year-old girl. Believing that herein lay the source of her delusional system, I seized on what I perceived to be an obvious factual discrepancy in her account: "If you have been here in the hospital for nine years, you couldn't have a six- and a three-year-old child!" My sense of being a local version of the prophet Nathan confronting David with the discrepancy between his words and his actions in the Bathsheba-Uriah-David triangle, and my perception of myself as junior psychiatrist, were both utterly shattered when the patient responded with obvious amusement: "You don't know much about this place, do you?" Then she proceeded to tell me about the underground tunnels that connected the hospital buildings and about the sexual activities that took place there between patients and members of the hospital staff. Ever since, I have tried to point out what I perceive to be discrepancies in other persons' communication in a very tentative and provisional way, for what may look discrepant to the observer may prove to be not only consistent but also an occasion for personal enlightenment. The minister who is careful in this regard has a right to expect that others will be similarly circumspect in their confrontations toward her.

Immediacy. The final condition for facilitating listening is immediacy, which refers more generally to how both persons are experiencing the relationship between them, but more particularly to the willingness of the helping person to use the present relationship—right here and now—to help the other person understand her own feelings and behavior in the relationship itself. As Switzer points out, "This requires a great deal of sensitivity, since the helping person must recognize expressions on the part of the other that in various disguised forms might be referring to the relationship between the two of them" (1979, p. 92).

For example, a parishioner might begin to be very critical of other ministers, noting that ministers like to be the "object of attention," but they never seem to have time to pay attention to anyone else. As Switzer notes, empathy alone may prompt the minister in this case to sense the other person's feeling that she does not receive the attention she desires and perhaps feels that she deserves. The fact that she has singled out ministers for special criticism in this regard, however, would suggest that she may well have in mind the very person she is speaking with at the moment. Thus, the condition of immediacy will lead him to recognize and comment on his impression that she may be feeling that *he* has not been paying enough attention to *her,* and that she may even be experiencing this neglect as they are talking together. Perhaps she has felt that he seems distracted, or that he has not been very empathetic or respectful toward her. Maybe he has not arranged the social environment (for example, his office) so that their conversation was not subject to interruption. Whatever the actual case may be, his recognition that her comment has immediacy—not merely ministers in general or not simply his behavior in other contexts, but right here and now—and his communication of this recognition to her will enable them to focus on what is going on between them. Are her feelings, for example, justified? If he has been taking phone calls during the conversation, they undoubtedly are. If he has seemed distracted—thinking about the sermon he needs to write—her feelings are clearly justified. If, on the other hand, she left a message at his home saying that she needed to talk with him and the issue was urgent, yet has been talking about rather insignificant matters for twenty minutes or so, her feelings are not particularly justified. In the latter case, her raising of the issue about his inattentiveness allows him, in turn, to express his dismay over the fact that he has responded to her request for a meeting to discuss an urgent matter and instead she has been talking about what seem to him to be rather insignificant concerns.

It was something of an inside joke among those of us who were trained in the client-centered method of counseling that if we were ever stumped for something to say to the client, we could always fall back on, "That's what you're feeling *now*." We might have little if any clue to what the "that" in this instance might be, but at least our comment would keep the focus on the immediate. While this was a response of last resort, it makes the point that immediacy is important because there is always the possibility of the helping person's being "out of sync"—in thoughts and emotions—with where the other person's thoughts and emotions are at this moment. Sometimes (as noted in the previous discussion of impatience as a sign of disrespect) the minister is way out ahead, having already anticipated where the conversation is likely to be leading. Other times, the minister is far behind, still mulling over in her mind what the other person said several minutes ago. These timing or temporal discrepancies often occur in conversations between friends (where we can hardly wait for the other person to complete a story so that we can tell a story of our own) or between spouses (where the husband is still asking himself, "Now, what did she mean by that remark?" while his wife has already moved on to a different topic).

The fact that this is a common occurrence should be an encouragement to the minister to acknowledge her failure to stay in temporal sync with the other person, and to ask him to go back to something he had previously said but which hadn't fully registered with her because she was still mulling over something he had said even earlier or about where the conversation might be heading. Instead of being disruptive, or a cause for resentment ("You're not listening to me?"), these acknowledgments and accompanying requests are almost always viewed positively by the other person, as they communicate to him that one *does* want to understand what he is saying. The opportunity to revisit his earlier comments may also enable him to explore them more deeply, to see some features in them that he did not see on his earlier account.

A different and perhaps less defensible—though understandable—type of immediacy loss is when the minister finds himself thinking about something unrelated to the conversation. In the case noted above, the woman who complained about inattentive ministers may have been aware that the minister was not listening to her but was thinking about something else entirely. She may have realized this when she asked a question ("Do you think I was wrong to speak to her that way?") and he didn't answer. Ironically, this problem has bearing on Switzer's acknowledgment that it is "not entirely clear to me as to how this condition may be effectively furnished with any regularity in preaching, especially right at the moment that it seems to be called for" (1979, p. 93). The irony is in the fact that parishioners often find themselves thinking about unrelated matters while "listening" to the preacher!

In both cases, the listener's distractibility may or may not be "meaningful." A parishioner may have tuned out on the sermon merely because there is something she considers more important on her mind (such as a report that she needs to have finished and on her boss's desk first thing Monday morning). Or she may have "tuned out" because the sermon topic, or the way the preacher was approaching the topic, made her "upset" ("What does *he* know about motherhood?"). Similarly, the minister's distractibility during a conversation where she is providing counsel may be because there is something more pressing on her mind (the funeral she must conduct this afternoon for a high school boy killed in a car accident). Or she may not be listening attentively because the subject or the way the person was approaching the subject stirred unpleasant emotions ("How can she talk so blithely about her plans for an extended vacation with her boyfriend in the Bahamas while leaving her children at home to fend for themselves?"). "Tuning out" is a mild form of dissociation, and dissociation is an available defense we all have at our disposal when the situation is too threatening. What the minister owes to herself and to the other person is that she enter empathetically into her own experiencing in order to discover why she is having difficulty attending to this conversation: "Why does the other person's unconcern for her children not only evoke moral indignation in me but also the need to, as it were, escape the scene altogether?"

It is possible, of course, that the minister is neither distracted by some other more pressing concern or defending against the anxiety the conversation has evoked in her, but that she is simply thoroughly bored by this particular individual. She wants to be empathetic and respectful, but she finds the conversation dull and tiresome. There is a character in a Monty Python routine who believes that he is "invisible" because no one responds to what he has to say. What he does not realize is that the things he has to say are so dull and uninteresting that it is amazing the others do not leave the room altogether. A general understanding in psychotherapeutic circles is that if a therapist finds a particular client boring, this is an appropriate basis for referral, as this is not only likely to be fatal to the success of the therapy but also, and more hopefully, another therapist may find this individual interesting. As William James once noted, we believe in that which we find interesting and disbelieve in that which does not interest us (James, 1984).

The minister may not enjoy the luxury of referral, especially if the problem is that the parishioner's conversation is dull and tiresome. Ministers usually make referrals when they find that the problem is beyond their competence. A parishioner whose issues produce boredom in the listener is probably not experiencing problems that are beyond the minister's competence. Rather, she may feel that they are *beneath* her competence! I suggest, therefore, that the minister may want to become a student, as it were, of the problem of boredom, as this may provide insight into her own experiential world and perhaps that of many of her parishioners.

The psychoanalyst Otto Fenichel wrote an essay in 1934 on the psychology of boredom. He defined it as an unpleasurable experience of a lack of impulse and noted its connection with depression, loneliness, and restlessness. He also noted that boredom may be a state of tension in which instinctual aims are repressed. Prisoners and patients in long-term care facilities may become bored because of having to repress sexual desires. (Later, in the chapter on boundary issues, I will discuss ways in which ministers' lives are similar to those of prisoners and patients). Fenichel distinguishes between "pathological" and "normal" boredom, noting that while in both states "something expected does not occur," the difference is that in pathological boredom this expected event fails to occur because one "represses his instinctual action out of anxiety," whereas in normal boredom it fails to occur because the external world does not give what "we have a right to expect." Thus, in pathological boredom, the inadequacy lies within, while in normal boredom, the inadequacy is external.

The minister who finds a particular parishioner boring is probably experiencing normal boredom, as the parishioner is apparently not providing sufficiently interesting material, whether because it seems rather trivial (she is describing her cat's sleeping habits, or he is explaining how he reduced the font size so that his paper would not exceed the ten page limit), because they have been over the same ground several times, or some similar reason. If, however, the minister is experiencing boredom where these reasons do not apply, he should consider the possibility that his boredom is pathological, due to the repression of instinctual aims. If this view of the matter seems overly psychoanalytic, consider the following story related to me by a preschool teacher. A four-year-old girl informed the teacher that she didn't want to go on the field trip that was planned for the following day because "field trips are boring." The teacher was about to tell her about all the interesting things they would see on tomorrow's field trip when a boy, overhearing their conversation, said to the girl, "Oh, you just miss your mama!" His comment was immediately followed by another boy's reassurance, "I used to miss my mama too, but I got over it." These boys knew nothing about psychoanalysis, but they had very perceptively put their finger on why the little girl was "bored" by field trips. Separation anxiety was behind her boredom, and the boys not only picked this up, entering into her experiential world because they knew it only too well themselves, but also assured her that she, too, could "get over it." Thus, the minister who experiences boredom while listening to a "tiresome" parishioner or student *may* be experiencing normal boredom—the other person is *truly* boring—but may instead be dealing with boredom that is more pathological, that is, due to instinctual repression out of anxiety (anxiety about what would happen if he did not repress the instinctual needs in question).

I realize that a discussion of boredom may seem to take us far afield from immediacy as a condition of effective listening. But immediacy, like respect, can often be best understood by identifying situations in which it is conspicuous by its absence. As Switzer observes in the case of preaching, immediacy is not something that we can readily put into words. The times that a minister can interrupt the sermon to say, "I see a number of you smiling as though you know exactly what I am talking about," are relatively rare, and drawing attention to the immediacy of the moment may have the effect of undermining it. The counselor *can* say, "That's what you're feeling right now" on occasion, but if he said this often in the course of the counseling hour, the client would certainly become suspicious ("What is this, a favorite mantra of yours?"), and the immediacy of the conversation would be lost. The minister should therefore be attentive to signs–largely within herself–of the absence or loss of immediacy, and search in her own experiential world for the possible reasons for this.

An interactive system. The foregoing discussion of the seven conditions for facilitating effective listening indicates, much like the traditional model of the seven deadly sins, that they are not merely a list of discrete characteristics but an interactive system. Certain conditions reinforce others, and the relative absence of one or more of these conditions will affect the quality of the whole. The experienced therapist does not think of them individually, though she may from time to time take inventory on her therapeutic work in order to ensure that she has not neglected or allowed one or more of these conditions to atrophy. In the pastoral counseling literature, by far the most attention has been given to the first condition–the accurate communication of empathy–and there *is* a sense in which its absence *will* undermine the whole, thus perhaps justifying the general perception that it is the chief of the seven conditions (even as pride is often declared to be the chief of the deadly sins).

As we have seen, however, an exclusive emphasis on empathy, important as it is, can lead to a very skewed understanding of what makes for effective listening. In Underwood's formulation, empathy, confrontation, and respect go together, thus suggesting, perhaps, that in addition to viewing the seven conditions as a system, we should consider how certain conditions form different subsystems. I leave it to the ingenuity of the reader to work these out in greater detail, with the cautionary note that these subsystems are not static, but dynamic; that is, the fact that these three conditions, empathy, confrontation, and respect, may operate together does not preclude their being involved in other dyadic or triadic relationships, such as my own observation that there may be a strong link between confrontation and concreteness.

Concluding Comments

In this chapter I have explored the anxieties that, if they go unrecognized, may inhibit good listening, but, if recognized, may actually contribute to effective listening. I have also discussed the attitudes and conditions that contribute to good listening. These certainly do not cover all the conditions, circumstances, and influences that affect, positively or negatively, the creation of a good listening environment, but they do, in my view, make a strong case for the need to create such an environment. The assumption that lies behind this chapter is that one needs to create a listening environment that is potentially good or helpful in order for conversation to occur regardless of who the minister's conversation partner happens to be. In this sense, the listening environment sketched out here is intended to be generic. Of course, if some students find it difficult to learn in what others may consider an optimal learning environment, and if some students have special needs for which the learning environment provided them is inadequate, the same applies to the listening environment created by the minister. Some will find that the listening environment sketched here is not good or helpful for them, and some will find that it is inadequate for their particular needs. (The latter is usually discussed in the pastoral counseling literature under the heading of "referral.")

These exceptions and special needs, however, do not invalidate the claim that the attitudes and conditions presented here are conducive to a listening environment that will be helpful to the vast majority of the persons who have asked to be listened to. As in the educational environment, some will make more or better use of this resource than others. Among those with whom the minister works, some will never ask for it. Also, unlike the regularly scheduled worship service, class session, or committee meeting, the listening environment presented here has a more "occasional" use. Still, when we take a larger view of the minister as one who provides counsel—not only private one-on-one conversations but also brief, informal encounters in more public settings—we also make the case for a more expansive view of the listening environment itself as one that surrounds and permeates the larger organism in which the minister enacts her professional calling. In this sense, Switzer is exactly right to suggest that the conditions that make for good listening in the private pastoral conversation are conducive to good preaching. This application may, however, be broadened to include the worship service, the classroom, the committee meeting, because the same values that inform the minister's counseling role should also permeate these other environments.

We need, therefore, to heed Nichols' warning that we are ever in danger of losing the "art of listening." Instructive in this regard is his own self-disclosure that the requirement of writing a book on the art of listening threw him into a state of panic and despair, as he realized that just as he began to feel that he was "learning to listen better," he would experience a "setback" that took him all the way back to square one: "But, fortunately or unfortunately, I had a commitment to finish writing this book, and so after a while of brooding in hurt silence I'd go back and try to talk to the person I'd quarreled with—only this time with a firm resolve to listen to his or her side before telling mine" (1995, p. 4).

It is frequently observed that women are better listeners than men. In her article "Female-Friendly Pastoral Care," Carolyn Stahl Bohler (1996, pp. 27–49) places listening at the top of her list of guidelines for counseling and then tells a distressing story about a role play in a counseling course in which a forty-year-old student, the mother of two teenagers, was relating to the male student who had been assigned to "listen to her" that she was three months pregnant and worried both about her own health and that of the future child. She told him about having consulted with various professionals, all of whom verbalized concern about everyone in her family but her ("How would the older children adjust?" "What would be the effect of another baby on her husband's work?"). Yet, after hearing about her resentment and sense of vulnerability—even fear of dying during childbirth—the other student offered to pray "for her" and instead of focusing on her resentment and fear, he intoned, "Lord, help this baby, in this mother's womb." He was "stunned" when she pointed out to him after the exercise that he "had not listened to her at all" (p. 29). Because women are perceived to spend more of their time and energy in a listening role, this is often treated as a professional liability, as if the capacity to listen is a weakness, not a strength, in positions of leadership. On the other hand, men often complain that some women do not listen very well, that they are confrontational in an accusatory way, or that they talk to them in a patronizing manner. And, of course, there are men who are very good listeners.

Some children—both girls and boys—have discovered that listening is their only viable role in a family of talkers, or have had this role assigned to them by a parent who needs "someone to talk to." No doubt, many of these children are found among the ranks of ministers, who continue to accept the burden of listening to the troubles, trials, and tribulations of others. This time, however, they hope that they may be in a position to help other persons come to terms with their problems and not only, as when they were children, to listen helplessly. Could it be that the tendency of ministers to pray at the conclusion of a counseling session has roots in their experience, after listening to a parent pouring out her troubles, of recognizing their own helplessness and therefore asking God to make things better?

Nichols, however, suggests that friends make the best listeners because the relationship between friends is "voluntary and optional; you can leave if you want to, and therefore it's safer to be honest and take risks" (1995, p. 225). The novelist Henry James was considered by his friends to be such a good, fair-minded listener that a husband and wife would independently consult him about their marital problems, with full awareness that the partner would also be consulting him.

We can learn much from our friends' examples. In addition, it is possible to learn from those who have devoted their professional lives as counselors to reclaiming and refining the lost art of listening. Their experience has demonstrated that a good listening environment can be created—by anyone—and that good listening may be intentional, not happen merely by chance. As Noyce puts it, "listening is hard work," but this is true of any art in which one wishes to gain proficiency. In addition, this is precisely why a minister needs to create a good listening environment, so that the wheel does not have to be reinvented each and every time one is asked for counsel. In time, the attitudes and conditions for effective listening may, in fact, become second nature.

2

How to Construct a Conversation

As noted, Michael P. Nichols believes that friends make the best listeners. This is because the relationship between friends, being voluntary and optional, makes it safer to be honest and take risks. In addition, with a friend, "You can talk over painful and embarrassing subjects, reveal self-doubts, try out different sides of yourself, and be who you are" (1995, p. 226). Friends who listen also "make us feel interesting, and their interest inspires us to say more interesting things. Their receptivity is transformative: by listening intently to us, our friends make us feel larger, more alive. That's the glory of friendship" (p. 226). Of course, there is the downside as well. Nichols discusses situations where friends take sides when conflicts develop between friends, where a friend's offer of constructive criticism backfires, and where friends seem to outgrow each other. Explaining why she decided to write a book about gossip, Patricia Meyer Spacks, a professor of English literature at Yale University, relates a personal experience. It involved a close friend, a woman colleague, whom she met early every weekday morning for half an hour of "coffee and reinvigorating conversation" (p. ix). Sometimes a male colleague would come in, his expression seeming to convey contempt at their verbal trivialities as their talk moved from details of their own lives to speculation about others, or from discussion of novels to contemplation of friends' love affairs. Considering their frequently proclaimed, desperate need for time, their husbands could not understand why they counted these minutes together sacred. The two women had difficulty explaining to their husbands why they insisted on these early morning conversations, nor could they even fully explain it to themselves. Spacks concluded that it afforded them a chance to "gossip," and her book was written to redeem gossip from its ignoble connotations.

In *Slim's Table: Race, Respectability, and Masculinity* (1992), Mitchell Duneier focuses his attention on a group of working-class black men who would meet each evening in a cafeteria in the Hyde Park area of Chicago for coffee, dessert, and conversation. One of the men explained to Duneier, a sociology student at the University of Chicago, that this was one occasion in his life where he could participate in "intelligent conversation" (p. 111).

What these three authors—a psychotherapist, an English professor, and a sociology student—seem to agree on is that there is a great need for conversation among friends, a need so great that individuals will make significant sacrifices in order to have these conversations. I believe that Nichols is right in suggesting that conversations between friends should serve as a sort of ideal model for all the other conversations in which we become involved, including those between wives and husbands, parents and children, work associates, and therapist and client. Of course, these other conversations will have dimensions that are not found in a conversation between friends, and the injection of these other dimensions into a conversation between friends—for example, when a friend acts as if he were my therapist—may ruin the conversation, if not the friendship itself: "What are you trying to do, play amateur psychiatrist at my expense?" Even so, the more these conversations approximate a conversation between friends, the more satisfying they are likely to be.

I am especially interested here in Nichols' view that the conversation between therapist and client should have many of the features of a conversation between friends. If this is true of a therapeutic conversation, should it not be equally true of a conversation in which a minister is providing counsel? Several writers in the field of pastoral care and counseling have suggested that the best term for the counseling that ministers do is "pastoral conversation." (Carol Lakey Hess [1996] has made a similar proposal in the field of religious education.) Gaylord

Noyce has used this term to emphasize that the work of the minister is more of a seamless whole than we might otherwise perceive it to be (1981). Conversation is the glue that holds it all together. When we use terms such as "pastoral counseling" or "pastoral psychotherapy," the role of the minister as counselor seems to become more formal, more technical, and more official. In contrast, "pastoral conversation" communicates a less formal, technical, and official interaction between two or more persons, one that more nearly approximates a conversation between friends.

In chapter 5, I will discuss the dangers that are involved when the minister sheds the formalities of her office and asks the other person to think of her as "just a friend." In this chapter, however, I want to emphasize its positive aspects. I have titled this chapter "How to Construct a Conversation" in order to emphasize that a conversation in which the minister understands himself to be providing counsel does not simply happen by chance. It needs to be "made" or "created," and the minister bears primary responsibility for this. Several things should be taken into account as one goes about creating a conversational milieu. I will begin with the most obvious issue, which is, How does the minister respond to what the other person says or communicates?

Responding to the Other

One of the most—perhaps *the* most—pressing concerns that the very idea of assuming the counselor role raises for a seminarian is expressed in the questions, What will I say? What *should* I say? These questions, and the obvious anxiety behind them, are somewhat reminiscent of the rather shy teenager who is going out on her first date: "What will I talk about? What will I say?" If her mother says, "Just be your natural self. You talk with Bobby at school, and he has liked the way you talk with him or he wouldn't have asked you out," such reassuring words are likely to elicit the protest, "But, Mother, he's taking me to a party, and then we're going to Moondoggies after that. *This is different!*" If Eleanor's father happened to be listening in on this conversation, he might make the sage comment that mother and daughter are both right, which, while true, may not seem to be especially helpful. Still, mother is right to say that Eleanor should treat this as not fundamentally different from the other times she has talked with Bobby, and Eleanor is right to point out that there are some important differences. Also, her mother's reassurances are vitally important ("You already know how to talk with Bobby, and he wouldn't have asked you out if he didn't like the way you talk with him."). The anxiety that Eleanor is experiencing, however, suggests that it may be helpful for her mother (or father) to offer her a few "pointers" on how to navigate her way, conversationally speaking, through her first date.

Like Eleanor and Bobby, the minister and the person who has requested a meeting with her have most likely had previous conversations. This is an important difference between the minister and the pastoral psychotherapist (to whom the client was referred by a minister or other professional). These may have been friendly little chats, or they may have been more formal and polite interchanges. Unless the minister has good reason for thinking otherwise, she should assume that, at least initially, the other person wants the basic nature of the conversation to be the same. If Eleanor has come across to Bobby as a rather shy girl whom he has come to know and like, he will find a suddenly boisterous, wisecracking Eleanor more than a little puzzling. If the minister and the other person have been on friendly terms, there is no reason why the minister should suddenly adopt a more "official" style, as if to announce, "I am now your counselor, and you are my client." If, on the other hand, their previous interactions have been more formal and polite, the mere fact that the other person has asked to talk with the minister in private does not mean that she should suddenly become friendly in a folksy sort of way. A radical shift from the customary way in which the two persons have related to each other on other occasions is likely to be disconcerting to the other person, an unnerving distraction from his purpose in coming.

On the other hand, although the general demeanor of the minister does not change, there *is* a difference between the friendly little chats or the formal interchanges the two have had before and what is likely to transpire in *this* conversation. As we have already noted in chapter 1, the minister will be intentional about listening. Such intentionality may have been true of their previous conversations, but the very fact that this time the other person has requested an opportunity to talk with the minister means that this intentionality is not optional (as it may have been when they were engaging in light and friendly banter on previous occasions). Such banter will not necessarily be out of place, but it cannot be allowed to distract from the fact that the other person would not have requested this meeting if there was not something on her mind that she wanted to discuss. How the minister *responds* to what is being related will also be more intentional than in the friendly chats–or polite interchanges–they have previously experienced.

The pastoral counseling literature is filled with suggestions, together with snippets from actual pastoral conversations, for how—and how not—to respond to the counselee. Many of the same suggestions have been made a common feature of clinical pastoral education. Over the years, a rather broad consensus has developed on what types of responses are most likely to reflect and contribute to good or effective listening. A particularly useful formulation of these responses is the one Howard Clinebell presents in *Basic Types of Pastoral Care and Counseling* (1984, pp. 94–96). He cites Elias H. Porter's typology of five counselor responses and then adds a sixth of his own (*advising*):

1. *Supportive.* Responses indicating the intent to reassure and perhaps reduce the counselee's intensity of feeling.
2. *Understanding.* Responses indicating the intention to communicate understanding and in effect to inquire whether this understanding is accurate.
3. *Interpretive.* Responses indicating the intent to teach, to impart meaning, or explain why.
4. *Probing.* Responses indicating the intent to query, to seek further information or provoke further discussion along a certain line.
5. *Evaluative.* Responses expressing a judgment concerning the relative appropriateness, correctness, or effectiveness of the counselee's thoughts, feelings, or behavior.
6. *Advising.* Responses indicating the intent to recommend certain approaches, actions, attitudes, or beliefs (or to recommend against them).

Clinebell indicates that a *supportive* response seeks to reassure, undergird, or inspire; an *understanding* response reflects empathy for the counselee's feelings and attitudes; an *interpretive* response intends to teach or explain the dynamics (the why) of a person's thoughts, feelings, or behavior; a *probing* response is one that questions; an *evaluative* response carries a value judgment; and an *advising* response offers a constructive suggestion for coping with a problem. In his view, all six have a place in pastoral counseling, and a minister "should be able to use them all with flexible selectivity, depending on the needs of the particular counselee" (p. 95). He further suggests that *understanding* responses should predominate in the rapport-building phase of counseling, but that they should be present in all stages (and types) of pastoral counseling. He notes that ministers with little or no training in counseling seldom use understanding responses, and that the counseling style of many clergy tends to be weakest in this type of response. Different types of pastoral counseling call for greater use of some types than others. For example, in crisis counseling, *supportive* responses are especially important.

To illustrate these responses, Clinebell (p. 95) provides the following statement (which I have slightly modified) by a woman, age 19, to her counselor:

> I tell you, I hate my father. I hate him! I really hate him! I realize I have no good reason for this. After all, he is a minister, and a good man, and he has never laid a hand on me. Yet I have this strong feeling against him, and what makes me feel so terrible about it is that there really isn't any reason for it. I also know that the Bible says to love and honor your father, that hating your father is therefore a sin, and this worries me too.

Clinebell then provides examples that are reflective of six types of responses. Because several of these, as Clinebell notes, are negative examples of the response in question (i.e., what not to say), I have constructed what are, in my own judgment, better (i.e., more positive) illustrations of each type:

> *Supportive:* "It may seem as though having hateful feelings toward your own father is a terrible thing, especially a father who is a minister, but the very fact that you want to talk about these feelings with me and perhaps to discover why you have them is itself a step in the right direction. I know that it requires courage to talk with someone who is also a minister about these feelings."

> *Understanding:* "You are saying that your father is a good minister and hasn't struck you, and yet you have hateful feelings toward him, and the apparent absence of any good reason for your feelings concerns and troubles you."

> *Interpretive:* "You wonder why you could have hateful feelings toward your father when, as you say, he is a good minister and hasn't actually struck you physically. There seems to be a discrepancy here between your portrayal of him and your feelings toward him. Perhaps we should look at this discrepancy. It may help us to understand the feelings you have toward him."

Probing: "Perhaps you could tell me more about how these feelings toward your father emerge. For example, what is happening between the two of you when these feelings well up inside you? What situations trigger them? Do they begin with an argument or conflict?"

Evaluative: "I wonder if there are, in fact, some grounds for your feelings toward your father. That he is a minister and hasn't actually struck you physically doesn't necessarily mean that he hasn't done anything to warrant your hateful feelings toward him. If you consider some of the ways that he has possibly mistreated you, you may find that at least some of these feelings are warranted."

Advising: "Because you have feelings toward your father that you cannot explain, you could either simply try to get rid of these feelings or you could try to see if there is some explanation for them. I am willing for us to take whatever course you think best, though I tend to think the second approach is preferable because you and I find these hateful feelings of yours rather mystifying."

As noted, Clinebell believes that *understanding* responses should predominate in the rapport-building phase of counseling. If we assume that this is the first conversation the minister and the woman have had—that her hateful feelings toward her father are the main reason she requested the meeting—this would suggest, perhaps, that the understanding response identified above—which also happens to be the most succinct—would be the preferable one. This, however, is not necessarily the case, as this particular woman's tone of voice and physical demeanor may suggest that she is desperately in need of support (in which case, the *supportive* response may be the preferred one). On the other hand, it may be that this is not the first allusion she has made to her hateful feelings toward her father, and that the minister has already responded to the earlier ones with supportive and/or understanding responses. This being the case, she may be ready for, even anticipating, an *interpretive* response. The suggested interpretive response is, incidentally, a confrontational one, though stated in a very nonaggressive manner.

Conceivably, an *evaluative, probing,* or *advising* response would be appropriate as well, though I tend to believe that in this case, the *interpretive* response that was offered is likely to achieve what the *evaluative* response is intended to realize without the danger that she will defend her father against the suggestion that he has "mistreated" her. The *probing* response assumes that discerning how and why her hateful feelings emerge will help to explain why she has these feelings, and it guesses that these feelings have to do with arguments or conflicts. These assumptions and hunches may be on the right track, but the question here is whether the *understanding* response will achieve the same goal, and with less likelihood that she will deny that she and her father have any arguments or conflicts, which may, in fact, be true. Also, the *understanding* response refers to the "apparent" absence of any good reason for her feelings, and therefore invites her to consider whether there may *possibly* be a good reason or reasons for her feelings. The tone of the *understanding* response is therefore more conversational, whereas the *probing* response has more of an interview tone.

The *advising* response is one that is probably best saved for the end of the conversation when the two of them are trying to decide what to do next. The issue of her hatred of her father has been opened up in this initial conversation, but where do we go from here? If introduced later, the minister's advice would not have the controlling feel that it would have if it came immediately after her initial confession regarding her hateful feelings toward her father. Because the basis for her hateful feelings toward her father may, in fact, be *his* controlling ways, the *advising* response, if offered too early, might be reminiscent to her of the way her father has been treating her.

In other words, I would augment Clinebell's point about the importance of *understanding* responses in the "rapport-building phase" of counseling to say that *supportive, understanding,* and *interpretive* responses are likely to be more appropriate in what I would call the "tone-setting phase" of the conversation, whereas *probing, evaluative,* and *advising* responses are likely to be used more strategically as the conversation moves into what I would call its "exploratory phase." (Later, I will discuss the third or "resolution phase.") In addition, as Figure 1 indicates, there are certain correlations between the three primary (or "tone-setting") responses and the three secondary (or "exploratory phase") responses. These are *supportive-advising, understanding-probing,* and *interpretive-evaluative.* In each case, the second responses are more interventionist (or directive) and therefore carry greater risk, especially if employed early in the "tone-setting" phase. These correlations may be described as follows:

Figure 1

Types of Counselor Responses

Almost Always Appropriate	Used More Selectively	Inappropriate Responses
Supportive Responses ◄──►	Advising Responses ──	Controlling Responses
Understanding Responses ◄──►	Probing Responses ──	Impatient Responses
Interpretive Responses ◄──►	Evaluative Responses ──	Moralistic Responses

Supportive-Advising. If the *supportive* response is intended to reassure the other person, the *advising* response goes beyond reassurance by offering recommendations. Ministers who view themselves as *supportive* may find that their supportive role tends to shade over into an *advising* role. In this case, the minister goes beyond reassuring the woman that her desire to talk about her feelings toward her father is an expression of her courage (a *supportive* response) to making suggestions as to how she might deal with these feelings (an *advising* response). He notes two possible approaches she could take—try to get rid of these feelings or explore the possible reasons she has them—and recommends the latter course.

I have written the *advising* response in a way that presents advising in an essentially positive light. Over the years, whether advising has any place in pastoral counseling has been a much-debated issue. I share Clinebell's view that it *does* have a place, but I strongly oppose the heavy-handed advising that is advocated by some writers in the pastoral counseling field (i.e., those who believe that one has not provided counsel unless he has given explicit advice). The *advising* response indicated here is one that communicates to the woman that, even as it was her decision to come to the minister to talk about her feelings toward her father, it remains her decision as to how she wants to carry this conversation further. The minister states his own preference, but indicates that he is willing to take the other course. Also, by identifying these two possible courses, he also helps the woman to anticipate a resolution of her problem, and this in itself is inherently supportive or reassuring.

In short, advising is an extension of support, but it needs to be used with caution, as it can communicate that the minister believes that the other person lacks the necessary resources to address her own problems (with appropriate support from the minister). In other words, the dangers of advising are either that the minister will make himself indispensable or that he will force the other person into a position where she needs to reject his advice in order to maintain her autonomy. The advice itself may be good advice, but the advisory role of the minister is perceived as a threat.

Understanding-Probing. If the *understanding* response is intended to communicate the minister's understanding and, in effect, to inquire whether this understanding is accurate, the *probing* response takes this a step further and suggests that there are aspects to the problem or issue that are not yet understood or understandable. If the *understanding* response observes "an apparent absence of any good reason for" the daughter's feelings toward her father, the *probing* response wants to know why she has these feelings. It seeks an explanation for what so far has not been adequately explained. Ministers who are primarily oriented toward understanding, who see themselves as *understanding,* nonjudgmental persons, may find that their efforts to be understanding sometimes shade over into efforts to *probe* for explanations. They are capable of making *understanding* responses—"You are saying that…"—but they are also aware of a small, insistent voice in their minds that is saying to them, "I wonder why she has these feelings toward her father? What is causing this? Could it be that her 'reasons' for why she should not have these feelings are actually inadequate, that they are hiding other reasons why she *should* have these feelings toward her father?"

One reason why *understanding* responses have been so highly valued in the pastoral counseling field (as Clinebell's comment that they should predominate in the rapport-building phase indicates) is that ministers have had a tendency to move too quickly into *probing* responses. These responses, in turn, often cause the person who has asked for counsel to become defensive. As noted, a *probing* response, especially if it is made in the tone-setting phase of the conversation, is likely to be experienced as threatening. The *probing* response that I have offered here—"What is happening between the two of you? What situations trigger them? Do they begin with an argument or conflict?"—could, for example, threaten the woman's need to idealize her father, because her own positive self-image may be dependent on the fact that she is the daughter of a father who is a good minister and thus revered by others. An *understanding* response—"The apparent absence of any good reason for your feelings concerns and troubles you"—is more tentative, more provisional, more simply based on what she has already more-or-less said, inviting her to go in the very direction that the *probing* response suggests or implies, but at her own pace and in her own way.

It is true, of course, that a conversation consisting only of "What I hear you saying" responses can be maddening to the other. A good case in point is the following set of interchanges between a minister and a sixty-eight-year-old woman who had recently suffered the deaths of her husband and father (Cryer and Vayhinger, 1962, pp. 71–73).

> Mrs. O.: Living here alone doesn't seem to be working out at all. Ever since my father died and my husband, just a short time later, I've been left all alone. I don't know if I can take it. My children all want someone to stay here with me. I just don't know.

> Minister: The death of your father, then your husband, so close together, has left you feeling lonely, and your children all want you to have someone stay here with you, is that it?

> Mrs. O.: Yes, that's it. I just feel that the responsibility of taking care of a house is too much.

> Minister: The responsibility of caring for the house seems too much for you, is that it?

> Mrs. O.: It's all such a care and I am all alone, but I know that it is all up to me. It is such a hard task, and lonely, but I'll have to bear it alone.

> Minister: You feel that all of the care and responsibility is left upon your own shoulders and that the task ahead must be met alone.

> Mrs. O.: Yes, that's it, I must handle these things alone.

> Minister: You feel, then, that these things must definitely be done by you?

> Mrs. O.: Yes. No one can work them out for me.

> Minister: No one else can work them out for you, is that it?

This minister, obviously attempting to be a good, "client-centered" counselor, was pleased with the fact that he avoided the temptation to give "a good sermon on the fatherhood of God during those times throughout the interview that seemed to call for spiritualizing" and instead "managed to maintain the internal frame of reference," the latter being the term that Carl Rogers employed to convey the counselor's effort to "perceive the world as the client sees it" (Rogers, 1951, p. 29). His tendency to parrot Mrs. O. and then repeat the query, "Is that it?" (a phrase she soon finds herself adopting) belies this claim, however, and it also shows—by way of negative example—that good *understanding* responses help to move the conversation forward. A sign that one is using too many *understanding* responses, that there is insufficient variation in one's responses, is the sense that the conversation is not going anywhere, that the two parties involved seem to be spinning their wheels. When this happens, it is very likely that a *probing* response *is* called for, or that one should turn to a more *interpretive* mode.

Interpretive-Evaluative. If the *interpretive* response is intended to teach, impart meaning, or explain why, the *evaluative* response takes this a step further and expresses a judgment concerning the relative appropriateness or effectiveness of the other person's thoughts, feelings, or behavior. In effect, one communicates to the other: "This is what I think you are doing and why you are doing it (interpretive), and, on the basis of this interpretation, I think what you are doing is good (for such-and-such reason) or not good (for such-and-such reason)." Ministers who view themselves as primarily *interpreters* (for example, preachers or teachers) are likely to be most comfortable with this way of communicating. Some ministers can do this effectively without undermining the conversational milieu itself.

In the case of the daughter of the minister, the counseling minister's *interpretive* response notes (as does the *understanding* response) the seeming "discrepancy" between the woman's portrayal of her father and her hateful feelings toward him, and gently suggests that they might focus on this apparent discrepancy. Other words, of course, might have been used. Some readers might prefer "a disconnect," while others might prefer "a gap." The goal would be to note the issue itself while avoiding language that might seem judgmental or critical. "Inconsistency," "conflict," or "confusion," all of which may be true, are likely to seem more judgmental, and thus to provoke a counter-defense.

The *evaluative* response, however, *does* contain a note of judgment or critique, though it is directed not toward her but toward her father: "That he is a minister and hasn't actually struck you physically does not necessarily mean that he hasn't done anything to warrant your hateful feelings toward him. If you consider some of the ways that he has possibly mistreated you, you may find that at least some of these feelings are warranted." The suggestion that she may in fact have grounds for hating her father has been put forward, and the way has been opened for her to consider the appropriateness of her feelings toward him. Maybe he *is* subject not only to psychological critique (i.e., he has not been as faithful to the responsibilities of a father as he should have been) but also moral judgment (i.e., he is guilty of wrongdoing).

I assume that most persons who read the daughter's statement have much the same reaction as this *evaluative* response suggests, that they suspect that her father *has* done something to warrant these feelings of hers, that these feelings are not unprovoked. Some may feel this so strongly that they consider the evaluative response presented here to be too tentative or too tepid: "Her father's a tyrant!" In any case, because we tend to respond this way, we make, in effect, two evaluations, one of her father (whom we consider culpable, though we do not yet know why), and one of her (who seems unable to see that her explanations for why she should not feel this way leave many unanswered questions and open up many alternative explanations). We are probably correct in this initial judgment, but we *do* need to be aware that we have, in fact, made an evaluative comment based on very little empirical evidence. There is a chance, for example, that hateful feelings arising from some other cause or source have been displaced onto her father. If so, they *do* have an explanation, but not one for which the father himself is culpable. In that case, the *evaluative* response has taken a wrong turn, and, if so, the minister needs to remain open to correction.

In my experience, seminarians have a distinct tendency to make *evaluative* responses and to make them in the tone-setting phase of the conversation. Often these are simple expressions such as, "It's okay for you to feel this way," or "Good for you," or "I'm proud of you." These statements, explicitly or implicitly, offer an evaluation of the thoughts, emotions, or behavior of the other person. Although they may seem to the speaker to be a *supportive* response, one that offers reassurance, they carry some evaluative freight that may be detrimental to the conversation. Why? Because they substitute evaluation for understanding, and in doing so, they fail to enter into the experiential world of the other in its fullness or complexity. If the woman in this example were to be told, "It's okay for you to feel this way about your father," a large part of her experiential world would be denied, namely, the part that believes it is *not* okay for her to feel this way because it seems unjustified or wrong. Also, she may wonder on what grounds the person she is now talking with makes this ostensibly supportive (but actually evaluative) statement. Is the minister speaking on his own behalf? Is he speaking in the name of God? The very fact that it is possible to raise such questions as these supports the view that *evaluative* responses should be used selectively.

Another concern is that an *evaluative* response—"It's okay to feel this way," "Good for you," or "I'm proud of you"—*can* come across to the other person as paternalistic, maternalistic, big-brotherish, or big-sisterish. Some persons may react negatively to what they perceive to be a certain presumption that seems to inform such statements: "Who gave you the right to say that it is okay for me to feel this way or that what I have said or done is praiseworthy?" Some future ministers (perhaps especially those who are elder brothers and sisters or are the high achievers in their families of origin) may have developed the habit of praising others for their achievements and may not recognize that these others resent the presumption that stands behind these seemingly innocent remarks. Learning to create a conversation based on understanding may require these future ministers to abstain from such words of support and praise and to develop a way of communicating that is less likely to cause offense.

None of this means, of course, that the minister has no right to make evaluations as to the goodness or correctness of the other person's thoughts, emotions, or behavior. If psychotherapists make evaluative comments, then surely ministers may too. In fact, there has been a whole spate of literature on the minister as "moral counselor" (for example, Browning, 1976; Noyce, 1989) that argues this very point. My point here, though, is that an *interpretive* response—which, as we have seen, *can* be confrontational—is usually preferable to a more overtly *evaluative* response, as it allows the other person to make her own evaluations. The minister's suggestion that there is an apparent "discrepancy" between her portrayal of her father and her feelings toward him should be sufficient encouragement for her to make her own evaluation.

Inappropriate responses. The figure above also indicates three types of responses that are not conducive to a good, productive conversation between the minister and the person who has asked for counsel. These responses are on a continuum with the six responses already noted. As *supportive* responses may go a step further toward *advising* responses, so advising responses may go further yet and become *controlling.* Similarly, *understanding* responses may move toward *probing* responses, and these may go further and become *impatient* responses. In the same way, *interpretive* responses may move toward *evaluative* responses, and these may go a step beyond evaluation and become *moralistic.*

This movement across the continuum frequently occurs in communication between parents and children, teachers and students, and spouses. A mother, for example, may have a genuine desire to support her teenage daughter as she struggles to figure out what to do with her life. In the early stages of their conversation together, she may offer *supportive* reassurances, "I know that you'll find your way. After all, you are my daughter, and I've raised you to be strong and resourceful." As the conversation continues, and her daughter does not seem responsive to these reassurances–"Mother, I'm just so confused and mixed-up"–her mother may respond to her helplessness with an *advising* response, "Well, maybe you should go and see the guidance counselor and also talk with the youth minister at church. They may have some really good ideas." Her daughter may react to this advice, "I don't think it will do any good. They don't really know me, and they only care about the more popular kids who have promising futures." At this point, the mother–anxious about her daughter's low opinion of herself and unwillingness to act on her advice–may move to a more *controlling* response: "I'll tell you what I'm going to do. I'll call the guidance counselor first thing tomorrow morning and ask her to make an appointment to see you. Then, just to be sure she followed up on this, I'll call later in the day to find out how it went." In the movement across the continuum, the mother has gone from reassuring her daughter that she has the strength and resourcefulness to see the problem through to arranging the solution and checking to see if there was compliance with it. In effect, the reassurances at the beginning of the conversation have been nullified at the end.

With regard to the case that we have been discussing, the following illustrates what I mean by *controlling, impatient,* and *moralistic* responses.

Controlling: "You have feelings about your father that you wish you didn't have. I know a really great method for getting rid of negative thoughts and feelings. I'll help you work through the steps–there are seven of them, and you do one step per week. Sounds good, huh?"

Impatient: "If you are saying that there is no good reason for you to have hateful feelings toward your father, why don't you just get rid of them? If you let them fester as you've been doing, they will turn you into a bitter and unhappy woman."

Moralistic: "Your guilt is telling you that it is wrong for you to have these hateful feelings toward your father. As you yourself said, your father is a good person. He doesn't deserve these bad feelings you have for him from his own flesh and blood. Think of all he's sacrificed for you. Let's see what we can do to correct your feelings toward him."

I have written these responses so as to make the point that they are on a continuum with the other two responses with which they are related on the chart. Thus, the *controlling* response is ostensibly *supportive*, as it recognizes the woman's deep concern about the feelings she has toward her father and what they are doing to her and their relationship. This *is* supportive. But then it goes on to recommend a method that, with the assistance of the minister, should enable her to divest herself of her negative feelings in seven weeks. This recommendation is undoubtedly well-intentioned, but it puts the woman into the position of either accepting the minister's plan for dealing with these hateful feelings or leaving the conversation altogether. This is what makes it controlling. Conceivably, the very reason she has these hateful feelings toward her father is that *his* goodness is also of the controlling kind. She may feel, then, that in seeking this minister out, she has been confronted with simply more of the same. Her decision not to accept the minister's offer may therefore produce additional guilt: "There must be something wrong with me for resisting such kind, well-intentioned attention."

A clue to the fact that his response is controlling is that it has gone beyond his *advising* response, that her options seemed to be to either try to get rid of the feelings she has toward her father or see if there is some explanation for them. The *advising* response indicated his openness to taking either course she thought best, but expressed the opinion that "the second approach is preferable because you and I find these hateful feelings of yours rather mystifying." Now, the minister is taking the further step of telling her that there is one course that he would recommend and presenting the plan with no input from her whatsoever. It could, of course, be argued that if he knows a surefire method for solving her problem it would be unethical for him to withhold it from her. In this case, however, he is leaving her no choice in the matter. It is his way, or no way. He has not only blocked the option of "trying to see if there is some explanation" for her feelings but any other option—a possible third that he (or she) has not thought of—as well.

The *impatient* response is ostensibly based on *understanding,* for the minister does express concern that she will become "a bitter and unhappy woman." But the tone of the response undermines this attempt to express understanding. The genuine concern he has expressed over her struggle to make sense of the fact that her feelings are incongruent with her perception of her father has given way to a need to get the problem solved as expeditiously as possible. A clue to the fact that the minister's response is an impatient one is that it goes beyond the *probing* response, which asked her to tell him more about how these feelings emerge (What situations trigger them? Arguments? Conflicts?), by implying that such probing may take time and effort and may not, in any case, yield very much. Why not, then, simply cut to the chase and get her from point A to point B? The tone of the response—just get rid of these feelings; otherwise they will turn you into a bitter woman—suggests the need to act posthaste, that time is against her, and the sooner she gets over this problem and gets on with her life the better. There is also the implication that the relational dynamics between the woman and her father need not be considered, that the counseling minister—to save time and trouble?—is quite happy to take at face value her comment that she has no reason to have these feelings toward her father. If this is the case, these feelings serve no useful purpose. Conceivably, the impatience expressed in this response is shared by the woman herself. Perhaps she fended off his earlier *probing* responses ("I don't want to get into all that"), or previous experience has taught him that the persons who come to him for counsel resist, even resent, his desire to probe. "I didn't come here to be psychoanalyzed, I wanted you to listen and then suggest something I can do." But such experiences, no matter how discouraging they may have been, do not justify the impatient response presented here. Nor does the fact that the other person is impatient mean that the minister should accommodate her, especially if he knows that "getting rid of these feelings," even if successful, will have other consequences (for example, cause her to develop physical symptoms that appear equally mystifying).

As we will see later in this chapter, a strong case can and has been made that ministers should employ brief counseling approaches in their role as counselors. One can be an advocate of brief counseling, however, and not endorse the impatient "just get it out of your system" response indicated here.

The *moralistic* response is an extension of the *interpretive* mode, as it focuses on what the woman's guilt is telling her, and interprets this as an indication that her hateful feelings are wrong (and does not entertain the possibility that her guilt itself is wrong). It implies that an *evaluation* has already taken place, that is, that her statements about not having any good reason to hate her father are reliable, and that her feelings toward him are therefore inappropriate. What this moralistic statement adds is the judgment that her father does not deserve this, especially from his own daughter, and adds the caveat that he has made sacrifices for her: "Is this any way to repay your father for his kindness toward you?" A correction of her feelings is needed, and the minister offers to assist her in doing so.

The *evaluative* response presented earlier suggested that her father may have done something "to warrant your hateful feelings toward him." The *moralistic* response presented here places the onus on her. Does this mean that this response is moralistic simply because it makes a judgment against her and not her father? No. A *moralistic* response could also have been made by taking the earlier *evaluative* response a step or two further. It might, for example, suggest that she has every reason to have hateful feelings toward her father because she wouldn't have these feelings "unless he had mistreated you," adding, "We need to uncover these bad things that he has done to you." Where the earlier *evaluative* statement was cautious, suggesting that he has "possibly mistreated you" and that "at least some of these feelings are warranted," a *moralistic* response would condemn her father without any supporting evidence. What makes this and the other response moralistic is that character judgments are being made on the basis of few, if any, facts. Why assume that her father "doesn't deserve this, especially from his own daughter"? Why assume that he has done "bad things" to her? As noted above, what if her hateful feelings derive from the fact that his goodness and kindness are experienced by her as controlling?

Controlling, impatient, and *moralistic* responses are inappropriate in a conversation between a minister and a person who has sought her counsel. If a minister finds herself making these kinds of responses, she should ask herself why she is doing so, and whether she is doing this with only one or two of the persons for whom she is providing counsel or with several or all of them. It may be that one person simply evokes the worst in her. If so, this very fact may provide a valuable insight into that person, as it may be that he has a similar effect on other persons too. She should also, though, engage in introspection in order to discover why this person *does* have this effect on her. Specifically, "Why am I responding in a controlling, impatient, or moralistic manner to what this particular individual says?" Very possibly, these responses reveal anxieties (as discussed in chapter 1) that are activated by this individual and no other. If, on the other hand, the minister finds that he is responding controllingly, impatiently, or moralistically with virtually everyone with whom he has conversations in which he is in the counselor role, this also calls for introspection, but with a different question in mind: "Why am I responding in virtually all my conversations in a controlling, or impatient, or moralistic way?"

This question is especially important for the minister to ask himself if he is not typically this way. Some persons are controlling, impatient, or moralistic by nature, and, certainly, some of these persons are found among the clergy. Unless, through training and/or life experiences, they are able to change (working, as it were, from the right side to the left side of the chart), they are unlikely to make good listeners and good conversation partners. But if the minister is normally oriented toward the appropriate or selectively employed responses, the fact that she has changed invites exploration. Why has her usual tendency to offer *supportive, understanding,* or *interpretive* responses given way to *controlling, impatient,* or *moralistic* responses? What is going on in her life that is causing this alteration in her normal manner of responding to persons who have asked her to listen to them? Could it be that she resents being the listener all the time ("I wish someone would listen to me for once")? Could she be suffering from apathy, depression, fatigue, restlessness? To discover whether this is the case, she may want to conduct an "internal conversation" not unlike those she has with persons she counsels, and alternately assume the position of "listener" and "listened to." Or she may need to talk to a trusted friend about the problem, for a friend may be more willing to be honest and take risks than her husband or significant other, who wants above all to be supportive of her. (On the tendency of ministers *not* to be introspective when writing their own pastoral care cases, see Capps and Fowler, 2001, chap. 6).

I have given quite a lot of attention to the types of responses that ministers should—and should not—employ in conversations with persons who seek their counsel because responding, like listening, is integral to any good conversation, and the "pastoral conversation" is no exception. By identifying specific types of responses, even though this may seem rather artificial, readers may practice making the kinds of responses that have received great support over the years in courses in pastoral care and counseling and in clinical pastoral education programs. They may also find that the correlations presented in the chart are self-revealing, as they may discover that they tend to prefer one of these types of responses over the other two. This, in turn, may help them to identify their particular strengths but also the potential dangers in their preferred approach. No particular judgment is implied here regarding which "model" is the most or least preferable, though, understandably, some persons who seek a minister's counsel will prefer one over the other, and certain situations may, in fact, make one or the other the preferred approach. The minister who is able to employ the full range of appropriate and selectively used responses is likely to be more helpful, other things being equal. I have indicated by the use of arrows on the left side of the chart on page 63 that the minister should make every effort to use supportive, understanding, *and* interpretive responses, as these can often be mutually reinforcing.

Types of Conversations

Having discussed the types of responses that occur in conversations between ministers and those who seek or require their counsel, I now want to turn to Gaylord Noyce's suggestion that there are essentially four types of conversations (1981, pp. 9–11). These types are not limited to those that occur between a minister and a parishioner, as they are typical of all conversations, and perhaps especially of conversations between friends. What I want to suggest is that the minister can be especially aware of what type of conversation is expected or desirable, and thus allow or enable the conversation to take this form rather than one of the others. In this way, the minister shapes the conversation, giving it a form or structure, but in a way that is unobtrusive and, like the banks of a river, facilitates the conversational flow:

1. *Turning-point:* A person is at a junction in life, trying to make a decision, and feels that a talk with the minister may help to bring clarity and identify an appropriate course of action.
2. *Shared self-disclosure:* The minister and the person she is talking with move to a new level of mutual understanding because one or both reveals something about herself that was not previously known.
3. *Growing edge exchange:* The interests of one person and the competence of the other are in such resonance that both learn from the conversation.
4. *Rehearsal:* Conversation that enables the participants to share, celebrate, or remember certain events.

Because *rehearsal* not only has the connotation of recounting a previous experience (this is essentially how Noyce uses the word), but also, and more popularly, the connotation of a practice for a future performance, I suggest that we replace the term *rehearsal* with *recollection.* In this way, there is less likelihood of its being confused with the *turning-point* conversation, which is very likely to involve rehearsal of a decision that has not yet been made.

Noyce suggests that the *turning-point* conversation is not one in which "someone else tells us what to do but that the person facilitates our own decision, quite possibly not even realizing what a help he or she is being at the time" (1981, p. 9). He relates the time when he was making a professional decision—whether to move or to stay where he was. A single comment in a conversation with a friend was so helpful that he has often recalled it when faced with other tough decisions. When decisions are hard for him, he is tempted to think that one way is "right" and the other is "wrong," and he begins to fear that he will make the "wrong" one. Then paralysis sets in, and the decision gets even harder to make: "What if I make the wrong decision and regret it the rest of my life?" As he was struggling with the decision of whether to move or stay where he was, the friend said to him, "Gaylord, you'll be happy either way." For Noyce, "this was like a word of grace, lifting a hidden burden from my shoulders" (p. 10).

A turning-point conversation in which the minister is asked to give counsel often occurs when the other person has become, or is on the verge of becoming, paralyzed. It can be a decision, like Noyce's, about whether to take a new position or remain where he is. It might also be a decision about whether to remain in an unhappy marriage or to seek a legal separation. Or the adult child of an elderly parent may be struggling with the decision of whether to place him in a long-term care facility. These examples may imply that turning-point conversations are only about momentous decisions that will be life-changing for one or more of the persons involved, but what makes this a turning-point conversation is not so much the momentousness of the decision itself, but the fact that the other person (or persons) is feeling conflicted and hopes that by talking with the minister she will be helped toward resolving the conflict.

The response of Noyce's friend was a *supportive* one, as it reassured him that whatever he decided would turn out okay for him. This supportive comment arrested the paralyzing mode of thinking into which he had been sinking—right versus wrong—and offered the reassuring thought that, in fact, either course he took would be the "right" one. It is as if one were to revise the last two lines of Robert Frost's poem "The Road Not Taken" (Frost, p. 105) from "I took the one less traveled by, / And that has made all the difference" to read, "I took the one road rather than the other, / But I would have been happy either way." This revision replaces the original version's sense of the fatefulness of the decision to take the less traveled road and the implication that the other road would have been "wrong" for Frost, and offers the more reassuring—if less dramatic—thought that the traveler was choosing between two fine alternatives, either of which would have been "right" for him. That the response of Noyce's friend was supportive is reflected in the fact that it was like a word of grace lifting a hidden burden from Noyce's shoulders.

Note that his friend was content to offer a supportive response and did not take the additional step of advising Noyce what to do. He did not tell his friend that he should stay put nor did he tell him he should accept the offer to go elsewhere. Conceivably, Noyce's recital of the pros and cons of the two alternatives gave his friend the sense that one was better than the other, or that Noyce was already leaning one way or the other, but, if so, he did not advise him either way. Nor, of course, did he take the even further step of trying to control Noyce: "You need to stay where you are. Think of your obligations to your family and to your employer. To ask your wife to leave her job, your children to leave their friends, and to leave your employer in the lurch would not be fair to them. I really don't think you have any other choice." The fact that his friend's supportive response lifted his burden and has been invoked many times since is itself evidence that the further step of advising him what to do, much less a response that attempted to exert control, was unnecessary, and might well have been counter-productive, as it would have been an endorsement of the paralyzing right versus wrong mode of thinking about these matters from which he needed to free himself.

While the friend's response was a supportive one, it also expressed *understanding.* He could not have given Noyce this reassurance if he had not already understood what his friend was going through by entering empathically into Noyce's own experiential world of perplexity and immobilization. He was also, one suspects, drawing on his knowledge of the kind of person that Noyce was, the fact that his friend was not the sort of person to bemoan the decision he eventually made or to punish himself for it if things did not turn out as well as he had hoped. Thus, the friend knew that Noyce's own intentionality would play a role in making whatever course he decided on a "happy" one.

The response was also *interpretive.* "You'll be happy either way" is an interpretation based on what Noyce had already told him about his choices. If Noyce were not genuinely perplexed, but had already made his decision, he would probably have presented the two alternatives in such a way as to communicate that one was clearly superior to the other. That he had not done so is reflected in his friend's interpretation of what he had heard, "There are good things about both, and you are the type of person who will seize upon these good things and not let yourself succumb to regrets about what might have been." Incidentally, the friend here has employed the method of presenting a third alternative for breaking an immobilizing interpretive frame based on "either-or" thinking (see Capps, 1998, p. 105ff).

Thus, it may be that the friend's comment was so helpful to Noyce because it actually reflected all three of the almost always appropriate responses presented in the chart on page 63. As the arrows indicate, the response moved up and down instead of across, thus reflecting the supportive-understanding-interpretive atmosphere of the conversation as a whole. No advising-probing-evaluative responses seemed to be needed in order for Noyce to feel that a word of grace had been spoken.

Noyce illustrates the second type of conversation—*shared self-disclosure*—by referring to another conversation with a friend, one in which a friend said, with a happy note of surprise, "I guess I have just told you more about my present vocational ambivalence than I have told anyone but my therapist." Noyce adds, "This was no counseling session, but a walk along a city street" (1981, p. 10). Of course, this illustration indicates that, unlike the previous example, it was the friend and not Noyce who had made a significant self-disclosure. The fact that the previous illustration also involved self-disclosure indicates that self-disclosure is likely to be a feature of turning-point conversations as well, but here the emphasis is not on a decision that is hanging in the balance, but on the self-disclosure itself. As Noyce puts it, the disclosure leads the two persons to "a new level of mutual understanding" (p. 10).

This new level of mutual understanding is what a shared self-disclosure conversation is principally about. The friend in this case has entrusted Noyce with information about himself and his experiential world—that of vocational ambivalence—previously shared with only one other person, his therapist. That Noyce has remembered his friend's statement is itself evidence that he was honored, not made uncomfortable, by this self-disclosure. Noyce could have been saying to himself as the two of them parted, "He must view me as a pretty important friend in his life to have shared with me things he has only shared with his therapist." He might also have found himself thinking, "The fact that he mentioned his therapist tells me that the mutual understanding we have experienced is similar to, but different from, the relationship he has with his therapist." Noyce would be wise, in other words, to honor the difference and not use these disclosures as warrant for him to shift, however imperceptibly, from friend to therapist.

Noyce does not say what his response was to his friend's comment, but the fact that he suggests that the shared self-disclosure type of conversation leads to a new level of mutual understanding indicates that *understanding* responses are likely to be prominent in conversations of this type. Conceivably, Noyce responded to these self-disclosures wordlessly, or with a brief "I see" or "That's very interesting." One would expect, however, that he would have said something in return, indicating that he had understood the degree or depth of his friend's "present vocational ambivalence." He might have said, "You're really struggling with what you should be doing with your life," or "It's like being pulled in various directions at once," or "Your thoughts about your vocation in life are in something of a turmoil." The words *struggle, pulled,* and *turmoil* communicate the listener's effort to understand the speaker's experiential world from the inside, from where the feelings themselves reside.

Conceivably, Noyce might be prompted to go beyond understanding responses to probing ones, but, because he is a friend, and because they are walking along the street, he may well leave the probing to his friend's therapist, and remain content to respond on an understanding basis only. By responding with understanding comments such as these, he communicates his desire to be an interested, invested listener, thus forestalling any subsequent regrets his friend might have about having revealed so much about himself, while at the same time avoiding the questioning tone of a probing response. Also, as with our discussion of the turning-point conversation, in which a very supportive response proved to be one of understanding and an interpretive one as well, the understanding tone of these suggested responses would more than likely communicate support: "I feel your struggle, and I hope that *you* feel my solidarity with you." They are also likely to come across as mildly interpretive. These responses may, in fact, have led the friend to recognize, more profoundly than he had before, that his problem was one of "vocational ambivalence," that this was the interpretive framework within which this conversation could be viewed. Thus, as the chart on page 63 indicates, an essentially understanding mode of response may also shade into the supportive and interpretive.

Noyce illustrates *growing edge exchanges* with an account of an evening he spent with two biologists talking about evolution and genetic mutations. They also talked about the "necessary assumptions of causation that science makes and the limitations this process presents when it comes to understanding meaning and purpose–the science and religion issue." He concludes, "We helped each other learn through conversation in an exciting evening of talk" (p. 10). While this conversation differed from the previous two in that a personal struggle was not involved, it nonetheless indicates how a conversation between a minister and another person who seeks her counsel might be a *growing-edge exchange*. In *The Pastoral Care Case* (2001), Gene Fowler and I relate the actual story of a parishioner (Bob) who had listened intently to the minister's sermon on the Nicodemus story (John 3:1–21) and had requested a meeting with him so that they could discuss what it really means to be "born again." The initial meeting was followed by a second one, both of which were growing-edge exchanges for both men.

Because their conversation was prompted by a sermon on a biblical text, it was perhaps inevitable that the minister would be called on to make a series of *interpretive* responses. The questions that were in Bob's mind were not unlike those of Nicodemus himself. He wanted to know if what he had already experienced might qualify as having been "born again," though he doubted that this was the case. He also wanted to know if his "faith" was adequate as it was, though he acknowledged having a yearning for something more. As interpreter, the minister replied to Bob's questions with some theological distinctions that he had found personally helpful. In the give-and-take that followed, he did not take the further step of evaluating the quality of Bob's faith, though he accepted Bob's own perception that there was "something missing" or "lacking" in it. Nor did he resort to moralizing responses, suggesting, for example, that the present state of Bob's faith was "inadequate" or "immature." In response to the minister's theological interpretations, which centered on "born againness" being more a process than a single episode, Bob gave an account of what he took to be religious experiences–times of profound gratitude to God–that occurred in his walks in the Maine woods. These accounts prompted the minister to reread some essays by Ralph Waldo Emerson that he had read in college, ostensibly to learn more about where his parishioners were coming from, but also because he found something personally compelling in Bob's account of his experiences in nature. Like Noyce in his conversation with the two biologists, both minister and parishioner were enriched by these exchanges.

If the general mode of response in this case was one of interpretation–offering theological insights and clarifications–the two conversations they had about what it means to be "born again" were also experienced as ones in which the minister was supportive and understanding. His interpretive responses carried a note of reassurance ("There is nothing fundamentally wrong with your faith") and of understanding ("These are perplexing issues for me as well, and I will therefore draw on what our church teaches and how I have tried to understand these teachings in my own faith journey"). Thus, as in the two previous types of conversation, the minister in this *growing-edge exchange* moved up and down the left column, augmenting interpretive responses with expressions of support and understanding.

Growing-edge exchanges are not necessarily limited to those involving theological or explicitly religious issues. They may also be about child-rearing, education, health issues, political issues, and so forth. One would assume, however, that the parishioner would raise the subject because she is seeking information or knowledge about something that is currently troubling her. The ensuing conversation may, in turn, lead to new perceptions and insights that the minister might not otherwise have. For example, the minister who is asked by a gay parishioner for help in understanding his church's objection to same-sex unions (an issue that *could* have come up in the above exchange, because Bob's daughter had actually left the denomination because it did not approve of lesbian relationships) may, in turn, learn something about why gay and lesbian couples would want a ceremony celebrating and endorsing their unions. The two individuals may not come to a common understanding as a result of a single conversation, but, as in Noyce's exchange with the two biologists, one or both may leave feeling more energized and alive than he has felt in a long time.

Noyce indicates that what I am calling the *recollective* type of conversation is one in which common memories are shared, especially by those who were eyewitnesses to them but also by others who were not present at the time but who are presumed to be interested in what happened. He cites the experience of the Kennedy assassination weekend, or of growing up in the '30s, or '50s, or '70s. These conversations are significant "not so much because a decision is facilitated, a relationship suddenly deepened, or something interesting learned, but because life is shared through them, and life shared is good, even if the things talked over are painful or sad" (1981, pp. 10–11).

Conversations of this type involving a minister may be prompted by the anniversary of the death of someone the other person (or persons) cherished, or perhaps by an elderly person's desire to talk about events or experiences in her past. Some conversations of this type may be solely for the purpose of taking a trip down memory lane, but there are times when the recollective conversation has a note of urgency. For example (the following case is from Cryer and Vayhinger, 1962, pp. 60–62), a 68-year-old woman was dying of cancer. She had been a good church person, and apparently her minister was making regular pastoral visits to her home. But one Sunday after church, her son asked his own minister to call. She seems to have wanted her son's minister to visit her because she was preparing to relate an experience that she did not want her own minister to know about.

After he entered her room and sat down, she began, "I suppose you know I'm going to die?" Their conversation continued for a brief moment on how she would miss the beautiful things in life, and then she began to focus on her concern:

> Mrs. A: You know, Reverend, lying in bed waiting to die has some good points. I've been thinking. It's all so silly—I mean, life—its arguments, feuds, and all. It's all so silly when you think about it.

> Minister: It's easy to place the stress at the wrong point in life, I suppose.

> Mrs. A: Oh, how true. Sometimes I feel like laughing at my life. When I think of the heartaches and tears and worries, I just feel like laughing. Isn't it in the Bible, "Vanity of vanities! All is vanity"?

Their conversation shifted briefly to her awareness that she was dying and then returned to her past life:

> Mrs. A.: If we could only relive parts of our lives again.

> Minister: You feel there might have been times when you could have been different?

> Mrs. A.: Yes, I know you'll think it's silly, Reverend, but for a long time I've been president of our women's group, almost twenty years, I guess. And once, when the others were going to consider another president, I did a terrible thing. I let them think the other woman was not good enough. Now she's gone, poor soul, and I keep thinking about it. It wasn't very Christian was it, Reverend?

The minister agreed, but assured her that the greatness of our faith is that "there is always room for failures," for "forgiveness is part of God's nature." She replied in a tired voice, "I guess we all sin at times, and I suppose that forgiveness is ours." Sensing her tiredness and feeling there was not much more he could do on this visit, the minister proposed prayer and said the Lord's Prayer. When he finished, she responded, "Even the Lord's Prayer sounds different now." As he got up to go she added, "I hope I haven't bored you." He assured her that she had not.

This woman's recollection of the time when she defamed another woman in order to retain the presidency of the women's group raised for her the spectre of the vanity or absurdity of life, and it also seemed to be an episode in her life from which she sought some kind of peace or release before she died. The minister's response was meant to be supportive, providing reassurance that "failures" like this are encompassed by the forgiveness of God, whose very nature it is to forgive. One assumes that, as the Lord's Prayer was spoken, she heard the words, "And forgive us our trespasses, as we forgive those who trespass against us," and made this prayer her own. Thus, what may have seemed a rather unoriginal pastoral intervention–the recitation of the Lord's Prayer–appears to have offered the very support she needed.

This example is noteworthy, however, for its use of interpretive and understanding responses as well. When the minister says, "It's easy to place the stress at the wrong point in life, I suppose" or "You feel there might have been times when you could have been different?" he is attempting to respond in an understanding way, entering to the best of his ability into her own experiential world. And when he says that "being a Christian is very difficult" and "it seems to me that we are bound to fail once in a while," he is making statements that move, if ever so slightly, from understanding to interpretive responses. The most important interpretive response, however, is his observation that "forgiveness is part of God's nature," a statement that not only reassures but also teaches, imparts meaning, or offers an explanation.

Thus, here, as with the three earlier conversation types, the minister moves up and down the left column responses, sometimes responding supportively, other times understandingly, and still other times in an interpretive mode. Under other circumstances, he might have used one or more of the more selectively employed responses–advising, probing, evaluating–but this particular *recollective* conversation was not the time for that. Of course, until her own response to his recitation of the Lord's Prayer, we would probably have concluded that his efforts to be supportive, understanding, and relevantly interpretive had not penetrated her sense of life's absurdity and her guilt—and shame—for having defamed the other woman's character in order to win what seemed like such an insignificant prize. But even if she had not said that the "Lord's Prayer sounds different now," it would not mean that she would necessarily have been helped by his having taken a step in the advising, probing, and/or evaluative direction.

One important value of Noyce's typology of conversations is that it shows that the kinds of conversations that occur between friends are essentially the same kinds of conversations that occur when ministers assume the counselor role. Turning-point, shared self-disclosure, growing-edge exchanges, and recollective conversations compose the bulk of conversations between ministers and persons requesting or requiring counsel. There are, however, qualitative differences between conversations between friends and what Noyce calls "pastoral conversations." A major difference is that the minister makes a conscious effort to give pastoral conversations a structure that may not be present in conversations between friends.

The Structure of the Conversation

Having discussed types of responses and types of conversations, I would now like to consider how the conversation, whatever type it may be, might be structured. In a practicum in client-centered counseling in which I was involved in graduate school, a student asked, "What if a counselee begins to weep very late in the scheduled fifty-minute appointment? Is it appropriate to allow the session to run over so that she has time to regain her composure?" The answer that our instructor gave surprised us. He said, "It rarely happens. If the counselee weeps, she will almost always do so in the middle of the session so that she allows *herself* time to regain her composure." This response elicited several comments that indicated many students were not convinced: "Isn't it possible that she may be weeping late in the session in order to manipulate us into allowing her more than her allotted time?" "Isn't it possible that she will begin exploring some very deep issues toward the end of the session, and these cause her to lose her composure?" The therapist-instructor who was leading the session agreed that these things are possible and that they do happen on occasion. He contended, however, that, by and large, the students could count on the point he was making about the counselee's own sense of timing. The anxiety behind the original question was not without foundation but was probably exaggerated. Instead, we should trust the process.

I relate this story because it suggests that there is a natural structure to a conversation, one that both parties to the conversation are implicitly aware of. Yet, surprisingly little has been written in the pastoral care and counseling literature about the structure of the "pastoral conversation." Many resources deal with the structure of a worship service, and considerable debate has ensued over how the service should be structured. Normally, the conversation in which a minister provides counsel is of roughly the same duration as the typical Sunday morning worship service. This temporal similarity between worshiping and counseling suggests that attention should also be given to the structure of the pastoral conversation. (Premarital counseling is a possible exception. Stahmann and Hiebert [1997, pp. 51–52] recommend one and one-half- to two-hour sessions.)

I recall my first few conversations with parishioners in my first parish assignment. I had learned some things about responsive listening, but I did not have a clue as to how the conversation itself was supposed to unfold. I found myself asking rather helplessly, "What am I to do after I have listened attentively?" I recall one rather fumbling attempt to conclude a conversation: "I hope you have found it useful to have been listened to," which elicited the reply, "Oh, yes, it has been very helpful." Then there was an awkward silence during which several gambits came to mind: I could say a prayer; I could ask her if she wanted to talk again some time; or I could get up and begin ushering her to the door. I chose the latter, not because I had anything against prayer, or because I was reluctant to schedule another conversation at some later date, but largely out of some anxiety that, because we had already been talking a full hour, I really shouldn't keep her any longer. After she left, I said to myself, "Well, I guess I won't be seeing *her* again." Then I remembered something that one of the salesmen told me when I was washing cars at a used car lot: "The toughest thing in this business, sonny, is closing the deal!"

I assume that I was not alone in my confusion, that the readers of this book are likely to find themselves faced with a similar dilemma. Of course, a prayer *would* have achieved a certain closure that my rather awkward effort to usher the woman to the door failed to achieve. But even a prayer typically leaves some loose ends, issues unresolved, a lingering ambiguity about "what's next." I want therefore to make a suggestion that may, on the face of it, seem trite or unhelpful. This is that the conversation has a beginning, a middle, and an end. As the previous illustration about a student's query regarding a weeping client indicates, the therapist-instructor was very cognizant of these three phases. He said that crying was less likely to occur in the beginning or the ending phase of the conversation, and far more likely to occur in the middle phase. This suggests the usefulness of a conception of the pastoral conversation that has three identifiable phases—beginning, middle, and end.

Earlier in this chapter, I referred to the tone-setting phase, and noted that *supportive, understanding,* and *interpretive* responses are almost exclusively used in this initial phase. Then I referred to the exploratory phase, and suggested that while these three responses will continue to be predominant in this phase, *advising, probing,* and *evaluative* responses are likely to occur as well. Although advising, probing, and evaluation are likely to be rejected or resisted in the tone-setting phase, there is often more receptivity to them in the exploratory phase, especially if the beginning phase of the conversation was devoted to establishing a supportive-understanding-interpretive response milieu. (We should not forget that a favorable listening environment has also hopefully been established in the beginning phase.) I suggest that the third, ending phase be termed the "resolution phase."

Although this three-phase structure may appear to be rather arbitrary—why not two, or four, or five phases?—it has the weight of Christian tradition behind it. In his book on *The Poetry of Meditation: A Study in English Religious Literature of the Seventeenth Century* (1954), Louis L. Martz devotes a chapter to the structure of the meditative process that was developed in the fifteenth century by Jesuits and was then adopted, with some modifications, by the English Puritans. He notes that "the enormous popularity of methodical meditation...may be attributed to the fact that it satisfied and developed a natural, fundamental tendency of the human mind—a tendency to work from a particular situation, through analysis of that situation, and finally to some sort of resolution of the problem which the situation has presented" (p. 39). In a similar way, I am proposing that the structure of conversations in which the minister assumes the counselor role is a three-phase process, beginning with the formulation of the situation, continuing with the exploration of the situation, and concluding with "some sort of resolution of the problem which the situation has presented."

These three phases are not necessarily of equal duration, but I believe that both the minister and the person being counseled are at least subconsciously aware of a roughly equal duration between the three phases and that they sense the junctures in the conversation where they have begun to move from phase one to phase two, and from phase two to phase three. There is usually some awareness by at least one of the conversation partners—preferably the minister—if the expected shift from one phase to the other has not occurred at its more-or-less appointed time. If too much time is being spent in the tone-setting phase, where the situation that brings the other person to the minister is presented, or in the exploratory phase, where the problem or problems embedded in the situation are explored, this may indicate that anxiety is an important dynamic in the conversation, whether the anxiety is on the part of the minister, the parishioner, or both. On the other hand, it could also simply mean that the minister does not have the requisite skill in structuring the conversation. Conversely, there may also be awareness by at least one of the conversation partners—preferably the minister—if there has been a premature shift from the first to the second, or from the second to the third phase. Anxiety may be the primary culprit here as well, though again, the minister's lack of skill in shaping the conversation may be the primary cause.

The Tone-setting Phase

To illustrate these three phases, I would like to return to the case of the nineteen-year-old woman who has hateful feelings toward her minister father. All that we have to work with is the simple statement she made about these feelings not being warranted. However, the various responses that I constructed to illustrate the types of responses that are especially useful in counseling indicate my assumption that this statement is likely to have been made in the tone-setting phase, though not, I would assume, at the very beginning of the conversation. Assuming that this is the first time the counseling minister and the woman have talked about the situation, there must have had to be some prior discussion of the sorts of things that would constitute a baseline for her confession that she had hateful feelings toward her father. Some of these may have centered on facts about her background, her family, her current life situation (college student? working full-time? living at home? has own apartment?), the usual things that we say about ourselves by way of introduction. If these things were already known to the minister (who may have been the minister of the church she attends, a campus pastor, a professor in the religion department, etc.) and the woman knew that he knew these things, they may have been dispensed with, but something about her family would most likely have been discussed before she volunteered that she had hateful feelings toward her father. It is very unlikely that she entered the minister's office (or joined him at the lunch table) and immediately blurted out, "I tell you, I hate my father. I hate him! I really hate him!" If this had happened, I know I would have found myself rather taken aback and would have said something like, "Whoa, slow down, let's rewind the reel," or some such comment that would communicate the sense of being startled by what would seem, in that case, more of an announcement intended to be shocking than a thoughtful confession.

Also likely to have occurred earlier would be some indications, verbal or nonverbal, that she was struggling with the question whether to divulge these feelings to the minister. She may have felt that it was a betrayal of her father and her family to tell someone else about what she was feeling, especially when this someone else was himself a minister (and very possibly a professional acquaintance). In effect, this was to be a *shared self-disclosure* type of conversation, and we would therefore expect that she would have some initial resistance to making the disclosure. In fact, if the resistance was not present, we might wonder why. Had she reached the point of desperation where she simply had to tell someone about this? Did she have other motives for telling about her feelings toward her father, such as a desire to defame her father, but to do so by indirection, hoping that the listener would assume that her father *is* deserving of these hateful feelings toward him and, being a professional colleague of her father, would begin circulating the story? (The woman who wanted to retain her presidency of the women's group may have taken this very approach.) In any event, resistance to this self-disclosure would likely be present during the beginning phase of the conversation, and it would be incumbent on the minister to recognize the resistance while also recognizing her desire to be self-disclosive (on the matter of resistance, see the "counseling in the wilderness" case in Dittes, 1999b, pp. 139–48).

An implication of what I have said thus far is that the beginning phase of the conversation need not–should not–be idle or random chatter. One should expect that if a good listening environment is created, the beginning phase of the conversation will comprise the disclosure of the situation that prompted the other person to ask for this meeting. (In two earlier works [1979, 1980] I actually refer to this initial phase of the conversation as the "identification of the problem" phase.) Time spent in idle chatter in the beginning phase will be sorely missed in the third or resolution phase of the conversation, as this summary phase is the one most likely to be compromised by a poor use of time at the beginning. This does not, of course, mean that the minister should be inhospitable or demanding, asking, "What brings you here?" before the other person has even had a chance to sit down. Of course, a few pleasantries will be expressed at the beginning. What I mean by "idle or random chatter" is a five-minute discussion of the weather, the minister's vacation plans, the fact that her mother met his aunt at a national denominational meeting, and so forth. This is also not the time for the minister to provide a detailed commentary on the latest Garrison Keillor show or a film that "you have got to see." In this respect, a meeting in which the allotted time is fifty to sixty minutes differs from a conversation between friends. If the counseling is being done over lunch, there may, of course, be exceptions, but even then, the matter at hand should not be deferred until dessert is ordered.

Let us assume, then, that the woman has revealed in the beginning phase her hateful feelings toward her father, and let us assume that the minister has responded with supportive, understanding, and/or interpretive responses to this self-disclosure. He has either assured her that it is a "very good thing" that she has had the courage to talk about these feelings, or has noted that the "apparent absence" of any good reason for her feelings is really troubling her, or has noted that there seems to be a discrepancy between her portrayal of her father and her feelings toward him and has suggested that they look into this discrepancy in order to understand these feelings better. Quite possibly, he has said all these things, perhaps in this very order (from supportive to understanding to interpretive). In any event, all three comments invite her to talk more about this self-disclosure. They also signal the minister's perception that this is precisely the topic that they should discuss further, that he anticipates this will be the subject that is likely to take up the remaining minutes of their time together, and that this is, in fact, a very appropriate use of their time. (Some counselees wonder if what they are talking about in the counseling session is what they are "supposed" to be talking about in such a situation. Their anxiety about this is comparable to those students who want to make certain that they have not "misunderstood" the teacher's assignment.) Other issues may secondarily or tangentially arise, but this is deemed the focal issue, much as his friend's "vocational ambivalence" was the focal issue in Noyce's illustration of a shared self-disclosure conversation.

The Exploratory Phase

If there appears to be agreement about the focal issue, the conversation now moves into the exploratory phase. The word *explore* has several meanings, including "to look into a matter carefully," "to travel in a previously unknown or little known region to learn more about it," and "to examine or probe in order to make a diagnosis." While I believe that a case may be made for the diagnostic meaning of exploration (this case has been forcefully made by Paul W. Pruyser in his book *The Minister as Diagnostician* [1976]; I have also offered a version of it in Capps, 1980), the best meaning of exploration for our purposes here is the travel metaphor, as the minister and the woman with whom he is conversing are, in fact, going into a region whose character and contours are as yet unknown to them, but which they are open to learning more about. James E. Dittes calls this "counseling in the wilderness" (Dittes, 1999b). This is the region of the woman's hateful feelings toward her father and what they mean or portend. As noted in the introduction, Ludwig Wittgenstein has said, "A problem has the form: I do not know my way about" (Wittgenstein, 1958, p. 123). In this sense, both are making a commitment to explore a problematic region in this woman's life in order that she may in fact find her way about. (In Capps 1979 and 1980, I refer to this as the "reconstruction of the problem" phase of the counseling session.)

On the basis of what we know about this case from the single excerpt provided by Clinebell, we may assume that the exploratory phase will focus on the woman's feelings toward her father, and especially on the question of whether and in what sense her father has related to her in ways that have provoked these hateful feelings. Has he mistreated her (perhaps not physically, as she has pointed out, but verbally)? Or has his kindness toward her actually made it difficult for her to develop an independence of her own? These and other possibilities call for further exploration—this is the unknown or little known region that we want to learn more about. The primary issue, however, is not "getting at the facts," though this is certainly important, but to explore the counselee's own experiential world in relation to these facts. Her experiential world is the region to be explored. If, for example, he *has* mistreated her verbally by saying things that are demeaning, the issue is not primarily whether he has done this only once or twice or many times, but how she experiences these demeaning comments. A single demeaning statement may have been enough to confirm what she had long suspected, that her father had little respect for her. If so, the minister would not say, "Could it be that you are making a mountain out of a molehill?" or "Maybe you should cut him some slack. We all say stupid things once in a while." Instead, he would say, "What he said that night confirmed your suspicions that he never had much respect for you." (If she seems more tentative about her suspicions, he would say, "seemed to confirm.")

Although this would be an understanding response, we would anticipate that in the exploratory phase, the minister might also venture responses that are probing, such as asking her to reveal more about what she is thinking when these hateful feelings well up in her, or evaluative ones, such as suggesting to her the possibility that her father *has* said or done something that makes her feelings—some of them, at least—warranted. We cannot predict where this exploration might lead, but we would hope that out of it would come greater congruence between her perception of her father and the feelings she has toward him. As Carl Rogers points out in *On Becoming a Person* (1961), a shift from incongruence to congruence is a major goal of counseling. Congruence is reflected in an accurate matching of experiencing, awareness, and communication. Rogers suggests that the simplest example of such congruence is an infant. If an infant is experiencing hunger at the physiological and visceral level, her awareness appears to match this experience, and her communication is congruent with it. She is "a unified person all the way through, whether we tap her experience at the visceral level, the level of her awareness, or the level of communication. Probably one of the reasons why most people respond to infants is that they are so completely genuine, integrated or congruent. If an infant expresses affection or anger or contentment or fear there *is* no doubt in our minds that she *is* this experience, all the way through" (p. 339).

An example of incongruence is a man who becomes angrily involved in a group discussion: "His face flushes, his tone communicates anger, he shakes his finger at his opponent. Yet when a friend says, 'Well, let's not get angry about this,' he replies, with evident sincerity and surprise, 'I'm not angry, I don't have any *feeling* about this at all! I was just pointing out the logical facts.' The other men in the group break out in laughter at this statement" (Rogers, 1961, pp. 339–40). Rogers asks, "What is happening here? It seems clear that at a physiological level he is experiencing anger, but this is not matched by his awareness. In addition, his communication is actually ambiguous and unclear. In its words it is a setting forth of logic and fact, but in its tone and accompanying gestures, it is carrying a very different message—'I am angry at you'" (p. 340). Rogers indicates his belief that this ambiguity or contradictoriness of communication "is always present when a person who is at that moment incongruent endeavors to communicate" (p. 340).

One may argue that the woman in the case we have been discussing *is* experiencing incongruence between her visceral experiencing, her awareness, and her communication. The major absence of a match is between her experiencing of hateful feelings and her lack of awareness of any reasons for these feelings. Her communication reflects this disjuncture. On the other hand, there is a level of her experiencing of which she also seems unaware, and this is her apparent need to view these feelings negatively, as inappropriate or unwarranted. A major source of incongruence in her case, then, is her experiencing of hateful feelings toward her father and her judgment on this experiencing. This is an even deeper level of incongruence than the discrepancy between her portrayal of her father and her feelings toward him, as the incongruence here is between the feelings she has (and her awareness of them) and her tendency to view these feelings as ones she shouldn't have. She marshals support for this judgment by invoking the Bible, pointing out that "the Bible says to love and honor your father, that hating your father is therefore a sin."

From the perspective of Rogers' client-centered counseling approach, the goal should not be to try to get rid of these feelings, but to try to understand them and for the woman to be more accepting of them, thus admitting them into her perception of herself. No doubt the man in Rogers' example is unaware of his anger in part because he cannot admit into his perception of himself that he is a person who is no stranger to anger. The woman in Clinebell's case *is* aware of her hateful feelings, but she has not accepted them into her self-perception. She cannot say, "I am a person who has hateful feelings toward my father *and I can accept this fact about myself.*"

In short, we may view the discrepancy between this woman's feelings and her view of her father and the incongruence between her experiencing and her view of herself as two related, but different issues. Following Heinz Kohut, we might call the former a self-other issue, and the latter a self-self issue (Kohut, 1984, pp. 51–52), but the terminology we use is not the important thing. What *is* important is that the exploratory phase of the conversation should not become so focused on the issue of her father that the issue of her self-rejection is neglected. Or, if the exploratory phase *does* center only on the former, either because time does not permit exploration of the second issue or because this second issue is one whose exploration would take the conversation into terrain that requires a more experienced guide, the minister should make a mental note of this fact. This mental note will then have a significant place in the *resolution* phase of the conversation.

It should be noted that the exploratory phase is not merely one in which the minister would attempt to get the woman in this case to make more self-disclosures. Rather, the exploratory phase is one in which the various facts and meanings of the self-disclosure that have already been presented are themselves explored. More self-disclosures, such as her feelings toward her mother, would only add breadth to the conversation. Instead the goal in the exploratory phase is to achieve greater focus, to be both intentional and attentional. This is where the minister's constructive efforts are especially important, because what the conversation in the second phase is attentive to is, to a large degree, a matter of choice, and the minister plays a very important role in this choice.

Family therapist Jay Haley was once asked to be a consultant for a therapist in training who was having an especially difficult time with a particular family. Haley asked the trainee what the problem was, and was told, "The symbiotic relationship between the mother and daughter." Haley responded, "I wouldn't let that be the problem" (O'Hanlon and Wilk, 1987, p. 70). What he meant was that the problem, as stated, was much too global, and that it needed to be sharpened, more narrowly focused and circumscribed. What he also implied is that the therapist plays a major role in determining what will in fact be taken to *be* the problem. We usually assume that the problem is already known to the person who has come for counsel, that she may or may not reveal it right away (she might, for example, talk about something else entirely or offer what is sometimes called the "presenting problem," i.e., a problem that is likely to be related to the "real" or "deeper" problem, but is not in fact that problem), and that the minister's task is therefore to "figure out" what the problem is from the clues that the other person provides. In this view, the minister plays amateur detective, and it is therefore no wonder that the minister feels herself to be under considerable pressure and fears that she may not be able to rise to the challenge.

If, however, it is the minister's role to *participate* in the defining or framing of the problem to be explored, she is less likely to feel overwhelmed. It is *not* the minister's task to penetrate a mystery, but it *is* her task to help focus the conversation so that it does not become diffuse and go off in too many directions at once. This is not a privileging of "male-linear thinking" over "female circular or weblike thinking," nor is it a violation of what Mary Field Belenky and her coauthors of *Women's Ways of Knowing* call "connected knowing" (Belenky et al., 1986, pp. 101–3), for the point is not that the conversation is either linear or circular, but that it has a focus, providing both persons the sense and assurance that they are talking about the same thing, that they are not engaged in "parallel talk" (the adult version of the "parallel play" of two-year-old children).

By focusing the conversation in this way, the minister will be fully aware that there are other concerns or problems worth talking about, including issues that have direct or indirect bearing on the one that *is* explored. In this sense, the minister is fully aware that this conversation is limited in scope. This awareness, however, should not be cause for despair, for the hope is that in helping this woman explore the focal concern or problem (i.e., her hateful feelings toward her father), she will become more adept at exploring other concerns and problems, whether these are ones that she currently has, or ones that she will have in the future.

In emphasizing the importance of congruence, including the hope that this woman would experience greater congruence between her awareness of her feelings and her self-perception as one who should not have such feelings, I am aware of the fact that I have not yet had anything to say about her view that the Bible says to love and honor one's father and that hating your father is therefore a sin. The exploratory phase of the conversation may well include consideration of this view. If so, I would assume that this will have the same exploratory feel to it as their travels into the world of her feelings of hatred would have. This is perhaps a region about which the minister has greater technical knowledge than the woman does, but, at the moment, it is an experiential matter for her, and the minister should respect this fact. He should also be sensitive to the fact that, because she is the daughter of a minister, her father's voice and the "voice" of the Bible are both emotionally and cognitively interrelated. It is, therefore, not altogether surprising that she would invoke the Bible in support of her judgment that her feelings toward her father—especially her father?—are wrong.

The Resolution Phase

As Louis L. Martz points out, the mind has a natural tendency to work toward "some sort of *resolution* of the problems which the situation has presented" (1954, p. 39, my emphasis). The third, or resolution phase, of the conversation begins when both the minister and the other person begin to have a sense that their exploration has borne as much fruit as it is likely to bear on this occasion. It is the point where, as in my illustration of my first fumbling efforts to counsel parishioners, the other person looks at the minister with querying eyes. This query could be a simple "So what's next?" or it could be a more searching "So what do you think? Am I a despicable daughter?"

One definition of the word *resolution* is "a decision as to future action." The simple "So what's next?" question indicates that a decision *does* need to be made regarding future action, and this needs to be a mutual decision, one which both persons fundamentally endorse. If there is to be another scheduled conversation, the minister should indicate why he believes this *is* the "future action" to be taken. This is the point at which our earlier analogy between the pastoral conversation and worship breaks down, for there is no need at the end of the worship service to announce that there will be another one next week, much less to provide a reason why this will be the case. A second conversation between the minister and the person who has requested a meeting is optional, and because this is true, some rationale for scheduling a second one needs to be indicated. This rationale should also be agreed on by both parties.

In turn, this rationale gives the other person something to think about in the meantime. This is not "homework" in the sense that some therapists employ it, but it does sound an anticipatory note: "Next time, let's continue our exploration here, at this point." The most valuable exploratory work often occurs between conversations, and this may be as true for the minister as it is for the person who has requested a listening ear. An insight or discovery may be made by one or both as they review their earlier conversation in their minds. Often, the next meeting together begins with one or both reporting on what has been "discovered" in the meantime, and this frequently becomes the focus of conversation: "I've been thinking about why I have assumed that my hateful feelings toward my father are wrong. I have never questioned this assumption. This got me to thinking that I often make assumptions and then draw conclusions from these assumptions. Now I'm wondering what would happen if I looked at the assumptions themselves." Or, the discovery could be: "I thought that by talking about my hateful feelings toward my father I wouldn't be able to hold my head up in his presence, that I would go skulking around, feeling ashamed about what I had done, as though he would know that I had done this. Instead, I felt more free around him. I was actually less guarded than before. It was just the reverse of what I anticipated."

The insight or discovery might also be one the minister introduces: "Since we last talked, I've been wondering to myself why I didn't pick up on what you said about how you shouldn't have hateful feelings toward your father because he's a minister. This implies that the daughter of a minister can't allow herself to have the same feelings that the daughter of another father may have. I guess it was the special burden that you carry that I wasn't hearing, probably because of my own anxieties about this, being a minister myself." This discovery should not lead to a focus on the minister's struggles, but to the "invitation," as it were, for the woman to explore this "special burden" if she feels this would be helpful to her.

In light of the likelihood of these intervening discoveries, is a second conversation always warranted? This is not discussed much in the pastoral counseling literature, for even those who are advocates of "brief counseling" approaches and methods for ministers recommend three or more sessions. Because I will discuss these recommendations in greater detail in chapter five, I will not comment further on this issue here, except to note that a psychotherapist in New York City has a practice based on one session per client. He developed the approach as a result of a study he conducted in which he interviewed clients who did not return, as promised, for their second session with the therapist. While the therapist involved had assumed that the initial session must therefore have been a "failure," he found that two-thirds of the persons he interviewed felt that the session had provided them with the clarity they needed in order to deal with the concern or problem on their own. To them, the session had been a "success."

Of course, it could be argued that their expectations of what therapy could do for them were too minimalist and that if they *had* continued in therapy, they would have experienced growth in ways unforeseen to them. Still, this illustration supports my basic point that there should be a rationale for scheduling another conversation, and that this rationale should be made explicit and be endorsed by both persons. The minister assumes too much responsibility for the conversational process itself if he says, "In my considered judgment, we need to talk further," and does not reveal what this judgment is. The other person may be too timid to ask, but she has a right to know why another conversation is being recommended and should have an opportunity to indicate whether she endorses this reasoning or not. After all, in the vast majority of cases, it is the other person who initiated the conversation in the first place. The initiative should remain with her.

The converse is also true. The judgment that one conversation has been sufficient also should be supported. This should not be an arbitrary decision by the minister, and he should be aware of anxiety (for any of the reasons discussed in chapter 1) that may be inordinately influencing this decision. The woman in Clinebell's case might conclude on her own that she had reached sufficient clarity about her feelings toward her father that she does not need to have another conversation with the minister. Or she may decide that she simply cannot allow herself to explore these feelings further–they make her too anxious–and that this conversation has enabled her to see this. Her decision should, of course, be respected. But because this was a very troubling concern for her, the minister has every reason to suggest that they talk again. A two-week interval may be preferable to a one-week interval, however, as there is no pressing decision to be made.

Thus, if one meaning of the word *resolution* is "a decision as to future action," this particular case essentially raises the rather standard or routine question of whether a second conversation should be scheduled. Other cases would raise other decisional issues, such as what action should be taken to protect an abused spouse from further abuse, or whether the parishioner should be referred to another professional. These and other related issues will be discussed in more detail in chapter 5. For now, the point is that a decision as to future action, and rationale for this decision, is an important consideration in the resolution phase of the conversation. This is true not only of the initial conversation but of subsequent conversations as well.

Another meaning of *resolution* is "the passing (in music) of a dissonant chord into a consonant one." While this is a musical term, it has relevance for the conversational context as well. The desire to end the conversation on a consonant note is reflected in Noyce's illustration of his own *turning-point* counseling and his *shared self-disclosure* conversation with the friend who was experiencing vocational ambivalence. It may be too much to say that, other things being equal, a conversation between the minister and the counseled person should always end on a consonant note, but one important aspect of a "good" conversation is that both parties involved feel encouraged by what has transpired between them. Some years ago, I occasionally conversed with our academic dean in his office. After two or three of these conversations, I realized that, though I had anticipated these talks with considerable expectation—usually because I had some ideas I wanted to present to him or because I was flattered that he had summoned me—I left them feeling beleaguered and not a little demoralized. These, of course, were conversations about institutional, not personal matters, and are not entirely comparable to conversations between ministers and persons who have asked to talk with them. I believe, nonetheless, that pastoral conversations should be inherently encouraging. As I have argued in a previous book, ministers are "agents of hope" (Capps, 1995), and hope, in essence, is the anticipation that what is desired will happen.

Thus, in the case of the woman with hateful feelings toward her father, the resolution from the dissonant note struck earlier in the conversation to the consonant note near its conclusion need not be anything as premature and artificial as, "You have helped me rid myself of my hateful feelings," but it could well be, "I am not as troubled about these feelings as when I came in," or "I am not feeling as down on myself for having these feelings," or "I am beginning to realize that these feelings *do* have an explanation and that they are not entirely unprovoked." These resolutions, whether verbalized or simply expressed in her overall demeanor, are comparable to Noyce's feeling in his turning-point conversation of a burden having been lifted from his shoulders. It is perhaps too much to expect that she will leave whistling a happy tune, but there may be a certain spring in her step based, in large part, on her sense that she *can,* at least to a degree, "own" these hateful feelings and not see them as necessarily evidence that she is a despicable, ungrateful daughter.

A third meaning of *resolution* is "the act of solving a puzzle." As persons who are addicted to jigsaw puzzles well know, the "resolution" comes when all the pieces have been placed in their proper positions. As children, we would try to force the pieces to fit, but we found, in the end, that these efforts were counterproductive because it meant that the piece that was supposed to be in that position would have to be forced to fit somewhere else. If the conversation between the minister and the person who has sought her counsel is analogous to putting the pieces of a puzzle together, the attempt to "resolve" the concern or problem should not be "forced" on the other person. This is precisely where controlling, impatient, and even moralistic responses are most likely to arise, as the minister will be anxious to force a premature resolution or one that seeks to sidestep the problem's complexities.

Much is written in the pastoral care and counseling literature about the dangers of psychological reductionism, but there is also the danger of theological and moral reductionism, where complex psychological matters (such as the woman's hateful feelings toward her minister father) are reduced to ready-made theological formulae or simple moralisms. It is far better to confess to the other person in the concluding phase of an initial conversation, "I remain puzzled about some things," than to act as though one knows how it all fits together. As art historian James Elkins points out, one of the most anxiety-inducing experiences we have in life is when we are confronted by experiences or phenomena whose meaning is not readily apparent, or which may, in fact, have no particular meaning at all (Elkins, 1998, p. 16). He believes that he and his own colleagues have ascribed so many meanings to paintings—explaining every little detail—that the painting can barely stand up under their interpretive weight. Some paintings, in fact, do not need to be "understood," but simply "beheld." Thus, of the three meanings of *resolution* thus far discussed, "solving the puzzle" is the one that we should be most wary about. The minister especially should be aware of the sense of incompletion that he feels within himself and accept this ambiguous state of affairs for what it is. This very acceptance may be, in fact, his best means of entry into the counseled person's experiential world.

A fourth meaning of *resolution* has medical connotations, referring to the "subsidence or disappearance of a swelling, fever, or other manifestation of disease." While this use of the word is a relatively unfamiliar one to most of us, the idea behind it is not. We know the relief that comes when a child's high fever begins to break, or when the symptoms of a disease begin to disappear, indicating that the patient is on the road to recovery. A minister is not a doctor, but she is one whose impressions and judgments matter to the person with whom she has been conversing, and, therefore, she should be aware that the other wants these impressions and judgments to be verbalized. Since client-centered therapy came on the scene, considerable debate has ensued in the psychotherapeutic literature about "diagnosis," whether it has a place in psychotherapy and, if so, in what sense. Carl Rogers opposed it if it meant that the therapist would be making judgments from an external frame of reference, but allowed for its qualified use if the "diagnosis" derived from the therapist's empathic participation in the client's experiential world (1961, pp. 223–25). Because he believed that the word *diagnosis* would invariably connote the assigning of a label or description deriving from a more general population, he discouraged its use. I have argued that the "theological themes" that Paul W. Pruyser views as diagnostic (see Pruyser, 1976, pp. 60–79) may be useful for understanding and interpreting the deeper dimensions of a person's experiential world (see Capps, 1979, 1980), so I am more disposed to take a positive view of diagnosis. In fact, the theological themes that Pruyser sets forth have evident relevance for the case of the woman we have been discussing throughout this chapter.

Even so, we should not be distracted by the medical term *diagnosis* from the other very important fact that the best doctors attempt to be reassuring and understanding when they present their impressions and judgments at the conclusion of an exploration into the patient's problem. For the conversation in which a minister has been asked for counsel, this means that the types of responses that were predominant in the two preceding phases of the conversation–supportive, understanding, interpretive–should continue to predominate in this third phase, even if there has been a noticeable shift toward some offering of advice. In fact, though in some situations advising is especially appropriate, the conversation should not be judged a failure if it does not conclude with a word or words of advice. As previously noted, in Noyce's turning point conversation, his friend did not advise him on which course to take. If there ever was a perfect opportunity for giving advice, this was certainly it, as it was clear that there were two courses of action that Noyce could take. His friend could have weighed the merits of both in his mind and could have advised Noyce to take the one that he himself would have taken: "If I were you, I'd stay put. You have too much to lose by leaving, and new situations always look rosier than they really are." Instead, the friend offered an observation that was supportive, understanding, and interpretive–"either way, you will be happy"–and demonstrated his respect for Noyce by recognizing that Noyce was capable of making his own decision.

Some readers may ask: Why this caution against giving advice? Some reasons for this have already been noted in my comments on the supportive-advising-controlling continuum, but another very practical reason is that the other person may decide *not* to take the minister's advice and, as a result, may feel reluctant to talk with her again about this and perhaps other issues as well. Put otherwise, if the minister *does* offer advice in the resolution phase of the conversation, it should be expressed in a sufficiently tentative way that the other person will feel free to raise questions about it (preferably at the very time it is offered), give reasons for why he has misgivings about accepting it, or propose some modifications while accepting the basic idea.

If, for example, the minister advises the woman with hateful feelings toward her father to talk with him about these feelings in order to get them out in the open, she should be given the opportunity to raise questions ("You mean, just go up to him and blurt it out?"); give reasons why she does not think this is a good idea ("He will simply tell me what I already know, that the Bible says to love and honor your father"); or accept it in principle but with modifications ("What if I suggested that we go to a restaurant, just the two of us, so that we can talk about my future? This way, we might be able to have a conversation that builds a better relationship between us, which in turn will help to reduce my hateful feelings toward him"). In other words, advice should not have a "You must do this and do it this way" tone to it, but should instead provide a basis for further discussion. In this sense, it may contribute to the ultimate resolution of the concern or problem, but in a way that communicates respect for the other person and for the problem-resolving capacities this person already possesses. The "modification" that she proposes grows out of the idea that she should "try to get rid of her hateful feelings," but does so in a way that takes account of the facts that arise out of her relationship with her father.

Concluding Comments

We have seen that certain *types* of response can be especially helpful in moving a conversation through the tone-setting and exploratory phases on to the resolution phase. The reader may have noticed that, in all the illustrative material employed in this chapter, the minister did not make use of what might be called "psychological jargon." Students who enroll in courses in pastoral counseling often assume that they will be encouraged to use "psychological" words and phrases, and some of these students are already prepared to mistrust such a class because they have been warned that the professors who teach these courses want to replace faith language with psychological language. This chapter makes clear, however, that the minister does not need to adopt a special form of discourse when adopting the counselor role. Instead, he should use the same conventional language that he uses in other contexts.

Interestingly enough, I have often found myself in such conversations being the one who uses *more* conventional language because the other person has adopted the psychological jargon of our society to a greater extent than I have. (Note that Noyce's friend speaks of his "vocational ambivalence.") The use of such jargon has often meant that I have needed to ask for clarification: "When you say that your parents are 'codependent,' what do you mean by this?" Or, "Could you explain to me what you mean when you say you suffer from 'low self-worth'?" It is not that I do not have any understanding of these words, but that I want to know what they really mean for this particular person, how *she* understands or experiences them. For this, a more conventional descriptive statement is needed, which is typically provided in the form of a "for instance" that can then be discussed in more detail.

I realize, of course, that we all have our "specialized" vocabularies or ways of speaking that derive from the ways of life we have chosen and that the minister, as part of his concern to be understanding, should try his best to enter into the "language world" of the other person. In a recent conversation with a friend who has "made it big" in the corporate world of finance, he related how his son wanted to go to Venezuela for a year after college graduation rather than enter immediately into the profession for which he had been trained. With a note of resignation in his voice, my friend said, "So, once again, 'deep pockets Dad' anteed up." I realized I rarely heard these words—"deep pockets" and "anteed up"—in the academic setting where I spend my working days. In my professional world, a father might have said, "We knew it would be an expense we could ill afford, but we felt it would be a broadening experience for our son, as it would deepen his understanding of other cultures."

To the extent possible, the minister should enter into the "language world" of the other, as language is the primary means by which the other communicates what it is like within his own experiential world. This does not necessarily mean, however, that she needs to be able to use it herself as a way of demonstrating her concern to know the other's experiential world from the inside. In the actual conversation mentioned above, I said something like, "You say that with a bit of resignation, as though you preferred that Jack would get on with his career." He answered, "Yes, but that was then. Now, I realize this was just what Jack needed." Thus, what I had taken to be "resignation" in the here and now—the immediate—was actually "resignation" as he reflected back on the experience. What I had missed was the current note of pride in his voice, that "deep pockets Dad" was instrumental in enabling Jack to have this invaluable experience. As he concluded, "It was money well spent," I responded, "And Jack was grateful?" "You bet your life he was!"

In the next chapter, I will discuss the background thinking that a minister should engage in during the types of conversations we have considered in this chapter.

3

How to Think Systemically

When students enroll in a pastoral care course, they often believe that they will be asked to leave their minds—their capacity to think—at the door on the assumption that the course is only concerned with emotions or feelings. Some (especially those who did not want to take the course in the first place) believe, therefore, that it will be much less intellectually challenging than courses in theology, Bible, and church history. These students often sit in the back of the room and look bored, even a little defiant, as if to announce that they do not "go in for that touchy-feely sort of stuff."

I understand this perception of pastoral care courses, and I try my best to "convert" these cultured despisers because I am a convert myself. Until I actually began to read books in psychotherapy, I assumed that the counseling profession was constituted of persons who, though well-intentioned, were mental lightweights. To my surprise, I discovered that many had excellent training in philosophy (a field in which I had done graduate work) and that they were using their philosophical training to theorize about the nature and objectives of counseling. I also discovered that most of the disagreements between counselors were owing to the different philosophies to which they adhered. This should not have come to me as such a surprise, for, after all, in the mid-nineteenth century, it was philosophers with an empirical bent who developed the field of psychology, and the major psychologists of the late nineteenth and early twentieth centuries, such as Sigmund Freud and William James, were trained in philosophy. While the two fields are now much more distinct from each other, many of the most influential counseling theories of the late twentieth century were formulated out of philosophical theories current at the time (for example, existentialism, phenomenology, Wittgensteinian philosophy of language, structuralism, hermeneutics, and pragmatism).

In this chapter, I will discuss one of the ways in which a minister may use her mind when engaged in the role of counselor. I will propose that perhaps the most valuable form of thinking a minister can do in this situation is to think systemically. There are other ways to think in counseling, and they have their advocates. Some, for example, would suggest that thinking psychodynamically is more important than thinking systemically. I believe, with Michael P. Nichols, that these two ways of thinking are ultimately reconcilable, but for practical reasons that I hope to make clear as the chapter evolves, systemic thinking is especially valuable for ministers to know about and to be able to adapt to their own situations. In the course of this chapter, I will also take note of criticisms of the systemic way of thinking, and will indicate ways in which these criticisms may be taken into account through appropriate modifications and revisions.

Before I discuss the systemic way of thinking, however, I want to address the more preliminary question, "How can I talk and think at the same time?" and the related question, "If I am thinking during the conversation, won't I jeopardize the immediacy that is one of the conditions of good listening?" The answer to the first question is that, while it may be difficult to think while one is talking, it is much less difficult to think while one is listening. Since the minister does more listening than talking in the conversation, these listening periods afford him the opportunity to think about what is being related to him by the counseled person. To return to an example discussed in chapter 2, by the time Gaylord Noyce's friend said to him toward the end of their turning-point conversation, "You'll be happy either way," he had been doing a great deal of listening, and during that time he clearly had also been doing some thinking.

If we were to ask Noyce's friend, "When did this thought that Noyce would be happy either way occur to you?" he might not be able to recall the precise point in the conversation when it happened, but we can be quite certain that it occurred to him while he was listening to Noyce talk about the pros and cons of the two situations or options before him. We can also be relatively certain that he did not think this—that Noyce would be happy either way—before they entered into the conversation. Conceivably, he viewed his friend as such a happy soul by nature that he could safely say this even if Noyce were trying to decide between staying at Yale or going to live on a deserted island, or between going on a Caribbean cruise and going to the hospital for surgery. But this is doubtful. Rather, he arrived at this thought during the conversation itself, and this very fact is partly why Noyce found it so liberating: "*On the basis of what I have told him,* he has concluded that I would be happy either way."

Now, we might not feel that the friend's statement, "You'll be happy either way," is a particularly profound thought. We might even say, "Well, anyone could have said that." This may be true, but according to Noyce's own testimony (which is really all that matters here), *he* had not seen it until his friend pointed it out to him. It often happens that the person who is the recipient of another's counsel will say, "What you just said seems so obvious. Why couldn't I see it?" The person giving the counsel could respond, "I guess I could see it because you were doing the telling, and I was doing the listening."

What about the issue of immediacy? Doesn't thinking about what the other person is saying distance oneself from the other? This may be true of some ways of thinking, especially those that attempt to be "objective." The thinking that I will be arguing for here, however, is more akin to what Erik H. Erikson, in his well-known essay on "The Nature of Clinical Evidence," calls "disciplined subjectivity." He notes that the "psychotherapist shares with all clinicians the…requirement that even while facing most intimate and emotional matters, he must maintain intellectual inner contact with his conceptual models, however crude they may be. But more than any other clinician the psychotherapist must include in his field of observation a *specific self-awareness* in the very act of perceiving his patient's actions and reactions." This means that "there is a core of *disciplined subjectivity* in clinical work…which it is neither desirable nor possible to replace altogether with seemingly more objective methods" (Erikson, 1964, p. 53). Thus, intellectual contact with one's conceptual models (here, the systemic model) and an awareness of how one is experiencing in oneself the other person's words and reactions are the ingredients of the counselor's "disciplined subjectivity."

Thus, the thinking that occurs when one is engaged in the counselor role is the kind of thinking that arises out of, not in contradistinction to, the conditions of good or effective listening (as presented in chapter 1). This, after all, was true of Noyce's friend's observation that he would be "happy either way." This comment was not based on an objective assessment of the two options that Noyce had laid out, but on impressions derived from listening carefully to what Noyce was saying and how he was saying it. In a sense, it was Noyce who was being the more "objective" in that he was trying to think in terms of "right versus wrong choices," and it was his friend who brought him back to the more subjective, back to Noyce's own experiential world.

There is another way to make this point. As noted in chapter 2, one of the more common ways in which a counseling session is brought to a resolution is for the counselor to offer a "diagnosis." As we saw, Carl Rogers opposed diagnosis if it meant that the therapist made judgments from an external—purely objective—frame of reference, but he allowed for its qualified use if the diagnosis derived from the therapist's empathic participation in the client's experiential world. In this case, the diagnosis involves noting the incongruence between the client's experiencing and her awareness of this experiencing, or between her awareness of the experiencing and her communication of it. Noyce's friend's statement—"You'll be happy either way"—was diagnostic in this sense, as it noted the incongruence between the way Noyce was talking about the problem of deciding between staying put or going elsewhere (talk that treated the decision as a "right versus wrong" choice) and his deeper awareness that he would in fact be happy with either outcome. This "diagnosis" was also more liberating than Noyce's "right versus wrong" assessment had been.

In short, the thinking that I am advocating here grows naturally out of good listening. It is not incommensurate with the conditions of listening (as presented in chapter 1) or with the tone-setting responses (as discussed in chapter 2). In fact, the thinking that will be presented here is much more reflective of the supportive-understanding-interpretive response modes than the advising-probing-evaluative ones. Although we tend to view the former as more emotion or feeling oriented, and the latter as more thinking oriented, this is itself a false distinction. As William James argued more than a century ago, our thoughts are always informed by our emotions, and our emotions are mental as well as visceral phenomena. To say, for example, that anger is a feeling and doubt is a thought is inaccurate, for anger and doubt are both simultaneously combined of emotions and thoughts (James, 1950, pp. 185–91).

Precursors to Systemic Thinking

Before I discuss systemic thinking itself, I want to take a brief look at its precursors, focusing on a book by Russell J. Becker that reflects ministers' growing awareness in the 1950s that families need the minister's counsel as much as individuals do. I have argued in *Living Stories* (Capps, 1998) that the greatest influences on the way the counseling role of the minister was conceived in the latter half of the twentieth century were client-centered (or "Rogerian") therapy and family systems therapy. While there were advocates of other approaches, these two were the most influential. They were taught in the seminary classroom and presented in workshops for ministers. The client-centered approach tended to focus on the counseling of individuals, while the family systems approach, as its name implies, involved the counseling of families. Over the years, the client-centered model has continued to be influential in the teaching of "listening skills," but it has been augmented and sometimes replaced by other approaches that are considered to be more "directive," for example, cognitive-behavioral models. Meanwhile, the family systems approach has expanded to include pastoral counseling of individuals, and it has spawned several newer approaches. Some of these are extensions of the systems model, while others are more deeply critical of the systems model.

The idea that the minister is a family counselor preceded the family systems approach itself. Although Rollo May's *The Art of Counseling: How to Gain and Give Mental Health,* published in 1939, did not discuss family counseling per se, it did include a discussion of "the family constellation," which focused primarily on the characteristics of firstborns, secondborns, the youngest child, and the only child. Also, while the book is largely informed by a psychoanalytic (Freudian) theory of the personality, it is a clear precursor to client-centered therapy in its emphasis on the need for counselors to "learn to empathize," for "it is in this profound and somewhat mysterious process of empathy that understanding, influence, and the other significant relations between persons take place" (May, 1939, p. 75).

In one of the first books on pastoral ministry to families, John Charles Wynn's *Pastoral Ministry to Families* (1957), there is no mention of family systems theory. This, of course, is not at all surprising, as general systems theory had been formulated only a few years earlier, and the first applications of this theory to families were published at the very time Wynn's book was in press. This is important, because we tend today to so identify the emphasis on the pastoral care of families with the family systems model itself that we fail to realize that this emphasis preexisted the family *systems* approach.

In the 1960s, however, the systemic model began to provide a much-needed theoretical foundation for what Wynn had termed "pastoral ministry to families." Russell J. Becker's *Family Pastoral Care* (1963) is an early example of how systemic thinking was just beginning to influence thinking about ministry to families. In a section of his chapter on "Persons in Families" devoted to "the family as the matrix of persons," he cites a study by Robert D. Hess and Gerald Handel from their book entitled *Family Worlds: A Psychosocial Approach to Family Life*, which describes five different patterns of family life to illustrate that "all families develop unique interactional patterns" (Becker, 1963, p. 72). He also cites a research study by Erika Chance reported in her book *Families in Treatment* that found in the case of a family with a "problem child" that "the mother's concerns acted as a 'regulator' for the father and the child in specific areas" (Becker, p. 72). Walter Garre, another writer whom Becker cites, made the case for the family as the developer of its mentally ill member: "Family members protect themselves against the 'basic anxiety' evoked through any nuance of hostility by requiring one of their number to bear the weaknesses of each of the others" (Becker, p. 72). Becker adds, "It is a theory of scapegoating developed not as a tribal phenomenon but as a phenomenon within the family while all members continue to live and interact with the scapegoated member...That certain families may need to have one of its members be sick so that the rest may be well indicates the high price that one member may be required to pay for the well-being of others" (Becker, p. 73). This "scapegoat" was later to be termed the "identified patient."

Becker also notes the growing literature on family treatment, which is based on the premise that "if the unit of disturbance in living is the family rather than the individual, the unit which should receive psychotherapeutic help is the family" (p. 73). He cites the "breakthroughs" that are occurring in family treatment with the most severely disturbed individuals, those afflicted with schizophrenia. He notes especially the work of psychodynamic theorists (i.e., persons with an essentially Freudian orientation) such as Nathan W. Ackerman, whose book *The Psychodynamics of Family Life* appeared in 1958, and psychoanalyst Martin Grotjahn, whose *Psychoanalysis and the Family Neurosis* was published in 1960.

Finally, citing *Mental Health in the Metropolis*, by Leo Srole and Associates, published in 1962, Becker makes the point that the family cannot be viewed in isolation from the larger social environment. In an intensive study of lower-class families in midtown Manhattan, Srole and his colleagues found that "where infrequent employment at substandard wages puts a family in constant peril of disruption and dislocation, the mother assumes the deadly role of disparaging the adequacy of her breadwinner husband" (Becker, p. 73). The male child, in turn, joins her in this rejection of the father's claim to family respect and authority, and he carries this rejection of social authority into rejection of school, law, and society. Becker concludes: "The authors of this study are bold to say that society itself by substandard wages and its irresponsibility about the costs of poverty casts the first stone against the lower socio-economic family" (p. 73). It should also be noted, however, that this analysis of the internal family dynamic implicitly blames the mother—whom Erika Chance calls the "regulator"—for the antisocial attitudes and behavior of her male children. While Becker does not critique this feature of the analysis, subsequent authors in the field of pastoral care, writing from a feminist perspective, have issued strong challenges against it, noting that the mother is no less a victim of the socioeconomic system than her underemployed husband.

In his discussion of how the minister should go about family counseling, Becker says that the family should be seen as a group. This especially includes the father, mother, and the "difficult" child, and may include other siblings depending on the proximity of ages and "the degree of parental pressure being placed on more than one child" (p. 75). He adds: "Working with the family as a group is a bright change from isolated and repetitive individual appointments. Normally something significant and helpful is accomplished in a *single* session" (p. 75). Becker's rationale for single-session counseling is based on his understanding of the *family problem* and the *purpose of family counseling*. The *problem* usually means that a child has become incomprehensible to the parents. Becker's previous years of study and work with Carl Rogers are evident in his view of why such incomprehensibility has developed: "The images which each holds of self and others are disparate rather than congruent. Communication between parents and child is blocked because 'who one is talking to' is not the same person as he holds himself to be" (p. 75). In effect, Becker has taken Rogers' concept of congruence (as discussed in chapter 2) and has applied it to the perceptions that we have of ourselves versus the perceptions that others have of us. This, in turn, becomes a basis for helping the family "unblock" its communication processes. The *purpose* of family counseling, then, is to "open up communication between family members by finding the points of incongruity in the images of self and others and by helping the parents to see the way in which the behavior of the 'mysterious child in their midst' is a function of their own expectations and demands" (p. 75).

Becker has two responses to the objection that this purpose could not possibly be achieved in a single session. One is that family counseling helps to free the family "to a new readiness to hear the Gospel of God's reconciling work in Jesus Christ" (p. 75). In effect, it frees the family from its "costly preoccupation with its problem" so that it can "return to the larger community of the church" and participate in "the work of human reconciliation" to which the church itself is witness. The second is simply that the single session runs well beyond an hour's length. It is divided into four parts:

1. Meeting briefly with the family as a group (2–5 minutes)
2. Speaking with the child alone (10–20 minutes)
3. Conversation with the parents alone (15–30 minutes)
4. Meeting with the family as a group (30–60 minutes)

These time indications (ranging from one to two hours) are approximate and flexible, and are intended to suggest the proportions of each part of the session to the other parts.

Why would a minister get involved in family counseling in the first place? Shouldn't the minister simply defer to other trained professionals? Becker's response is this: "Too often parents encountering difficulties in family living want to locate the problem in the child and hustle *the child* off to a specialist. Most child guidance centers by their very existence implicitly encourage this" (p. 77). Even if these clinics have begun to recognize the problem, it nevertheless amounts to a *stigmatization* of the child, and Becker believes the minister is in a position to intervene against this: "The pastor stands at the point where he can stop some of this stigmatizing of the child as a 'problem child' before it snowballs and does its damaging worst through the process of seeking help itself" (p. 77). By means of the pastor's proximity to the family, "he can head off the process of singling out the child as a 'problem'" (p. 77).

Thus, against a prevailing view among clergy at the time that their task was basically to refer their own parishioners to other trained professionals, Becker here argues that the minister may assume the opposite role, that is, one of discouraging parents from "hustling" their child off to a specialist on the assumption that the child *is* the problem. As he puts it, "If stigmatization is to occur, the parent is to share in it fully" (p. 77). In light of our earlier discussions of confrontation, we could say that what Becker was proposing here is subtly confrontational. The minister not only encourages the family members to focus on the incongruities between perceptions of self and others, but also confronts the parents' assumption that the child is the problem and therefore needs to see a child specialist.

How does the minister conduct the session itself? Becker provides an extensive transcript of an actual session that was arranged following the pastor's attendance at one of the Couples Christian Concern Groups, which had been held that evening in a couple's home. As the pastor was leaving, the couple said they were having a problem with their eleven-year-old daughter, so a meeting was set up that would include the parents and the daughter. Their younger son was not included. I will not discuss this case, but instead simply note that Becker uses it to illustrate his view that the minister's counseling work should focus on (1) finding the role incongruities; and (2) facilitating parental insight. He refers to these as "two process flow stages," the first comprising parts two and three of the session, and the second comprising part four. Regarding the discerning of role incongruities, he points out that a family with a problem is "a family of *eccentrics*," by which he means not that they are a group of odd characters but that they are "off-center" with respect to the images of self and other that each person holds. The initial task, therefore, is to find where the weight of the eccentric pull is located, and this is "an exploratory responsibility." The questions asked of the child and the parents in parts two and three of the session are aimed at finding the present image held of the others. He cautions: "It is not depth, analytical exploration. It is exploration in terms of role images" (p. 77). Thus, the minister asks the child when they are alone together: What do you think is the problem in your family? How do you think your parents see you? How do you think your parents see themselves? Similar questions are asked of each parent when they are seen without the child. Becker emphasizes that the *mode* of inquiry is not interview style but is one of empathic interest in the world revealed in the image of each person.

Facilitating parental insight is the second stage of the session, and it brings everyone together. The minister's first task is to report on the incongruities that have been disclosed in the separate segments of the session. In so doing, the minister "enters into the thick of things" and is drawn into the center of the family disturbance (p. 79). Becker indicates that this report is not presented in an evaluative tone, but an interpretive one, and that even these interpretive comments are "essentially matters which previously each parent has come to on his own. They are not strange or mysterious judgments from on high" (p. 129). These points of interpretation are designed to help the parents toward an understanding of persons "as interacting social agents" so that they can each become "a more responsible person to the other" and act in "greater awareness" of "certain perceptions already held dimly" (p. 129). In his discussion of the case noted earlier, Becker notes that the parents' understanding of their own agency in regard to their daughter "pulses like an alternating current." First the light glows on the mother, next on the father, as the minister and mother see what the father does not perceive as the moment, and then the minister and father see what the mother has not yet perceived. The hope and expectation is that the parents will be able to carry on this dialogue, in which they supplement the awareness of the other, in the absence of the minister.

The child's own agency and responsibility in relation to the parents is also dealt with realistically. While the primary concern is to facilitate the parents' understanding of their part in the family problem, the daughter (in this case) is not exempted. On the other hand, by speaking to the child first, the minister hopes to have established a rapport with her that carries over into the second stage of the session where all have reunited, and thus to be in a position to model a way of communicating with the child, the effectiveness of which is perceived by the parents and which they may therefore emulate.

As described so far, the session has comprised the "tone-setting" and "exploratory" (or beginning and middle) phases described in chapter 2. As the session moves rather naturally into what I have called the "resolution phase," the minister in this case offers a suggestion for how the parents might "reverse the vicious cycle" that their over-expectations of their daughter have set in motion. He indicates that there are accomplishments that are "right" and "appropriate" at different levels of ability and maturity, and that if they accept this fact, their daughter is likely to surprise them with what she *can* do once she is free from the expectation that nothing she does is going to be "right" or "acceptable" in her parents' eyes. He suggests that they try this for a while and then, in two to three months, let him know how things are. If things are going well, they won't have another session, but if not, they will.

In his own comments on this resolution, Becker says that a subsequent session in a week or so *could* be appropriate, depending on "the degree of resolution and congruence which is achieved in a single session"

(p. 131). This may especially be indicated when the minister is aware that, for one reason or another, he has been unable to "enter fully into both the parents' and the child's shoes," or, in other words, has compromised his "objective-empathic perspective and become a protagonist for a cause," perhaps because of related problems of his own (p. 131). He may also want to follow up with an informal pastoral call two or three weeks later to see how things are going. The important point, however, is that the family now returns to the status of one of the parish families seen in various activities, and "the channels of communication between the family and pastor return to the ordinary contacts of parish life" (p. 131).

In short, the minister has entered "briefly but strategically into the world of this family," helping them relate the points of discrepancy in role perceptions (and expectations) to the points of difficulty in the family relationship. An effort toward greater role congruity has also been made: "Then having done this much he steps back from the family, leaving them the responsibility for their continued life and work with each other" (p. 130). What has he done for the child? He has accorded her "some means of appraising the whole situation in terms of its interpersonal complexities. At the very least the child is assured that family problems are *family* problems" (p. 130). In this particular case, this means that scapegoating the child for the parents' needs for perfection is checked, as are parental fears that she will become a wild teenager if these parental needs are relinquished. Of course, "All the problems of family living are not resolved by this one session. But the family is helped to see that theirs is a mutual responsibility for whatever problems they may have" (p. 130).

The Family Systems Model of Pastoral Counseling

In spite of the fact that Becker views the family itself as the problem and proposes a pastoral counseling approach that brings several members of the family together in the room, he does not use the word *system*. He thinks systemically, however, even though he makes no explicit use of systems theory itself. In the course of the next two decades, systems theory was increasingly used, both to challenge the individual-centered pastoral counseling based on the client-centered model and to advocate for the pastoral counseling of families. In addition, systems theory was applied to congregations.

A good example of the systems approach to the pastoral counseling of families is J. C. Wynn's *Family Therapy in Pastoral Ministry* (1982). A comparison of the tables of contents of his *Pastoral Ministry to Families* (1957) and this book indicates how much his thinking changed in the intervening years. Chapter headings in the earlier book included "The Church as the Family of God," "The Family in Common Worship," "The Pastoral Care of Church Families," "The Pastor as a Family Counselor," two chapters on "Christian Marriage," a chapter on "Three Special Problems in Pastoral Care" (these were aging persons and their relatives, children with disabilities, and childless couples), and a concluding chapter on "The Pastor as a Family Man." In the 1982 text, the chapter headings include "Today's Families Confront the Pastor," "Games Families Play," "Family Therapists You Should Know," "Interviews and Interventions," "Therapies and Theories," "Seventeen Often-Asked Questions About Family Therapy," and "Pastoral Theology and Family Therapy." The "Church as the Family of God" focus of the earlier text had been replaced by a concern with "Pastoral Theology," and there had also been a very noticeable shift toward therapeutic theory. Perhaps even more revealing, Wynn's acknowledgments in the 1982 book include a "group of therapists" with whom he had had informative conversations or from whom he had received tutelage in family therapy. These include many of the important names in the family systems approach, including Salvador Minuchin, Virginia Satir, Carl Whitaker, Jay Haley, John Weakland, and Paul Watzlawick.

In his 1982 book, Wynn argues that there has never been any question whether pastors ought to be doing family counseling, because in this matter they really have no choice. Their involvement with marriage conflicts and dysfunctional families is inevitable. The real question is how well they do it and to what extent they are adequately prepared. There are intrusions in the normal course of a family's life, such as accidents, unemployment, and illnesses, that prompt the minister to respond. To bring comfort, aid, and healing in such emergencies is to participate in family therapy. But, "To go still farther and assist family members in working through their altered relationships as a result of these intrusions is a deeper level of therapy," and this is the level that he addresses in the book (p. 19).

His goal is to help pastors begin to think in "a new and wholistic way about people *within the family context,* rather than as isolated individuals...Most clergy still tend to deal with family problems as if they are idiosyncratic, caused by a particular person" (p. 19). Systems theory, he notes, "may be either unknown or still unconvincing to most clergy." They tend to see the fact that a boy can't read and hates school as a personal difficulty rather than the outward expression of a family tension that is otherwise hidden from an outsider's gaze, and "the tragedy of the 'kitchen alcoholic' tends to be diagnosed as a peculiar, isolated behavior of the woman rather than one strand of a complex system of family relationships in which her husband's attitudes and her children's behavior also assume a large role" (p. 19). Family therapy, then, is "the practice of treating a family as a whole unit and taking into account the system in which the family members interact" (p. 22).

In his chapter entitled "Games Families Play," Wynn quotes the following from Augustus Napier and Carl Whitaker's *The Family Crucible* (1978): "It didn't seem to matter what the complaint was, or the traditional diagnosis. Troubles, it seemed, came in families. If the problem was the family, the family should be the focus of therapy. The family, in fact, should be the patient" (Wynn, 1982, p. 26). He illustrates this point with an example of a family with a predictable pattern: Whenever their marriage was on the verge of dissolving, the two parents were pulled back together by a new emergency. Once their fifteen-year-old daughter ran away from home. Once their son was arrested for smoking pot in a public square. Another time the father's serious automobile accident after a drinking bout laid him up for several weeks. This pattern was clear enough to a therapist, but not to the parents or any of the children. It was a clumsy attempt at self-styled therapy. A member of the family would create a crisis so that the family would have to work together to solve it, and this way the dissolution of the parents' marriage was forestalled.

What does this illustration tell us about the family as a system? Wynn notes three things. First, the family operated as a *system* because whatever one person did affected the behavior of the others, and this, in turn, doubled back and affected everyone again in a new way. Second, the crisis invariably brought the family back into their familiar but uneasy balance, a state called *homeostasis.* And third, they were playing by a set of *rules* that required one player to make a disastrous move whenever a family breakup was threatened. I would add that, on the basis of the evidence provided, the wife (and mother) did not precipitate a crisis. What does this mean? If her role is not to create a crisis, what *is* her role? This leads, then, to Wynn's fourth point, that the individual members of the family play *roles* that are assigned or ascribed to them by the system. These are roles that may be related to their official status (parent, child, sibling) but are not necessarily defined by these official statuses. Notice that the father is as likely to precipitate a crisis as the son or daughter. This leads to a fifth point, that the father, son, and daughter form a *subsystem* of crisis precipitators. The wife and mother may then be the permanent member of another subsystem, which others may join in order to pull the family out of its current crisis and return it to its former homeostasis. Still another subsystem is the parents, who get into a "let's break up" mode, which leads the crisis precipitator subsystem to go into action.

Central to this analysis is the idea of the family as a system. What, then, is a system? The dictionary suggests that it is "a set or arrangement of things so related or connected as to form a unity or organic whole," such as a solar system, school system, or system of highways. In *Pragmatics of Human Communication* (1967), Paul Watzlawick and his coauthors adopt the definition that a system is a set of objects with relationships between the objects and between their attributes. The objects are the components or parts of the system, attributes are the properties of the objects, and relationships tie the system together (Watzlawick, p. 120). As Wynn points out, the family system provides an *environment* whose totality is greater than all its individual components, and this environment is *interrelational,* with each individual viewed in relation to her or his *function* in the family. Because the family is greater than its individual components, an individual family member—or even all the family members—may be *defeated* by the family's power. Thus, a family can undo the work of therapy with an individual client, or an individual may be able to escape his designated role, only to find another member of the family being drawn into this vacated role. Wynn also notes that single persons who live alone are not free from the system because the family in which they grew up continues to influence their attitudes and behavior (Wynn, 1982, p. 28).

Features of the System

Wynn discusses the features of the family system, noting that there are three basic characteristics that nearly all family therapists refer to and use for diagnosis, description, and treatment. The first (already noted in the above illustration) is *homeostasis* (the Greek word for "same place"), which concerns the family's effort to maintain an equilibrium. In a healthy family, this is a good thing, but in an unhealthy one, it is achieved in ways that are harmful to individual family members. In such cases, the therapeutic goal is *neostasis* ("new place"), which is achieved by "jolting the system, altering its communication patterns, or teaching fresh methods of problem-solving" (p. 37). The very idea that the family *is* the problem, an idea established very early in the history of family therapy, led naturally to a "problem-solving" approach to the realization of a neostasis.

The second feature of the system is *the identified patient.* This is the family member who is designated as "the problem," who owns the problem, or who is likely to become the family scapegoat, bearing the guilt of others. This member may be the "symbol bearer" who takes on the shame of less-approved behaviors the others would like to adopt, but are too sophisticated to exhibit, such as belligerency, sexiness, or rebelliousness (p. 37). By refusing to confirm the family's judgment that it would be healthy if only the "identified patient" could be straightened out, the family therapist shifts the focus to the system itself. The question then becomes, What is wrong with a system that requires an identified patient, someone to bear the burden of its dysfunctionality? Wynn cites the case of family therapist Don Jackson, who worked with a family in which one of the sons was schizophrenic. Jackson focused on the question of what the family would do and how they would cope if the son were to become well. The family members resisted the question, but as Jackson persisted, the son was making more sense than he had before, and toward the end of the session he told Jackson that he thought his family needed him to be sick so that they could feel well (pp. 38–39). Deemed the member of the family who had a mental illness, the son proved to be the most perceptive of them all.

The third feature of the system is its use of *double-binding communication,* or a compulsorily confusing communication that cuts across two levels in a relatively contradictory style. For example, the mother who speaks of a tragic event but smiles throughout is sending a double-bind message, or the father who takes his son to the circus, but grumbles, "You'd better have a good time or I'll never take you to another circus" places the boy in a double-bind position. The famous story of the mother who gives her son two shirts for his birthday—a blue one and a brown one—and then says to him when he appears the next day wearing the blue one, "What? Didn't you like the brown one?" is using double-binding communication. Wynn relates a colleague's account of how his mother would set the table, cook the dinner, and clean up the dishes afterward while he and his father watched television. She would call to Stanley, "Would you like more ice cream?" He would say no, he wasn't hungry, but she would persist, "But it's your favorite—chocolate," and he would again refuse. Then she would call out, "Stanley, I'm dishing it up and putting it on the table." When he would resignedly go to the table to eat the ice cream he didn't want, his mother would say, "See what I mean? My work's never done!" These stories indicate that it is typical of some problem families to keep each other confused and defensive through double-binds, and this is the way they maintain the homeostasis of the family (p. 40).

There is one additional feature of the system that Wynn does not discuss under this heading, but that almost all family systems therapists refer to and use for diagnosis, description, and treatment. He discusses it, however, in his chapter on "Family Therapists You Should Know," specifically in his comments on Murray Bowen, whom he identifies as an "intergenerational theorist" (other categories are "problem-oriented," "psychodynamic," and "behavioral" theorists). This is the familiar concept of *triangulation,* a common form of which is where parental conflicts are "detoured" through the children. As Monica McGoldrick explains: "Often a parent who cannot deal with his or her spouse can more easily react against the same characteristics when reflected in a child" (McGoldrick, Anderson, and Walsh, 1989, p. 250). Or, as Jay Haley puts it, triangulation typically involves "coalitions across generation lines," as when father and son join against the mother, sabotaging her efforts to maintain a well-ordered household, or when (as in Becker's example), mother and child join in belittling the father for his inability to sustain the family financially (Haley, 1987, p. 115). As the child is often an unwitting participant in the triangulation, the parent bears the primary responsibility for continuing and maintaining destructive triangles. Children may not realize until they reach adulthood that one parent made them accomplices against the other parent, and this realization is likely to make them feel resentful for having been used without their awareness.

As Wynn points out, however, some triangles involve nonmembers of the family, while others may involve inanimate objects. Bowen "searches out the triangles of family relationships, the father-mother-scapegoated child," but he also focuses on "the husband-wife-lover, or perhaps the husband-wife-bourbon bottle" (p. 70). Wynn cites the case of a minister and his wife in which the third "member" of the triangle is initially his work (in which he becomes overinvolved) and, secondarily, her illness (which temporarily succeeds in countering the initial triangle). In some ways, triangles involving an object, behavior, or cause are more difficult to identify and to reverse. The husband's bourbon bottle may be a more difficult opponent for his wife to counter than a lover would be because it has no emotions of its own.

A student once came to me with the complaint that her husband's dog was causing conflict in their marriage. She indicated that though she doesn't especially like dogs, she accepted her husband's dog as the "price" she was willing to pay to be married to him. Now, however, he was working long hours to support them and was often away from home in the evening. Although she understood that he needed to make extra money to support them, she was becoming resentful of the fact that she had to care for his dog in his absence. On top of this, when her husband returned home late, the dog rushed to greet him and he would fondle the dog affectionately before he got around to greeting her. The triangulating party here was the dog, and the fact that her husband's relationship to him preceded his relationship to her contributed to her resentment. She didn't feel that she should issue an ultimatum, "Either he goes, or I go," because she realized how much her husband loved his dog, but she admitted that she was beginning to treat the dog rather harshly, and it disturbed her that she, a peaceful and compassionate person, would do this to a harmless old dog. She also admitted that she had never dreamed that she might one day be "jealous" of a dog. Other women, perhaps, but surely not a dog.

I related to her a story I had heard family therapist William Hudson O'Hanlon tell at a workshop about a woman who came to therapy because her husband was no longer demonstrative toward her. She complained: "He is more affectionate with his dog than he is toward me!" When the therapist asked her to explain, she said that when her husband came home from work, the dog would run to the door to greet him and soon the two of them were rolling around on the floor together. She paused for a moment, then laughed, "I have it! Next time, I'll listen for my husband and outrace that old mutt to the door!"

Of course, in the case of the student, there was the factor of her husband's working late hours, an economic necessity, perhaps, but a major part of the reason that the dog had become a matter of increased resentment. Thus, this illustration supports an aphorism that I have found rather useful over the years, that "triangles come in pairs." Behind the husband-wife-dog triangle lies the husband-wife-work triangle, and exploration into this triangle revealed that her husband was doing the extra work for a woman client of his. She did not suspect marital infidelity, but this obviously contributed to her frustration and resentment, for which the dog was both scapegoat and symptom bearer. (I will return to this case in chapter 4.)

The Family Process

In addition to these features of the system itself, Wynn also discusses the features of the *family process*, which is the sum total of all interactions in the family. In effect, this process provides the answer to a therapist's customary query, "What's going on in this household?" You would be telling about the family process if you were to say about a family, "They don't seem happy. They don't do anything together, the kids are all in trouble, there's lots of yelling, and the place is a wreck" (p. 43). Recently, my wife told me about a mother in her preschool who was reluctant to have her third son go to the child guidance center to be tested because her two older sons had been diagnosed as having learning and behavior problems and she wanted to believe that at least the third boy was "normal." My wife related that the father was away from home a great deal on business and that the mother, who had previously relied on physical punishment to keep her boys in line, had been trying, though not very successfully, to "communicate" with them instead. The struggling mother, the frequently absent father, and the three troubled sons—this is a statement about this particular family's process.

However, more specific features of the process may be identified, and Wynn identifies several. First, there are what we may call "the three R's of the process," *rules, roles,* and *rituals.* Every family has *rules: Never* interrupt father when he is talking, or *always* ridicule the awkward child, whatever she says or does. Perhaps the most frequent use of rules is in decision making, an aspect of family life that may precipitate considerable disputation. Families who have sensible rules for how decisions are made and who live by those rules have a better chance of living in harmony than those where the rules are arbitrary and thus always subject to being contested and challenged. Rules also determine how power is distributed in the family (p. 43). For example, the mother may be the one who sets and enforces rules about proper behavior inside the home, while the father sets and enforces the rules when the family is at church, eating in a restaurant, or on vacation. This clear division of power may work if all the family members understand and support it, but it can be quite dysfunctional if the parent in the "submissive" position subverts the rules that have been set by the one in the "dominant" position, as when the father intimates to a child that he doesn't have to keep his room as neat as mother says he does, or when the mother complains in front of the children that the father has led them to a pew that is too close to the front of the church.

Rules may also govern what topics are discussable in the family. A tragedy (such as the accidental death of a son or daughter), an event about which one parent is especially defensive or sensitive (such as the father's error in judgment that has produced economic hardship for the family), or an addiction (the mother's excessive alcohol use), are just some of the many situations where a silence rule may prevail.

Wynn suggests that disagreements about rules can be "adjudicated rather promptly if it is possible to focus on the rule rather than on the people involved, thus saving dignity for those concerned" (p. 44). Open negotiation of rules also has the value of making implicit rules explicit, which, in turn, gives members of the family ownership over them: "We make the rules; the rules don't make us."

Roles are the parts or functions that members of the family play in their relations with one another. One of the children may play the role of mediator, another the tension-reducer, and still another carries the family pride and honor. A parent may play the role of arbitrator between two of the children, or the family martyr, or the hapless fool who makes everyone else in the family feel competent. As already noted, one common role for one of the children to play is the identified patient or symptom bearer. Because families have subsystems, members of the family often have multiple roles. In one subsystem, a person may play one role, in another subsystem, another role. Wynn notes that "Mature or healthy people are capable of choosing and adjusting to several roles," whereas "dysfunctional people may be stuck in one role, incapable of change" (pp. 44–45). The occasion may call for the martyr to be responsible, or for the clown to make a serious statement or commitment, but they are unable to rise to the occasion. They are like the actor who can play only one type of character and then complains that he is being typecast. On the other hand, individual family members may find that the family is highly resistant to their efforts to break out of their assigned roles, and this resistance can continue long after they have become adults and left home. The sister who clowned around a great deal as a child and is now an effective trial lawyer remains the clown in the eyes of her adult siblings.

Family therapists place considerable emphasis on the roles that family members play, as these are not only an important key to their interrelationships, but also the point at which the therapist is able to help family members understand these relationships and to begin to take steps to modify them. In the case that Becker discusses, the mother's willingness to relinquish her role as the enforcer of high, nearly impossible standards frees the teenage daughter to relinquish her role as the rebel against these standards. As a result, both can claim roles that are more congruent with the decent, capable persons they are.

The third R, *rituals*, are the routines or set patterns that a family has developed in its interactions together. They include how members say goodbye, how they move about the house, who gets up early, who stays up late, and so forth. An example of a more complex ritual, however, is the one of the family mentioned earlier that averts the breakup of the parents' marriage by "arranging" for someone to get into serious difficulty. This is a set pattern, and it manifests itself whenever the need for it arises. So, too, is the set pattern of the pastor's wife who, in protest of her husband's overinvolvement in work, develops an illness that prevents her from carrying out any of her customary activities. To this, he responds with contrition and compassion, which allows her to berate him until he feels cleansed and she feels better (p. 45). This ritual is a predictable feature of their family process. If there are children at home, we can well imagine that they are drawn into this ritual as well. Thus, there are family rituals of which the family members are relatively conscious and do not need an outsider to point out to them (e.g., the order in which family members get up in the morning). These are not unimportant, for changing these sometimes resolves a family problem (I discuss such a case in Capps, 1990, pp. 68–69). The rituals that most interest family systems therapists, however, are the ones that are more hidden and dysfunctional. These are rituals of which family members are not as conscious. They are so involved in them that they cannot see them. An outsider is often required to point these patterns out to them.

In addition to the three R's of family process, Wynn discusses the three "spooky" influences of the process: *secrets, ghosts,* and *mystification. Secrets* involve things that are never talked about (a family rule), such as a family member's pregnancy outside of marriage, prison sentence, alcoholism, gambling debts, difficulty holding a job, or mental illness. Secrets are usually kept in order to maintain a mythic view of the family (for example, as morally superior to other families, as a model of harmony, or as self-reliant). Wynn indicates that secrets can make therapy an extremely difficult task at times, but that a child may reveal the secret or an adult may begin to tell it with obvious relief (p. 46). In *Prairie Reunion* (1995), Barbara J. Scot relates her effort as a middle-aged adult to find out why her father left her mother for another woman and subsequently committed suicide. By attending a family reunion in her hometown of Scotch Grove, Iowa, and asking her surviving relatives questions, she was able to piece together a story that was kept secret from her during childhood, and that she had not inquired much about when she was older and her mother was still living. She learned that her father had been "defeated" by the farmland that her maternal grandfather had given her mother at the time of her marriage. Her father's effort to establish his family on his own terms—a precipitous move to Colorado—did not succeed, and her mother returned to her farm in Iowa, taking her children with her.

The famous psychoanalyst and developmental theorist Erik H. Erikson was an illegitimate child from whom the identity of his natural father was withheld by his mother. One of his aunts speculated that Erikson's mother may simply not have known who the father was. He once confided to a young minister "that his personal religious concerns were connected heavily to the mystery of his paternity" (Friedman, 1999, p. 439). Several years ago, a student told me about the trauma she suffered when she discovered that the woman she had been told was her aunt was really her mother, and that the woman who was supposedly her mother was in fact her mother's sister. This, too, was a case of a pregnancy outside of marriage, and the family "handled" it by arranging for her aunt and uncle to raise her as their own child. In Erikson's case, not only was the identity of his natural father withheld from him but the man his mother married when he was three years old was represented to him as his natural father. Erikson later wrote that his mother and stepfather "apparently thought that such secretiveness was not only workable (because children then were not held to know what they had not been told) but also advisable, so that I would feel thoroughly at home in their home. As children will do, I played in with this and more or less forgot the period before the age three, when mother and I had lived alone" (Erikson, 1975, p. 27).

Ghosts are family expectations passed on from generation to generation. These may involve roles, such as the wife's expectation that she will handle the finances because her mother did, or the husband's assumption that he will not have much to do with the children because his father had little to do with him and his siblings when they were growing up. These may also involve behaviors. Father beat his children, so his sons beat their children. When family expectations in the husband's family and those in the wife's family conflict, misunderstandings develop. She may have grown up in a family where a fair degree of chaos was tolerated and even valued, whereas he may have been raised in a family that placed a high premium on order and decorum. These expectations can play themselves out in myriad ways, as both persons may assume that the way they were raised is the best way, or one (or both) may prefer the way the other was raised. One may hold her family up as exemplary in this regard and not reciprocate the other's willingness to recognize flaws in his family, thus creating resentment. Wynn suggests that ghosts can be "persistent and insidious" and notes that the exorcism of these family ghosts "is often a difficult challenge for the family therapist, and requires delving into the family of origin to begin the process" (p. 46).

Mystification is where family members mask their own interests by representing them as if they were to the advantage of someone else in the family or as if they reflect the other person's true desires (of which that person is currently unaware): "It will do you good to spend your first year of college here in Peoria instead of going off to Chapel Hill." Or, "You'll feel much better if you include your sister in your travel plans." Or, "Working in the family business this summer will be a much better learning experience than traipsing off to Alaska to work in a fish cannery." The issue here is not whether the speakers are factually correct, but that they have spoken in such a way as to disguise their own self-interest. Mystification is therefore a subtle form of influence and control, one that leaves the one who is spoken to feeling manipulated and defenseless to do anything about it (except, perhaps, to rebel). The therapist's task, according to Wynn, is to get the family member to use "I-messages," a straightforward communication that states the speaker's own views and reasons for it: "I would feel so lonely if you left Peoria to go to college," or "I worry about whether you will behave yourself, living in a college dorm and all." "I won't worry nearly as much if the two of you have each other to depend on in case something unforeseen happens." "Since you were a little boy it has been my dream that you would someday take over the family business. So when you said you wanted to go to Alaska with your friends, my heart sank." These are more straightforward communications, which then invite dialogue between parent and teenager.

Summing up his discussion of those family processes, Wynn cautions that there is less difference between healthy and dysfunctional families than we might suppose, which means that we should be careful not to engage in the scapegoating of families, or of their individual members, that seem more troubled than others. He notes Bowen's observation that much of the early family research focused on families with a schizophrenic child, so it was assumed that the relationship patterns that were being discovered, especially the use of double-binding communication, were characteristic of these families only. Only later was it discovered that the same features were present in families with neurotic (not psychotic) level problems, and in normal families as well (p. 50). Every family engages in mystification at times, and all families scapegoat on occasion. Therefore, it is best to think of families as located somewhere along a continuum between the extremes of the healthiest and the grossly dysfunctional. For an account of a highly dysfunctional family, I recommend Mikal Gilmore's *Shot in the Heart* (1994). Gilmore is the younger brother of Gary Gilmore, who was executed in 1976 for double homicide. The Gilmore family lends itself to systemic analysis employing the ideas presented here.

The Counseling Process

Wynn believes that "As clergy, we can indeed derive from the family therapists valuable methods to adapt in ministry" (p. 81). In his chapter on "Interviews and Interventions," he describes "the process of interviewing" (which literally means "seeing between"). This process begins with watching how the couple or family enter the office, listening to how they address each other, seeing how they look at each other, noting who speaks first and who habitually answers, noting whether they choose chairs in a pattern of relating to or distancing from certain others, and so forth. He emphasizes that the minister who engages in couples and family counseling does more than listen and observe; she needs to enter the family system—as a kind of "honorary relative"—in order to enable the family to make changes more efficiently (p. 83).

Wynn recommends a process for couples' counseling that is very similar to Becker's four-stage model for family counseling. In the first stage, with both parties present, he immediately takes the initiative, noting his recognition of the pain and awkwardness they feel at having to come for aid in their marriage, asking if they have sought help elsewhere, and then centering on whether the problem they have come to see him about is one step in a long series of crises or whether it is something more recent. He then briefly tells them how he works (his methods and philosophy) and what they can expect in the roughly ninety minutes ahead. He promises a tentative evaluation at the end.

Then he moves to the presenting problem: "No one ever phones me the first time they become troubled about their marriage. It usually takes a special jolt. Tell me what happened before you picked up the phone to call me." This will uncover the presenting problem that, while not the underlying relational difficulty, will need attention during the first session: "Positive attention to the opening complaint can open the way to working in depth" (p. 85).

Next, he queries them briefly about their history together (how and where they met, how long they knew each other before marriage, whether their families approved of their marriage, how long they have been married, if they have children and what their ages are, and anything else the couple thinks is pertinent). Other matters (such as family of origin issues) will naturally emerge as the conversation continues. Then he asks about the present: "What is going on in your marriage right now?" Following this, he asks them what remedies they have already tried. This question is sometimes met with resistance, for they may have turned to rather self-defeating measures (physical coercion, alcohol or drugs, mate-swapping), but the answers are illuminating because they enable him to avoid suggesting something they have already tried that hasn't worked. This question also communicates his belief that they are resourceful persons, that they came to him only after the things they had tried on their own didn't work.

Following this, he talks with each of them alone, so that they can say things they believe can't be said in the other's presence (for example, express anger and resentment, reveal a secret he or she is not yet ready to divulge to the partner, or simply receive personal attention without the tension felt in the presence of the other). After these individual conversations, he brings the couple together for a closing session that consists of summary, evaluation, and an assigned task. The summary is not his alone, but one in which all three participate. From this summation, he pulls together a tentative evaluation that touches on the seriousness of the conflict, the chances and methods for its correction, arrangements for further sessions (if needed), and some word of hope (if at all feasible). Finally, he leaves them with a task to fulfill and, assuming an additional session or more, asks them to report on this task the next time. This could be a communication exercise, a dinner date, or some other appropriate assignment that requires them to work on their problem. Finally, he takes their hands or touches each on the shoulder, bids them goodbye, and ushers them to the door (p. 88).

In *Rewriting Love Stories* (1991), Patricia O'Hanlon Hudson and William Hudson O'Hanlon offer this illustration of a task assignment: A couple who complained that they were no longer communicating were asked by the therapist to recall the circumstances in which they had previously communicated with each other. They both recalled that it was usually when they were on walks together. The assignment, then, was to walk together at least twice before the next session. They reported a positive change in their relationship, as they were "talking much more easily both on walks and at home" (p. 48). These talks also led to the insight, mutually shared, that the real problem was the wife's dissatisfaction with her job.

In another case, a couple who were both active in their careers and "swamped with church activities" realized that they "had left their relationship on the back burner for a long time" (p. 48). Again, the problem was one of not communicating. In their case, however, they had previously had their best talks while riding in the car. So the therapist recommended that they take a rather long trip (from Omaha to Salt Lake City) so that they could have time for conversation "and that they use shorter car trips, such as a trip to a neighboring town for apples in the fall, to keep the good momentum going" (p. 48). (The authors' use of the phrase "good momentum" suggests that, for this couple, a car ride symbolized forward progress.)

Family therapists Stephen R. and Carol H. Lankton (1986) employ a variation on the task assignment. They call this an "ambiguous function assignment." They developed this idea from reflecting on the stories that their mentor, Milton H. Erickson, told about his therapeutic work (I discuss Erickson in Capps, 1998, chap. 2). This assignment always involves a physical object because this helps to "solidify the imagination a little bit and externalize some of the mental stimulation that is going on" (Lankton, p. 138). For example, a couple having marital conflicts had the "ambiguous function assignment" of rearranging the pictures on the walls of their home. When they returned for their next session, the therapist asked them the standard question, "Why do you suppose I asked you to do this assignment?" They responded, "Because you recognized that our marriage is fundamentally sound but that some 'rearrangements' were needed. Just like the pictures on the walls." While this type of assignment may seem manipulative—despite the fact that the therapist has no preconceived idea as to what the prescribed activity is supposed to "mean"—it makes the valuable point that most couples relate through physical objects, and these objects have symbolic meaning for them. An activity involving the rearrangement of pictures on the wall may also be a reminder of the symbolic nature of the marriage itself, and may, in fact, be reminiscent of their wedding day, with its emphasis on rings and gifts. In fact, the Lanktons commonly use rings in these ambiguous function assignments. In one case, Stephen Lankton gave a client a ring to use in the assignment that he had purchased for $9.75. This, he notes, "was an investment in her future" (p. 138).

Wynn points out that an initial interview with a family group is different from one with a couple only, in part because parents' and children's coming together presents a mixture of greater complexity. However, as with couples, the way they enter the room, how they conduct themselves, and how they arrange themselves on the chairs provides insights that mere questioning would take a long time to reveal: "Keys to their family system will soon be shown by who talks to whom and how, whose remarks habitually follow someone else's, which person corrects the reports of others, those who comply and those who disagree" (p. 88).

Wynn begins the session with a query to which everyone is asked to give a response: "Tell me how you see the problem this family is having." This is first directed to someone who is likely to be reticent (if possible, an adolescent) and not to the most articulate (who could drown out all the others in a sweeping report). Nor is it directed to the identified patient (which would seem to confirm the family's scapegoating), nor to a young child (who may not be ready for such a challenge until she has observed how others handle the question). Next, Wynn shifts gears, and asks the family members to talk about "the better side," the good times the family has had, and its strengths. By directing this question to the children and firmly restraining the parents from any promptings, he learns not only where the strengths lie but also the "methods of amelioration" that have appealed to the family (p. 89).

From this, Wynn moves to asking the question of what remedies they have already tried. As noted in connection with couples counseling, this question eliminates from consideration approaches that have been tried and failed, and alerts the family members to the realization that they have already been working on the problem. Thus, it may kindle hope that there is a solution if they are able to change their methods.

The purpose of this initial meeting is "to be of support to these anxious parents and to establish rapport with their pained and resistant children" (p. 90). Much more than this is unrealistic, especially if the number of people is rather large or members of three generations are present, but Wynn nonetheless emphasizes the importance of making some intervention into the family difficulty. This usually involves a simple assignment—such as a shared activity—that they have not tried for some time.

Finally, Wynn emphasizes the need for the minister to take firm hold of the proceedings. Otherwise, the prognosis for change is poor. There is no standard interview model for a family because every family is different, but the minister's role is to guide the session through the topics chosen, the questions asked, the subjects terminated, the order in which persons are called on, and the persons whose interruptions or domination of the conversation are checked. The two major goals of the initial interview are (1) to gain a clear picture of the major problem behind the conflict; and (2) to ascertain what family members wish to change. A congruence between the two is desirable, but family members may not agree either on the picture itself or on what changes they would like to see. The minister should not be surprised or alarmed if these disagreements surface during the conversation and if some of them remain at the end. Disagreement "is easier by far to deal with than an apathy that excludes both dissonance and resolution" (p. 91). Wynn also notes that emotional catharsis is not necessarily to be sought, and is certainly not the primary gauge of whether the session has gone well or not: "This session can be kept on an intellectual level, minimally contentious and at moderate depth until some understandings are squared away and some principles established" (p. 91).

Subsequent interviews are almost always scheduled, though Wynn notes, "Family therapy tends to be short-term treatment. The Family Service Association of America reports that their family cases average only about six interviews" (p. 93). The second interview centers on what has happened in the interim, how well (or poorly) the assignment worked out (and whether it needs some adjustment), and consideration of the family background and history. The purpose of the latter is to discover homeostatic patterns and to enable the family members to appreciate that nothing has happened by accident. This history-taking usually comprises three generations, which enables the children to make new discoveries about their parents (and grandparents), even as the parents come to new understandings of their own parents. During this discussion, Wynn tries to keep the focus on the family's "patterns of interaction," which should now be apparent to the family members themselves. This discussion may evoke revised estimates of what they want to see changed, may provide new resistances, and may elicit new ways of relating to one another.

The third session centers on helping the family redefine the presenting problem in relational terms. This "systems move" sidelines the identified patient and gives focal attention to the family itself as the patient. At this point, the therapist moves to a new stage, which involves the entire family in working for change, with the parents put in charge of this change. More resistance is likely at this stage, and this is countered by encouraging every member to be flexible, as change is unlikely to occur without flexibility. Flexibility is precisely what dysfunctional families tend to lack, as the homeostasis they have established is typically a rigid one. Flexibility is possible, however, if members remain open to one another as they interact.   Positive feedback is vitally important at this stage. This "working through" stage, initiated in the third session, tends to effect a "resolution and termination in those cases that succeed" (p. 94). Another session or two may be required, however, to ensure that the gains that have been made are not "sabotaged" by one or more family members, and to make any necessary modifications in the plan for change.

The goal of therapy is, of course, to free the family from the need for a therapist: "When the family has shown some progress in handling its presenting problem and growing toward the change that will make repetition unlikely, it has reached a stage where it can arrest therapy for the present" (p. 94). In unsuccessful cases, options include the decision to continue in a new series of interviews or referral to another type of therapy.

Resistance and Referral

At various points in his discussion of the counseling process, Wynn uses the term resistance. Later, in his chapter on "Seventeen-Often-Asked Questions," he explains what he means by resistance, and notes that a fundamental principle of resistance is that the person or persons who have asked for help say and do things that hurt their prospects of getting such help. In this sense, they act against the very desires that brought them to therapy. In Rogerian terms, this is an instance of incongruence. This resistance, then, is different from a reasonable objection to an inaccurate and incorrect interpretation by the therapist, or a theraputic intervention that merely reveals the therapist's incompetence. Obvious forms of resistance are canceling an appointment at the last minute, refusing to carry out an assigned task, coming late for the appointment, and refusing to participate in the conversation. More subtle forms are bullying the therapist, showering compliments on the therapist (which usually signals the beginning of noncooperation), showing helplessness that plays directly into the hands of the minister-as-rescuer, trying to use anger to intimidate, distancing to control others, and making threats to drop out of therapy because "it isn't doing any good" (pp. 134–37).

Wynn is aware that family therapy is inappropriate in some instances and that some approaches and interventions used by family therapists are inappropriate for use by ministers. The situations in which family therapy is not the treatment of choice are ones in which a member of the family is a confirmed criminal or psychopath or has a progressive paranoid condition (this would have eliminated the Gilmore family, noted earlier, from family therapy); a key person in the family cannot participate because of illness or disease; or there is a mixture of family members who are incapable of honesty or who deal in deceit as their way of interaction (p. 126). Although I have not presented Wynn's discussion of the various interventions that family therapists employ (pp. 94–102), it is worth noting that some are inappropriate for ministers. These would include complex paradoxical directives, methods that escalate stress, and the psychotherapy of the absurd. These are either too difficult or they put at risk the relationship between the minister and the couple or family that exists outside the counseling setting. Interventions that are usually appropriate for ministers to use are reframing and similar techniques (see Capps, 1990).

There are several reasons that a minister would refer a couple or family to another professional. Because he believes that ministers *should* be doing counseling work with families, Wynn does not include the lack of interest in such counseling or of competence to do it among the valid reasons. Nor does he consider the argument that the minister has so many other obligations and responsibilities that there simply isn't time to provide counsel to couples and families. He believes, instead, that providing counsel is central to what it means to be a minister, and time should therefore be found for it, especially when it is requested. He does, however, recognize that there are valid reasons for referral that go beyond those already indicated, that is, reasons that family therapy itself is contraindicated. One is when problems surface in the course of the conversation with a couple or family that the minister simply cannot help with. When these arise, the minister need not terminate the counseling, but may instead say that there is someone she knows who can help with this particular problem (pp. 139–40). If, for example, the parents suspect that their child has a learning disability, or if a member of the family has a serious gambling problem, or if the couple's problems are exacerbated by a sexual dysfunction, a referral would be in order. But this should not replace the counseling that the minister is providing.

Ministers in the past often assumed that "it's either me or them," and they usually decided on the "them." This well-intentioned deferral to other professionals, however, may communicate unintended messages to the couple or family, such as a lack of interest in their problems, that the Christian faith is only relevant for the little aggravations and frustrations in life and not for the larger ones that prompted this couple or family to seek the minister's help, or that the minister has little confidence in the combination of personal counsel and corporate life that the church provides for helping a couple or family overcome its present difficulties. Also, ministers have deferred to other professionals because these professionals insisted on a single form of treatment—the one *they* provided—and therefore felt that any parallel counsel the minister might provide a couple or family was inherently counter-productive and would undermine their own therapeutic work. Increasingly, this insistence has been breaking down, and the various mental health professionals are working more collaboratively. A referral therefore need not mean that the minister ceases to have conversations with the couple or family. In fact, the minister and the therapist may confer together and develop a collaborative plan.

On the other hand, there are some families that a full-time family therapist would work with that a minister might not. Wynn does not say much about this, as the referrals he has in mind are primarily those where a family member has a problem requiring psychiatric evaluation and treatment (for example, a chemical dependency, suicide risk, unmanaged schizophrenic and paranoid disorders, or given to antisocial acts or violence). Clues as to when referral to a marriage counselor or family therapist is indicated are when the minister feels he has not been able to "take command" of the process—members of the family are clearly in control—or when the couple or family are being too dependent on the minister and are unable to take what they have learned from dealing with the presenting problem and apply this learning to other problems as they arise. At these junctures, it *is* appropriate for the minister to consider his other responsibilities and obligations and to weigh the costs of continuing to have frequent conversations with the couple or family.

In some instances where a referral to a marriage and family counselor has occurred, however, one member of the family may ask to continue to meet with the minister on an individual basis because he is finding these conversations personally valuable. There is no inherent reason why the minister should not agree to this request. Early in his career, Carl Rogers' primary therapeutic population were teenagers who had been declared delinquents. In one case, he found he had to inform the mother of a teenage boy that very little progress had been made and that he recommended that the treatment be terminated. The mother and boy left his office. A brief moment later, there was a knock on his door, and the mother poked her head in. "Do you take adults?" she asked. When Rogers said that he did, she asked him to be her counselor, and he agreed. In chapter 4, I will report on a somewhat similar case of individual counseling provided by Michael Nichols. It reflects the fact that, over the past decade or so, systemic thinking has been used increasingly by marriage and family therapists in counseling individuals.

In presenting Wynn's model for family counseling, I am aware that many readers of this book will feel that, in spite of the various qualifications and exceptions he makes for ministers, counseling families is still a formidable proposition and one for which they feel totally unprepared. After all, Wynn writes as one who has engaged in family therapy for many years. In contrast, the seminarian who is the primary reader of this book is likely to view the prospect of sitting down with a family as a very daunting one. "Is it realistic to assume, for example, that I will be able to 'take command' of the process in the way Wynn asserts that I must in order for the counseling to succeed?" This is a very reasonable question to ask, and, in my view, there is no simple answer to it. I believe, however, that the beginning minister *can* gain a sense of how family counseling works by engaging in the practice—quite common among ministers in congregations—of gathering as many family members as possible together after the death of a family member for reflection on what this person meant to them, what they valued about this person, and perhaps what also caused them irritation or even pain. In this situation, the minister "takes command," inviting each member to say something about the deceased person, and usually draws some conclusions from the conversation, which are communicated at the end of the session (and reiterated or refined at the funeral itself). Although this is a very different situation from one in which a family is having troubles, the session itself is not very different from what transpires in the initial session in family counseling. It may therefore be viewed by the beginning minister as a "rehearsal" for family counseling.

When my father died, the minister invited my three brothers and me to come to his office to "reminisce" about our father. This was a very helpful session, but it also underscored the value of the insights of systemic theory presented here. Instead of beginning with one of the more inarticulate brothers, the minister moved in chronological order (from oldest to youngest). By the time we got to the younger brothers, the overall tone of the conversation had already been set. I recall especially that our father was represented by the older brothers as a man of depth, especially when it came to religious matters. The contrary view, that he was something of a skeptic, held by the two younger brothers, while verbally expressed, did not seem to register with the minister, nor was it reflected in his homily at the funeral. A more nuanced picture of our father—one that recognized the truth in both perspectives—might have been presented if greater care had been taken with regard to who was asked to speak first. As systems theory suggests, the voices of the more powerful can drown out the voices of those who are less so.

By and large, however, the most typical use a minister (in whatever context she may be) will make of systems theory is in thinking systemically while giving counsel to a single individual. The nineteen-year-old daughter who says she hates her father is a good case in point. As I indicated in my comments in chapter 2 on the *tone-setting phase* of the conversation, there was likely to have been some discussion of the woman's family during this phase before she made this declaration of her hatred toward her minister father. It is unlikely that this declaration came out of the blue. Or, alternatively, the minister already knew some facts about the family, such as how many children there were, where she fit in the sibling birth order, and so forth. Perhaps she had told him a little about her family on a previous occasion. However this information was acquired, the minister could be thinking about the woman's role in the family system as they talked together about her feelings toward her father.

What is her family role? Standard-bearer? Tension-reducer? Symptom-bearer? Does she resent this role? Is her view that she has no basis for hating her father possibly related to the family's use of double-binding communication (which seems benign on the surface, but is actually destructive)? Is she part of a family triangle? We have heard only about her hatred toward her father (a dyadic relationship). Is this connected, however, to a third family member in some way (her mother, a sibling)? Or might it be related to a third person outside the family (such as a male or female friend whom her father rejects, or a career goal she would like to pursue to which he objects)?

The issue may relate to family rules that she accepted before but now, in her late teens, finds oppressive or arbitrary. Perhaps there are "spooky" things about the family that are having a negative impact on her life, especially in her relationship with her father. Suppose, for example, that her male friend comes from a religious tradition that her father (and his father, also a minister) considers dangerous or pernicious, and that her older siblings complied with this family "ghost" by marrying persons of the same faith as their parents and grandparents. She, however, is threatening to break out of this standardized routine, and to do so in a way that challenges the very foundations of the family legacy. There may be a "secret" attached to this "ghost," a great-aunt for example, who had married a man of this dangerous or pernicious tradition who abused her and then left her in disgrace for another woman.

Of course, these "maybes" *could* be dismissed as the figment of a fertile imagination. Still, they illustrate how a minister may "think systemically" in the course of giving counsel to an individual. For any given case, some, perhaps most, of these systemic considerations will not bear fruit. Yet in my own experience, there will always be something to which systems thinking directs one's *attention* that proves illuminating. Often, the "for instance" that the minister asks for—"Tell me what it was that your father said or did that aroused these hateful thoughts?"— becomes the means by which a systems concept is discovered to be relevant. If the episode that provoked these feelings was an argument, then most likely it was an argument about someone or something. This almost automatically raises the question of triangulation (or a triadic relationship).

Another avenue, which may involve some probing, is for the minister to ask himself, "What's missing in the story she tells?" For example, where is her mother in all this? (This is the very question one might ask about Jesus' story of the prodigal son.) This *could* reveal a father-mother-daughter triangulation and *could* lead the minister to conclude that there can be no real resolution of the problem unless this triangular relationship is addressed.

The Self-differentiation Factor

It was perhaps inevitable that the systems model would eventually be applied to the congregation itself. After all, a common understanding of the congregation is that it is a "family of families" (which has the negative effect of marginalizing single adults and childless couples). I will not discuss these extensions of the model in detail, but I would like to draw attention to an early contribution, E. Mansell Pattison's *Pastor and Parish–A Systems Approach* (1977), and then comment more fully on Edwin H. Friedman's *Generation to Generation: Family Process in Church and Synagogue* (1985). Pattison, an ordained minister who became a psychiatrist, brings systems theory to bear on the structure and function of the local congregation. His particular emphasis is the *subsystems* that make up the total system of the church, which he calls "a living system of identity." He suggests that the congregation has the following subsystems: proclaiming, symbolizing, moralizing, learning-growth, sustaining-maintaining, and reparative. Each subsystem is part of the total system, and the church as living system "is most effective when its efforts in all these areas are mutually reinforcing" (p. 47).

Pattison views the minister as "the shepherd of the church system," which means that she "functions to nurture and guide the subsystems of the church." This requires, among other things, giving up her narcissistic satisfaction of pointing to "what I accomplished" and instead finding "one's narcissistic reward indirectly through seeing the accomplishment of a *system* in which one's own role is *not* seen" (p. 65). While Pattison does not assign specific functions of the minister to specific subsystems, it seems clear that "the reparative subsystem" is the locus of the counseling role. He chooses the word "reparative" to avoid "too clinical an overtone," and instead emphasizes how all of us experience "being torn apart in our lives" and our need for help in "putting it all together" again (p. 45).

Edwin Friedman's *Generation to Generation* is a much more elaborate application of systems thinking to the church and synagogue. A rabbi, Friedman was a student of Murray Bowen, who, as we have already noted, is an "intergenerational theorist." Friedman's use of systems theory to understand the families within the congregation, the congregation as a family system, and the personal families of the clergy, is far too extensive to discuss here, but there is one particular issue in his chapter on "the idea of a family" that we have not yet considered. This is his discussion of Bowen's view that "self-differentiation" is the key factor in a family's ability to change.

The question of change may be put this way: What resources are available within the family for helping it overcome its own homeostatic resistance? Friedman makes a distinction between inanimate systems, and human systems. Unlike inanimate systems, animate systems (including human ones) possess will and mind, while the individual members of a human system like the family have, in addition, "the capacity for some self-differentiation," or "the capacity for some awareness of their own position in the relationship system, how it is affected by balancing forces, and how changes in each individual's functioning can in turn influence their homeostasis" (p. 27).

The recognition of this "self-differentiating" capacity on the part of individual family member is, for Friedman, a way of "trying to preserve the value of a systems orientation, yet not let it become totally deterministic" (p. 27). He attributes this insight to Bowen, who has suggested that "a key variable in the degree to which any family can change fundamentally is the amount of self-differentiation that existed in previous generations in the extended families of both partners" (p. 27). This reflects Bowen's "transgenerational approach" to family therapy, which, as Wynn points out, is especially reflected in how "the nuclear family emotional system repeats the interplay of elements from previous generations" (Wynn, 1982, p. 70). This also explains Bowen's strong advocacy of the *genogram,* a pictorial device used in taking the family history.[1]

Friedman centers on Bowen's "scale of differentiation," noting that differentiation means "the capacity of a family member to define his or her own life's goals and values apart from surrounding togetherness pressures" (p. 27). It includes the capacity to maintain a relatively nonanxious presence in the midst of anxious systems and to take maximum responsibility for one's own destiny and well-being, and it is measurable, in part, by the breadth of one's repertoire of responses when confronted with a crisis. It is not to be confused with autonomy (in the sense of becoming a separate individual). Rather, it means the capacity to be an "I" while remaining connected.

The individual members of a family may be placed on a scale of self-differentiation where 100 would be the highest degree of differentiation possible and 0 would be the lowest. A family composed of individuals toward the bottom of the scale is not necessarily sick, nor would it necessarily have more problems than other families. It would, however, be less well equipped to deal with a crisis, and if the predictable pattern was disturbed in some way, it would respond more quickly and forcibly to redress the balance and return to its homeostasis. This would be especially true if the disturbance were caused by one of its members' trying to achieve a higher level of self-differentiation.

A family at the highest end of the scale would, conversely, be marked by "infinite elasticity." If the father said he was taking the son

---

[1]An especially valuable text on the genogram is *Genograms: Assessment and Intervention* (1999), ed. Monica McGoldrick, Randy Gerson, and Sylvia Shellenberger. McGoldrick's *You Can Go Home Again: Reconnecting with Your Family* (1995) illustrates the uses of the genogram for interpreting transgenerational family systems through the use of historical materials relating to the Beethoven, Dickens, Freud, Kafka, Roosevelt, Kennedy, and other families.

to the movies, the mother and daughters would not feel insulted that they were not invited to go along. On the other hand, if the father and son invited the others to come along, the others would feel free to turn down their offer and the father and son would not feel that they should abandon their own plans. There would also be a maximum of "I" statements that define one's position and a minimum of "you" statements that blame others for the family's condition. Of course, there is no such thing as a family with "infinite elasticity." The goal of family therapy (or of couples therapy) may, however, be defined as helping the family move up the scale. Friedman adds: "The farther down the scale any family is located to start with, the more automatically this principle [of homeostasis] will operate, and the more difficult it will be to find a family member who can maintain the kind of nonanxious presence needed to keep the family on a course for change" (p. 29). He suggests, however, that one should support the strengths in their family (as manifested in the differentiating member) by coaching that person to stay on a committed course. This will bring more healing to the entire family than would result from focusing on the family's weaknesses manifested in the dysfunctional or recalcitrant member. This does not mean coaching the more differentiated member (or members) to leave, but to continue to maintain their self-differentiation while remaining a part of the family.

I would add to Friedman's discussion the following points: If the more self-differentiated member is an older sibling, she models the values of self-differentiation to her younger siblings. This is also the case when the more self-differentiated member of the family is one of the parents. In either case, the more self-differentiated member bears a heavier burden for the essential health of the family, especially in its response to crises, but this is the natural burden the self-differentiated carry in any human system. The self-differentiated member should not be expected to assume the superhuman task of "repairing" the family single-handedly, but she *can* play a major role in sustaining healthy relationships between individual family members.

Friedman indicates that the minister can gain invaluable insight into this matter of self-differentiation by looking to himself. Most decisions to enter the clergy are influenced by multigenerational forces. Many clergypersons are the sons, daughters, or grandchildren of clergy, or a parent or grandparent was influential in their decision to enter the clergy. Thus, clergy understand the role that multigenerational forces play in vocational decisions. Even those who came to their decisions through nonfamilial influences are likely, perhaps by virtue of their sibling order, to have assumed the role of "standard-bearer" in their respective families. Furthermore, entering the ministry is to enter a very traditional–or multigenerational–profession. A minister friend tells me that he has little idea what his son does for a living, because he works for a computer company. Conversely, his son knows a great deal about what his father does for a living, how he spends his time, what his activities are, and so forth. Thus, the clergy are well-acquainted with multigenerational influences, and they have chosen a profession in which, systemically considered, the scale of differentiation is more toward the bottom than the top.

For Friedman, then, the challenge is for ministers to "obtain more differentiation within that transmission process" so as to "increase our flexibility to function within the parameters of our 'calling'" (p. 296). This increased differentiation usually carries with it "more latitude for facing crisis, and provides satisfaction rather than stress" (p. 296).

Pattison addresses this issue of self-differentiation–though he does not call it that–in his chapter on the need for clergy to shepherd themselves. For Pattison personally, the issue of self-differentiation centered around the problem of pretense (a problem that a family system may also have). He felt he was presenting himself as one type of person when doing therapy and another type when he spoke publicly or preached in church. In the course of time, he came to realize that he was "simply being false to myself" and was engaging in an act of "self-betrayal." What he discovered "through search and effort" was "a new freedom–the freedom not to pretend, nor to have to pretend" (p. 83). His advice to ministers, "the shepherds in the system," is to "give up the pretenses of what you are not" and "in so doing you will discover the freedom to be what you are. Being yourself, you no longer need to feel exposure as you live and interact in the system of the church" (p. 83). This is self-differentiation, and it is much to be preferred, in Pattison's view, to escaping to times and places where ministers "can indulge themselves and not act like a pastor," for this is also a form of self-betrayal. There may be emotional release in such indulgence, but it cannot compare with the self-differentiation realized through being a "nonanxious presence" in the system itself.

Concluding Comments

In the next chapter, I will expand on Friedman's recognition of the importance of self-differentiation in human systems by considering the work of family therapists who are critical of certain aspects of the systems model. I hope, however, that the present chapter has demonstrated the value of thinking systemically, and that it has shown some of the ways in which this is done. Because systems theory was first introduced by therapists who worked with families, and, conversely, contributed to the view that the only way to effect change is to counsel families, not individuals, this theoretical model has been strongly identified with family therapy. In addition, from a sociocultural perspective, it was closely associated with the "normative" family headed by two parents (not a single parent) who are heterosexual. Wynn was not unaware of this bias when he wrote his *Pastoral Ministry to Families* (1957). In it, he endorses the then current effort to give primacy to the family in religious education, but cautions that this creates "the danger of the Church neglecting the problems of people outside 'average family' life." He warns against the church's stereotypical thinking that leaves no place for "the atypical family" and says that a church education program organized around the "typical" family configuration of father, mother, and children "will certainly increase the loneliness and isolation of those who already feel the want of close family ties: the unmarried, the widowed, the divorced, or in some instances unwed mothers" (p. 25). He also mentions those who have married outside the faith in which they were reared but want to maintain contact with it.

Of course, Wynn says nothing about the "blended" family (where previously divorced parents are raising two sets of children together), families where the two parents are gay or lesbian, or other less typical configurations (for example, where an unmarried or divorced but childless person marries a divorced parent with children). Nor, for that matter, does he discuss differences in family configuration due to socioeconomic class, race, and ethnicity. As he notes in his later book, however, "theological teachings about family have usually grown out of problems and polemics" as these are perceived by those who offer these teachings (1982, p. 158). The prophet Ezra, for example, discusses interfaith marriage in the context of anxiety about Israel's survival as a people, while the church father Jerome's view that the good of marriage is that it produces new virgins for the world occurred in the context of anxiety that the church was in danger of losing its spiritual direction. These men wrote, he says, "out of the pressures of their particular times. How could they have done otherwise?" (p. 159). Noting that our theories about the family derive from our current problems, Wynn cites philosopher John Dewey's observation that "We don't even bother to think until we are challenged by a problem" (p. 160).

For Russell Becker, the problem to which his book was addressed (1963) was the "crisis of intimacy" in family life due to the separation of work and home and the emergence of the isolated conjugal family (and decline of the extended family). This crisis was reflected, on the one hand, in the prevalence of "spouse phobia," or the irrational anxiety-tinged avoidance of the marital partner (p. 17), and, on the other hand, of the popularity of "spouse swapping" as a means to reinvigorate the marriage. From our vantage point several decades later, we might assume that "spouse swapping" was rare, perhaps even nonexistent among Christian couples. However, a minister once lamented to me that the "sensitivity group" that he had organized in the late 1960s became the vehicle through which couples in his church arranged spouse-swapping activities.

Becker notes that in the late 1940s, Phoebe Anderson, the director of the church nursery school in the Glenview Community Church outside Chicago, and her minister-husband gathered the parents of the nursery children in an evening group, doing so on the grounds that the problems the parents were having with their children were not primarily due to a problem in the child but were a reflection of parental conflicts to which the child was reacting. Parents who joined the group for the purpose of understanding their nursery-age children discovered that they were learning something about themselves. Before long, the groups were expanded to include couples other than those with nursery-age children. The Friends' (Quakers') term *concern* was adopted, and these Couples Christian Concern Groups, as they were called, were no longer limited to the parent-child relationship, but included any "concern" that might arise "at the point where one is fully engaged with life" (p. 41).

This was the sociocultural context, then, in which the systems view of the family gained prominence in pastoral counseling. Thus, the texts that we have been considering in this chapter were written with specific perceived problems in mind. Our problems today are not necessarily the same (though they may bear certain resemblances), and I assume that texts addressing today's problems will be selected to supplement this introductory guide to the minister's counselor role. This does not mean, however, that the systems theory itself is automatically outmoded. Instead, what it means is that we need to continue to test its applicability to present realities and the problems that we perceive to be most in need of attention today.[2] What is undeniable, in my view, is the continuing value of thinking systemically in one's work and role as counselor. As Wynn's work especially demonstrates, it is difficult for the minister to "take command" of the process unless she has a generative theory that enables her to find some meaningful coherence in the things that are being said to her. Systems theory helps one to listen more effectively, to hear things that would otherwise be unattended to or missed.

---

[2]In *Taking Care: Monitoring Power Dynamics and Relational Boundaries in Pastoral Care and Counseling* (1995), Carrie Doehring indicates that she originally approached pastoral situations from the perspective of family systems theory, but came to realize that this theory gives inadequate attention to the empowering and disempowering agencies of the larger society. She uses novels, such as Toni Morrison's *Beloved*, the story of a black woman in the post–Civil War South who kills her daughter as a means to ensure that the child will never have to go back to the hell of slavery, to show that power dynamics and relational boundary issues are contextualized, shown to be embedded in the larger social, political, and cultural dynamics in which the local events depicted in the novel are implicated. This is but one example of efforts in our own day to expand on the systems model.

4

How to Interpret Stories

In chapter 2, I identified "interpretive responses" as among the three "tone-setting" responses in a conversation in which the minister is providing counsel (the others being "supportive" and "understanding" responses). I also noted that interpretive responses may shade over into "evaluative" ones, and that these, in turn, may become "moralistic." In this chapter, I will be making the case for ministers as "interpreters" of the stories that are told to them by the persons they counsel.

The word *interpret* means "to explain the meaning of or make understandable," "to translate," "to construe" (as in interpreting someone's silence as contempt), or "to bring out the meaning of," especially in the sense of offering one's own conception of a work of art, whether in performance or criticism. The sense of *interpret* that is perhaps most central for our purposes is "to bring out the meaning of," though the other meanings may also hover in the background. Sometimes the minister, as interpreter, does need to explain or make understandable, or to translate into another form of discourse, or to construe the meaning of a behavior whose meaning may not be obvious or explicit. The central meaning of *interpret* for our purposes here, however, is "to bring out the meaning of," a definition implying that the "meaning" is already there in what the other person (or persons) is saying, but that it needs to be drawn out or made more explicit. The interpreter offers her own conception of what is being presented to her, but this is not a *pre*conception that she formed before listening to the other person; it is a conception that is drawn from what is being said–or presented–to her.

A case in point is the interpretive response in our discussion (in chapter 2) about the young woman who has hateful feelings toward her father. After listening to her, the minister says:

> You wonder why you would have hateful feelings toward your father when, as you say, he is a good minister and hasn't actually struck you physically. There seems to be a discrepancy here between your portrayal of him and your feelings toward him. Perhaps we should look at this discrepancy, as this may help us to understand the feelings you have toward him.

This response is mainly concerned to "bring out the meaning" of her testimony that she has hateful feelings toward her father. There may be elements of explanation ("You wonder why") and translation ("There seems to be a *discrepancy*") here, but the primary force of this response is to "bring out the meaning." This, the minister implies, is something that is best done collaboratively ("*we* should look" and "this may help *us*").

The issue this chapter addresses, however, is not the use of one or more interpretive responses in a conversation. Rather, it concerns the fact that the minister who provides counsel is engaged, from beginning to end, as an interpreter of the other person's story. Listening, of course, is essential to being able to help "bring out the meaning" of the story. Also, as we have seen in chapter 3, thinking is important. A minister could hardly participate in the bringing out of the meaning of the story without engaging in some thinking as he listens (attends) to what is being said. We may therefore view interpretation as occurring at the confluence of listening and thinking. By listening attentively and thinking well, the minister is in a position to be a reliable interpreter of the counseled person's story.

I have used the word *story* here, and this word itself should be explained. The dictionary defines *story* as the "telling of a happening or connected series of happenings, whether true or fictitious." It then suggests that *story* is the word that is "broadest in scope" and that it refers to "a series of connected events, true or fictitious." *Narrative* is "a more formal word, referring to the kind of prose that recounts happenings."

Tale "usually suggests a simple, leisurely story, more or less loosely organized, especially a fictitious or legendary one." *Anecdote* "applies to a short, entertaining account of a single incident, usually personal or biographical." If the conversation in which the minister assumes the role of counselor involves, at least in part, "the telling of a happening or connected series of happenings," it makes sense to employ the broader term *story* rather than *narrative, tale,* or *anecdote,* for each one of these has a connotation that is incongruent with the very idea that what occurs between the minister and the other person (or persons) is a *conversation.* Narrative is too formal; tale comes down too much on the side of the fictitious; and anecdote is too much concerned with entertaining. In the case I will present later in this chapter, we will see that the "single incident" aspect of anecdote does have relevance. I would suggest, however, that *episode* expresses this equally well without anecdote's implication of being entertaining. According to the dictionary, an episode is "any part of a story that is largely complete in itself."

The purpose of this chapter, then, is to show how the minister, in collaboration with the other person (or persons), can be a good interpreter of the stories that are told to her when she is in the role of counselor. A related purpose is to show how being a good interpreter of stories is a way—perhaps the best way—for a minister to help the other person (or persons) become more "self-differentiated." To meet these objectives, I will first consider some of the criticisms that have been made of the systems approach to family therapy. These criticisms set the stage for the emphasis I will place on story interpretation.

Criticisms of Systems Theory

Criticisms of the systems model have mostly originated from within the field of family therapy itself. This being the case, the critics invariably express their personal debt to the model and to the persons who introduced them to it in their training to become therapists, and then they go on to indicate the degree to which they continue to subscribe to it. The more moderate critics believe that the systems model is fundamentally sound but that it needs to be modified or expanded, while the more radical family therapists have suggested that its time has passed, and that it is now incumbent on family therapists to replace it with a different model more attuned to the realities of the therapeutic profession and the sociocultural context in which we now find ourselves.

These debates reflect family therapists' awareness of Thomas S. Kuhn's argument (1970) that scholarly disciplines and professional groups undergo "paradigm shifts" from time to time. In effect, those who are calling for the replacement of the systems model with a new model are arguing that a paradigm shift is already underway, but that we simply do not yet know what the form of the new paradigm will be. Those who are more moderate believe, instead, that there is no compelling reason for the systems model to be replaced. Paradigm shifts usually occur when a discipline or profession knows that it is in a crisis and believes that the only way out of it is to change direction. These moderates do not believe that family therapy *is* in such a crisis. Few defend the early 1950s formulations of the systems model, based on theories of cybernetics, but many believe that the view of families as systems is simply too valuable to abandon.

This more moderate position is taken, for example, by Monica McGoldrick and her colleagues. A student of Murray Bowen, McGoldrick emphasizes his themes of the multigenerational transmission process and the use of the genogram. In *Women in Families: A Framework for Family Therapy* (1989), McGoldrick and coeditors Carol M. Anderson and Froma Walsh note that when they began their own development as family therapists in the late 1960s, Virginia Satir, author of *Conjoint Family Therapy* (1964) and *Peoplemaking* (1972), was the only major female voice in the field. Although one of the earliest and most influential pioneers in the family field, "she was often derided by both men and women for her emphasis on feelings (a 'feminine' concern) at a time when her male colleagues were presenting revolutionary models that downplayed emotions and emphasized 'masculine' priorities—such as rational planning, instrumental problem-solving, hierarchy, neutrality, and power" (McGoldrick, 1989, p. 5). They note that Satir's "experiential" mentality was almost embarrassing, as was the fact that she was "touchy-feely" rather than distant and conceptual in her orientation and practice.

Since the 1970s, increasing numbers of women have become therapists in their own right, and they, together with a small number of men, have drawn attention to the underlying assumptions about gender on which the field was originally based. This has led to a general criticism of systems theory for placing greater emphasis on generations than on gender, especially in relation to parents but also in relation to siblings, and to the more specific criticism of its emphasis on changing performance *within roles* rather than on changing the roles themselves. These are often roles that do not originate within the family crucible itself, but are a function of the culture—mothers do this, fathers do that. Furthermore, "Family therapists still tend to hold women primarily responsible for what goes wrong in families," while books on marital therapy "fail to discuss the different implications for men and women of questioning their commitment to the marital relationship" (p. 11). Most of the discussion regarding facilitating change in family therapy still occurs "without reference to the unequal division of power between men and women in families and in larger social systems" (p. 11).

These are very trenchant criticisms of the family therapy guild. In the view of McGoldrick and her colleagues, however, they do not challenge the validity of the systems model itself. One of the essays in this volume, for example, addresses the issue of women's relationships with "larger systems," such as welfare, public schools, body health care, and mental health care, which "serve as a culture's carriers of beliefs regarding women, minorities, social class, and appropriate family organization" (p. 335). The concept of system here is not itself under critique. Rather, an expanded view of systems is called for.

An illustration in contemporary pastoral counseling literature of the use of systems theory in relation to an issue that received little if any attention in the earlier stages of systems-oriented family therapy is Joretta Marshall's *Counseling Lesbian Partners* (1997). Marshall indicates that the "dynamics of particular partnerships reflect not only themes from families of origin but also the experience of living in many systems that are not open and affirming for lesbians most of the time" (p. 15). Her endorsement of systems theory is expressed, for example, in her contention that it is essential for counselors who work with women in lesbian relationships to assist them "to think about the systems of which they are a part, of their family triangles, and of the impact of their self-disclosure upon these relationships" (p. 107).

Her one specific criticism of a system theorist is directed toward Murray Bowen's scale of self-differentiation. In discussing the case of two women who depend on each other to meet most of their social and emotional needs, Marshall suggests that these two women's close relationship is likely to be misinterpreted as pathological or, at the very least, dysfunctional, on the grounds that, from the perspective of Bowen's work on family systems, they appear *fused*. That is, "one partner appears lost in the other's presence (or absence) and seems to deny her own needs and wishes" (p. 89). From this point of view, women whose relationships reflect fusion or enmeshment are those for whom maintaining the relationship becomes so important that individual development or differentiation cannot occur. In Marshall's view, however, "the concept of fusion as utilized in many traditional family therapy strategies is challenged by feminist therapists and, in particular, by persons working with lesbian partnerships. The concern is that the positive aspects of women's relationships are denied by an overemphasis on differentiation" (p. 89). McGoldrick and her coeditors make the same point when they note that, for traditional systems theorists, "enmeshment' has been regarded as bad; 'differentiation' as good" (McGoldrick, 1989, p. 10). I will return to this issue later in the chapter.

The more radical position of challenging systems theory itself is reflected in Jill Freedman and Gene Combs's *Narrative Therapy: The Social Construction of Preferred Realities* (1996). These family therapists express their indebtedness to Michael White and David Epston, authors of *Narrative Means to Therapeutic Ends* (1990). This book is based on the idea that "persons give meaning to their lives and relationships by storying their experience" (p. 13). Because persons are rich in lived experience, and only a fraction of this experience can be storied at any one time, "a great deal of lived experience falls outside the dominant stories about the lives and relationships of persons" (p. 15). This means that "those aspects of lived experience that fall outside of the dominant story provide a rich and fertile ground for the generation, or re-generation, of alternative stories" (p. 15). By identifying—thus externalizing—the dominant story, which is inherently problematic (otherwise, the person would not require therapy), one begins to "separate" from it and experience "personal agency" over it. When this happens, alternative stories become available and a "re-authoring" of one's life now begins.

A rather homely illustration of such "re-authoring" is a practice I adopted in reading The Hardy Boys books to our son when he was seven years old. When he climbed into his bed at bedtime, I would begin reading. After a few pages of straightforward reading, I would begin to embellish the story or even take it in a very different direction, and his "task" was to determine where the original left off and the alternative account began. Clues would be behaviors by Frank and Joe Hardy or their friend Chet Morton that were clearly out of character, as, for example, when the trio would enter not the soda shop, but the local tavern several doors down and order not malted milk shakes, but beer or gin; or when one of the Hardy boys talked back to his mother, calling her views "Neanderthal"; or when they gave their famous father-detective a false clue so that he would go down a very blind alley. Our son relished these departures from the original story, in part, I believe, because it enabled *him* to play detective, to listen for clues that the story was being "re-authored."

White and Epston do not discuss the systems model to any great extent, but they do express their profound debt to Gregory Bateson (often considered the originator of systems thinking for therapy) for his view that the interpretation of an event is determined by how it fits with other human events. This emphasis on the event in context, together with Bateson's emphasis on the temporal dimension of therapy, led them to begin focusing on the narrative quality of therapy itself (White and Epston, pp. 2–3). Despite their debt to Bateson, the relative absence of systems concepts in their book is itself an indication that, for the most part, they can get along without them in their therapeutic work.

Freedman and Combs, however, explicitly present the narrative as a replacement for the systems approach. In their introductory chapter, "Shifting Paradigms: From Systems to Stories," they suggest that *system* is simply a metaphor for how one may view the family, and, therefore, there are other ways to view it. They acknowledge that the systems metaphor has served the field well, providing useful ways to talk about the processes and patterns by which people interconnect: "However, just as the idea of individual minds in individual bodies once limited our ability to conceptualize and work with mind as an interpersonal phenomenon in family systems, the idea of 'family systems' now can limit our ability to think about the flow of ideas in our larger culture" (p. 2). They see their use of the "narrative metaphor" as, in part, an outgrowth of changes in the systems model itself, especially from the prevailing view in its early history of the "family system as a machine" and the "therapist as a repair person" to its later history in which the system was viewed more ecologically as a kind of "ecosystem."

At some point in the evolutionary process of the family therapy field, Freedman and Combs "realized" what they had known all along, namely, that two of the early pioneers in family therapy, Gregory Bateson and Milton E. Erickson, were profoundly interested in stories. Erickson was well known for his "teaching tales," which he used to teach young therapists how he did therapy. And, as Stephen and Carol Lankton have pointed out, "If one looks in the indexes of Erickson's collected writings, or article titles of any book written by Erickson (and co-authors), or any edited collection of articles authored by Erickson, not a single entry will be found entitled 'family' or 'systems'" (1986, p. 43). Their books, *The Answer Within: A Clinical Framework of Ericksonian Hypnotherapy* (1983) and *Enchantment and Intervention in Family Therapy* (1986), are designed, in part, to "project onto Erickson's work a set of ideas that will unite, all inconclusively, Erickson's [therapeutic] interventions in a suitable family therapy theory or framework," or to "place his work within the framework of a systems theory" (1986, p. 44). They acknowledge that the language Erickson used was not systemic but "psychodynamic" (p. 44). Evidence of Erickson's "psychodynamic" orientation was his emphasis on the unconscious, especially his use of "suggestions" designed to appeal to the patient's unconscious mind. Stories he told to the patient were one way in which he "planted" suggestions that he was certain the conscious mind of the patient would dismiss or reject.

Similarly, as Freedman and Combs point out, Bateson believed that "metaphor is the logic of nature." As such, "it is the means by which "this whole fabric of mental interconnections holds together," and "is therefore inescapable in living systems" (Combs and Freedman, 1990, p. 29). Bateson's early career as an anthropologist (he was married for a time to Margaret Mead, the legendary anthropologist) taught him the importance of storytelling. For example, when studying the Iatmul tribe of New Guinea, he encountered an adolescent boy and asked him if he would tell him the story of his life. The boy agreed and began with his birth, his childhood, and his adolescence. When he continued to describe his adulthood and his advanced years, Bateson surmised that he had misunderstood the request, and reaffirmed that he wanted the boy's *own* story. The boy indicated to him that this *was* his story, that for a man born into the Iatmul tribe, there is no alternative story (see Ernst Kris, 1952, pp. 83–84). This very story illustrates the fact that while Bateson was interested in systems, he was also invested in the stories that reflected these systems.

This realization that two major figures in the development of family therapy, Erickson and Bateson, were deeply interested in stories, together with the pioneering work of White and Epston, led Combs and Freedman to write their first book, which is about the role of metaphor in individual and family therapy, *Symbol, Story and Ceremony: Using Metaphor in Individual and Family Therapy* (1990). In this book, the authors explore strategies for "telling stories" designed to communicate understanding or acceptance and, thus, to develop rapport; to help the client gain greater access to his emotional states or attitudes; to offer ideas for the client to consider; and to embed suggestions in an indirect way. As indicated, Erickson often used stories to embed suggestions, either telling his patients about an incident in his own family or relating what another patient had done in comparable circumstances. The story I told the student who was distraught over her husband's dog about the woman who decided that she could surely "outrace that old mutt" to the door when her husband returned home from work (see chapter 3) would be an example of this storytelling strategy, its purpose in this case being to embed a suggestion in an indirect way (for other illustrations from Erickson's own therapeutic work, see Erickson 1982; also Capps, 1998, chap. 2).

In *Narrative Therapy* (1996), published six years later, Freedman and Combs write about the "shifting paradigm" in family therapy from systems to stories. They cite the "feminist critique" of the systems metaphor and note that it has led the two of them to believe that this metaphor, "at least as it has evolved and been applied in family therapy, is as much a hindrance as a help" (p. 13). Their criticism is that it invites the therapist to focus on rather small and tight "feedback loops" when she should be paying more attention to the "ideas and practices at play in the larger cultural context." In other words, the focus has been on looking *within* families for collaborative causation of problems instead of working with family members "to identify the negative influence of certain values, institutions, and practices in the larger culture on their lives and relationships, and to invite them to pull together in opposing those values, institutions, and practices" (p. 13). It is noteworthy in this connection that Russell Becker (as noted in chapter 3) viewed counseling with the family as a means to free them up in order to take full advantage of the church community and its nurturing and strengthening resources. In this sense, he was mindful of the very limits of traditional family therapy that Freedman and Combs, writing some thirty years later, are addressing. On the other hand, Becker does not consider the ways in which the church community is complicit in the negative values, institutions, and practices of the larger culture; this is an issue that H. Richard Niebuhr addressed in his classic text *Christ and Culture* (1951), which explores the various ways in which individuals and communities negotiate the relationship between being followers of Christ and participants in the surrounding culture.

While they are critical of Milton Erickson's emphasis on the design of "clever strategies" to induce clients to change (for Erickson, these had grown out of his use of hypnosis), Freedman and Combs note that it was through him that they first encountered the belief that people can continually and actively re-author their lives: "While the story of our relationship with the systems metaphor is one of change leading to an eventual parting of the ways, the story of our relationship with the re-authoring metaphor is one of constancy" (p. 11). They argue that

"If the realities we inhabit are brought forth in the language we use, they are then kept alive and passed along in the stories that we live and tell" (pp. 29–30).

They view therapy, then, as an occasion for "opening space for new stories" (p. 42). The problem, however, is that "it is hard for most therapists to learn to listen to people's stories as stories." This is because they are predisposed to "listen with our ears cocked and our mouths set to say 'Aha!' when we recognize a 'clinically significant item'– something that we know what to do with" (p. 43). Genuine listening means that, when we meet people for the first time, we want to understand the meaning of their stories for *them,* and this means turning our backs on expert filters: "Not listening for chief complaints; not 'gathering' the pertinent-to-us-as-experts bits of diagnostic information interspersed in their stories; not hearing their anecdotes as matrices within which resources are embedded; not listening for surface hints about what the core 'problem' really is; and not comparing the selves they portray in their stories to normative standards" (p. 44). Instead, "We try to put ourselves in the shoes of the people we work with and understand, from their perspective, in their language, what has led them to seek our assistance. Only then can we recognize alternative stories" (p. 44). The authors advocate an attitude of "not-knowing" on the grounds that therapy is a process in which we are always moving toward what is not yet known (p. 44).

Listening to another's story is not, however, a passive activity, for when we listen to it, "we *interpret,* whether we want to or not" (p. 45). This is not a contradiction of the point that one listens in order to understand the meaning of others' stories *for themselves,* for interpretation is impossible to avoid. What *is* rejected is the idea that we, as therapists, are the experts, and that "we know more about the person's lived experience than the person does" (p. 45). In order to avoid interpreting what is heard according to one's own "expert" interests (if pathology, to hear the pathological aspects of the story; if pain, to hear its painful aspects; if disempowerment, to hear the deprivation of power), the authors recommend "deconstructive listening," which opens spaces "for aspects of people's life narratives that haven't yet been shared" (p. 46).

What this means in practice is that the listening is guided by the belief that the stories clients tell have many possible meanings and that the meaning the listener notes is, more often than not, different from the meaning that the speaker has intended. (In other words, we "misinterpret.") In "deconstructive listening," one actually capitalizes on this very difference "by looking for gaps in our understanding and asking people to fill in details, or by listening for ambiguities in meaning and then asking people how they are resolving or dealing with these ambiguities" (p. 47). Thus, as a client tells his story, the therapist interrupts at intervals to summarize her sense of what he is saying, and this allows him to tell her if the meaning she is deriving from the story fits with the intended meaning. Significantly, even though the goal is to understand the other person's reality, this reality begins to change in the process of telling and being listened to: "In considering our questions and comments, people can't help but examine their stories in new ways. Our very presence makes their world a new and different reality" (p. 47).

Like White and Epston, Freedman and Combs are interested in dislodging the "dominant stories" in the other person's narrative, and they share White and Epston's view that a valuable resource in this regard are the "sparkling events" that contradict problem-saturated narratives. They "invite people to take such events and transform them into stories that they can live–and in the living know themselves in preferred, satisfying ways" (p. 77). The goal is to enable these events to move from isolated, idiosyncratic happenings to the formation of stories around them and eventually to performance in the real world, thus becoming real in a person's everyday life. The idea that "transformative stories are performed stories" was suggested to them by Milton Erickson's story about being on a road trip with a friend. As he was driving, Erickson told his friend about another trip he had taken years earlier on the same road. As he was relating the story, he began trying to shift the gears manually. Since the car he was now driving had an automatic transmission, and he had been driving an automatic for years, it was evident that he was unconsciously "performing" the story that he was relating to his friend (pp. 87–88).

The authors tell about Jessica, a counselee who recalled an event from childhood in which she sat on her grandmother's lap and sang her a song. She immersed herself in this memory and saw herself through her grandmother's eyes. Then she developed the story through time, authoring and experiencing a speculative history of what her life would have been like if she had lived with her grandmother (p. 88). After this conversation, she began to do a whole range of things that were unusual for her, from saying thank you to quitting smoking. According to her own testimony, she had gained an understanding of the kind of person she was, and "began *living* a new story, not simply telling it" (p. 88, my emphasis).

Freedman and Combs make a very persuasive case for a paradigm shift from systems to stories, using the evolution of their own thinking to explain why they abandoned the systems approach. In the original formulation of his theory of paradigm shifts, however, Thomas Kuhn contended that such shifts do not occur in an orderly evolutionary process, that they are in fact revolutionary, as the reigning paradigm in a scientific discipline is overthrown or rendered obsolete by the new, insurgent one. This typically occurs as the result of an "anomaly," a discovery or finding of which the original model is unable to take adequate account (Kuhn, 1970, pp. 52–65). Following a period in which this finding is tested and retested to verify whether it is a "true" finding or the result of a flawed experimental design, the resulting crisis creates the demand for a new paradigm, typically one that does not merely attempt to account for the anomaly itself but one that also directs the discipline in an entirely new direction, toward entirely new research problems.

An example would be the discovery of "imageless thoughts" by European and American psychologists in the first decade of the twentieth century. Attempts to dismiss this finding, which was inconsistent with the reigning paradigm (based on the study of human consciousness), were successful for a time, but this could not last. Finally, in 1913, John B. Watson proposed that consciousness is not a usable hypothesis—being too subjective—and argued that the proper focus of psychology should be behavior, which was clearly observable and measurable (Watson, 1970). While the old paradigm was still useful for investigating many issues and problems, it was swept aside, deemed obsolete by the proponents of behaviorism (see Bakan, 1967, pp. 94–97).

As we have seen, many family therapists have been able to assimilate feminist views into the systems model, expanding it rather than abandoning it. Thus, feminism per se does not appear to be the anomaly, or source of the anomaly, that has led family therapists such as Freedman and Combs to call for—even announce—the paradigm shift from system to story. In my view, however, there *is* such an anomaly. In fact, it is revealed in the subtitle of their first book, *Symbol, Story, and Ceremony: Using Metaphor in Individual and Family Therapy.* To the early pioneers in family therapy, the whole idea was that the family, or significant components thereof, should be seen together. By injecting himself into the family process—as "honorary relative"—the therapist's very presence would affect and alter this process. It was believed that very little could be accomplished by seeing one member of the family or of the marital couple alone, and the claims made for the greater effectiveness of family therapy over individual therapy were based on this very claim.

The anomaly, then, is that family therapists began to see individuals. At a national conference of family therapists that I attended in 1989, the convenor, when introducing the conference theme, referred to the "dirty little secret" that the caseloads of family therapists now comprised at least as many individuals as families. In light of this fact, Steve de Shazer, a well-known family therapist, suggested that the therapy situation itself be viewed as a system (1991, p. 24). The system, he argued, is constructed purposefully from the following elements: the therapist subsystem, the client subsystem, the problem/solution subsystem, and the interactions and interrelationships between and among the first three (p. 24).

In this way, the concept of system could be retained, but it need no longer apply exclusively or even primarily to the family system. He also proposed that, in light of the claim that the therapeutic situation itself is a system, one could view the system as comprising three elements: the therapist, the client, and the members of his team who were observing the therapeutic process through a one-way mirror (and whom the therapist would consult in order to construct together a strategic intervention). This redefinition of the system, however useful it has proven to be, is typical, in Kuhn's view, of efforts in scientific disciplines to adapt the original paradigm to the new realities (in this case, the fact that family therapists were seeing individuals and not confining their work to families). Oftentimes, it is a stopgap measure that buys time until a new paradigm has emerged.

Significantly, as Freedman and Combs indicate, the story paradigm has continuities with one of the early pioneers in family therapy, Milton E. Erickson, who, as the Lanktons point out, never used systems language to describe his therapeutic practices. As Kuhn also shows, this is one way in which paradigm shifts occur, namely, that current practitioners "realize" that there is something in the tradition of their field that falls outside the paradigm itself, but now becomes visible when the paradigm itself is under siege. This "something" may then provide the basis and legitimation for the new paradigm. Because it has the prestige of having been resident in the tradition—though unnoticed and unrealized—it may make a more persuasive claim on current practitioners than a paradigm based on something entirely new.

In this case, there is a direct analogy between Freedman and Combs's "retrieval" of this earlier emphasis on story and the view that they and White and Epston put forth that the person in therapy needs to gain leverage on the dominant story of her life in order to claim other aspects of her lived experience. In effect, this turn to stories was a shift from "process" to "content." The systems model had given little methodological attention to the fact that the family members were all telling stories, i.e., their versions of what was wrong—and right—about the family to which they belonged.

Challenging the Fatalism in Systems Thinking

The fact that family therapists were seeing individual clients was a powerful stimulus toward the story model. But does this mean that the systems model should be abandoned? I believe that the answer is no, but that its locus in the new paradigm is significantly altered. A key text in this regard is Michael P. Nichols' *The Self in the System: Expanding the Limits of Family Therapy* (1987). As its title indicates, an especially important factor in the reconstrual of the systems model that I will be proposing later in this chapter is Bowen's theme of self-differentiation. Although Nichols studied with Bowen, he does not explicitly mention this theme. This is probably because he derives his own theory of the self from psychodynamic (mostly psychoanalytic) resources.

In his "Epilogue," Nichols claims that family therapy has now come of age: "Like an adolescent who once turned her back on her parents, family therapy has now grown strong enough and self-confident enough to reconcile with the once rejected ideas of individual psychotherapy" (p. 289). In addition, family therapists today see family life in a broader perspective than its pioneers did: "Not having discovered the system and built family therapy on it as a foundation, we can never value it as much as they did. And so, we are free to bring back the psychological life of individuals and to take a more inclusive view than the pioneers did" (p. 289).

Nichols recalls his earliest experiences in seeing families in therapy. He found that "systems concepts and techniques were as clarifying as turning on a light in a dark room...Things get very clear very fast when you learn to see triangles and enmeshment and disengagement where formerly you saw only chaos and confusion" (p. 289). In time, however, he felt something was missing. This was the fact that, with many families, systems concepts and methods were sufficient for good therapeutic results, but with others he began to suffer boredom, a sure sign that something was indeed missing. To counteract the boredom, he began to pay more attention to individuals—it was, he says, "as simple as that"–and gave himself permission to use with families some of the psychological insights that he had been reserving for his psychotherapy with individuals. "This dual emphasis on system and psyche brought new excitement and effectiveness to my work" (p. 290). As his title indicates, he began "to include more attention to the self in the system" (p. 290). In order to explore what this means for the minister as interpreter of stories, we need to consider Nichols' presentation of the "basic postulates of systems theory." This will set the stage for a consideration of the "basic postulates of the story model" that I want to present. First, then, here are the basic postulates of the systems model.

Basic Postulates of Systems Theory

Nichols believes that three basic postulates of systems theory can be identified and that these have become articles of faith to most family therapists. Each postulate identifies something that is generally true of families, but each one also directs our attention to the *interactions* of family members and diverts our attention away from the stories of each individual member of the family. These postulates are (1) the family is the context of human problems and, as in other groups, families have emergent properties that make them different from individual persons; (2) process, not content, reveals what is most significant about family interactions; and (3) dyadic and triadic models of behavior are better than monadic ones.

Of the first of these core beliefs, Nichols agrees that families have properties that make them different from individual persons; unfortunately, this belief has led family therapists to give insufficient attention to the properties that individuals *do* have. He contends that individuals have internal realities, and that family therapy has tended to emphasize only the external ones (i.e., where the individual interfaces with the family). An individual's internal realities are an important factor because they often determine whether or not an individual family member accepts the role that the family assigns to her: "A woman whose husband and children pressure her into the role of selfless caregiver can either comply or refuse" (p. 34). Thus, "to act responsibly as selves and to encourage responsible action in our clients we must distinguish between that which individual persons *do* and that which merely *happens*, irrespective of their own agency" (p. 26). It is certainly "true that family influences are often obscure, but so also are our own intentions and our own actions obscure." Thus, the range and freedom of human action can best be expanded "by taking into account the two-sided reality of social influence and individual initiative. Moreover, these two realities (more properly, two ways of looking at reality) are never independent. Personal behavior and private states of mind have social antecedents and context, but the person is as much an organizer as an effect of those around him or her" (p. 26).

Because individual family members have their own selfhood, they have their own personal stories, many of which intersect with the stories of the other family members but many of which also have their own reality independent of the family. The wife and mother who volunteers her services to a local Head Start program, or the husband and father who enjoys restoring old cars, or the teenage daughter who belongs to a high school chemistry club–these interests have their effects on family dynamics, if only because they influence other family members' daily schedules or routines, but we can certainly imagine these interests being expressed and acted on even if the woman were not a "wife and mother," the man were not a "husband and father," and the girl were not a "daughter." We are family members, but we are much more than this.

Regarding the second core belief, Nichols agrees that process, the way the family members interact, tells us more about how they function as a family than does what they actually talk about. He also agrees that attending to the process of family conversations has a clarifying effect. Instead of getting lost in the details, we step back and see how the family interacts. But this emphasis on process over content carries the implication that "there is a superordinate group mechanism that is more significant and more powerful than the individual members of the group" (p. 27). When we take seriously the content of what individuals say–the opinions they express, the values they affirm, the feelings they confess to having– we then recognize each one's unique individuality.

Exclusive focus on process also denies the validity of the competing interests in the family and the real basis for conflict: "Family quarrels do not necessarily clear up when the combatants are taught how to communicate." While it is true that the way a mother and daughter argue may complicate their differences, "teaching them to fight fair will not automatically resolve the differences" (p. 27). Mother and daughter may not share the same beliefs, hold the same opinions, or value the same things. Thus, while they need to find ways to communicate so that they do not always end up arguing with each other, the views they express are important in their own right, and the therapist should not treat their account of a clash in viewpoints as merely illustrative of how mother and daughter always end up arguing.

For Nichols, an exclusive or exaggerated focus on process to the neglect of content is actually reductionistic as the personal experiences of each family member are treated as though they are not very important: "When we shift from content to process, we see the horizontal flow of family life, but if we ignore the vertical dimension of personal experience, what appears to be clarity is, in fact, reductionistic" (p. 28). In a moment, I will discuss one of Nichols' own cases in support of his claim that ignoring the vertical dimension of personal experience is reductionistic. Meantime, I would note that the complaint by one family member that the therapist is siding with another ("You always take her side") may not be due to resistance or recalcitrance, but to the fact that the therapist is much more attentive to the process than to the content of what is being said. This very attentiveness to the one and not to the other may be experienced as bias against one of the family members (i.e., the one who is more likely to believe that content *is* more important than process).

About the third core belief that dyadic and triadic models of behavior are better than monadic ones, Nichols agrees: "Family therapists discovered that the actions of one person can often be understood more fully in terms of interactions between that person and others. A child's fearfulness may not spring from anything inside the child as much as it does from the child's relationship with an anxious or punitive mother." This dyad may in turn be a part of a larger triad: "The child's behavior reflects the relationship between mother and child, which is related to the relationship between husband and wife. Most people think of relationships in two-person terms: husband and wife, father and son, I-thou. But, as Murray Bowen pointed out, when we have problems in a relationship, we tend, automatically, to triangle in a third person" (p. 28). Clearly, "such triadic thinking has practical as well as theoretical advantages. The quickest way to free the child from fear may be to free (or at least release) the child from the husband-wife tension" (p. 28).

Nichols does not dispute this basic insight about dyadic and triadic models being superior to monadic ones. But he argues that "regardless of the conflicting effects of social relationships, at times a person acts in part from personal habit and for private reasons" (p. 29). Of course, we are inherently social beings embedded in a matrix of relationships: "But we are also persons in charge of our own lives. Shifting to a triadic view often brings to light important and unsuspected factors in human problems. However, clearing up triangular complications may or may not solve the problem. Sometimes it only clears the social field so that a person may be better able to get on with his or her personal struggle with life and its problems" (p. 29). This struggle may have little to do with a dyadic or triadic relationship in the family. The child's fears, for example, may be related to peer relationships at school—other children are bullying her—or to doubts about her ability to keep up with her classmates academically. Or she may have come to the awareness, perhaps on the occasion of a beloved pet's death, that she herself will not live forever. Family conflicts may exacerbate these fears, and family solidarity may neutralize them somewhat, but these are fears that do not have their origins—or solutions—in the dyadic or triadic family relationship itself.

Nichols concludes that the three basic postulates of systems theory are all assumptions imposed on the data. In all these propositions is a nucleus of truth, "but they have been over-elaborated, leading family therapists away from clinical observation and into a realm of unexamined myths" (p. 29). Valuable as they are, these concepts lead the therapist to focus on the group at the expense of the individual, on process at the expense of the content, and on relationship conflicts over personal and private—intrapsychic—struggles. When the family's systemic features are overemphasized, the individuality of each family member is taken less seriously than it ought to be. This can lead to therapeutic failure in cases where the individuality of a particular family member makes it difficult for that individual to cooperate with the therapeutic plan. When process is overemphasized, the content of the family members' statements may be neglected or ignored, as though what they think or believe or value is irrelevant or unimportant. When the role that family relationships play in supporting a dysfunction is overemphasized, the fact that many of our difficulties in life are private or intrapsychic is overlooked. A by-product of this view that the cause of the problem is relational is that spouses are often unfairly accused of contributing to the illness, as when a wife is automatically judged to be a "co-dependent" of her alcoholic husband, or as contributing to her husband's suicidal behavior. Her attitudes and behavior may be a contributing factor, but the root causes of such illnesses are often physical disorders or are traceable to earlier experiences that are largely or entirely independent of family relationships, even his own family of origin. His alcoholism or suicidal tendencies may be due, for example, to his earlier involvement in military combat, where he saw and participated in unspeakable horrors, or to doubts about his ability to perform in his current professional work at the level that is expected of him.

Escape to Profundity

Nichols is also critical of the family therapy guild's effort to *systematize* its own insights and discoveries. It is as though the insight that families may be viewed as systems has led family therapists to place an excessively high value on systematic thinking itself. In Nichols' view, at least two motivating forces propel us from concrete observation to abstract theorizing. One is pragmatic, the desire to make sense of complex data with a systematic statement of principles that organize and clarify. The other is the sheer pleasure of contemplation, the delight we experience in exercising our reasoning faculties and the pride we take in our intellectual accomplishments. But theorizing also serves a defensive function: "Thinking about family therapy is often easier than doing family therapy. The urge to philosophize is impelled by a quest for predictable constancy. Abstractions are orderly and stable, less threatening than troublesome experience. When the going gets tough, we escape to profundity" (Nichols, 1987, p. 31).

Nichols believes that this escape to profundity is related, though inversely, to therapists' genuine desire to help others: "Those of us who choose therapy as a profession are drawn to the helping role that being needed conveys, but we sometimes shrink from the anxiety of connection. Neediness, from a distance, draws us to give succor; up close, we may find that neediness overwhelming. Seeking distance from full immersion in the painful experience of our clients, we use systems thinking as a tool that clarifies but also establishes a barrier against painful emotional contact with the personal present" (p. 31). Thus, to defend ourselves from the chaotic experience of our client families, we gravitate toward "experience-distant concepts," and, increasingly, we "accept traditional views that have become crystallized and resistant to change," and we pass them on "in undigested complexity to give us a sense of convergent validation in the shared views of our teachers and colleagues" (p. 31).

Nichols implies that "systems thinkers" are especially susceptible to this escape to profundity because they are the most likely to allow form to masquerade as substance. Even the word *systemic,* which originally had quite precise meanings, has become something of an abstraction:

> When family therapists want to show the flag, they say "systemic." We are systemic thinkers, practicing systemic therapy; we ask systemic questions, and expect systemic answers. "Systemic," like "psychodynamic," is a fine word which, because

it is positively valued, has been appropriated by a major portion of the mental health profession. (If one isn't psychodynamic, one is likely to be systemic; some enterprising souls are both.) *Psychodynamic* is a perfectly valid term, meaning psychoanalytic, though not necessarily Freudian; it has been corrupted to mean, roughly, a psychology that recognizes that all motives are not transparent. Likewise, *systemic* is often used to mean merely, having to do with families. (pp. 31–32)

Nichols complains that much writing by family systems theorists today has become jargon. Especially is this true of those who link "systemic" with "epistemology." Among the terms currently being used to describe a family systems perspective are "cybernetic epistemology," "circular epistemology," "ecological epistemology," and "ecosystemic epistemology." Nichols comments: "These puffed-up phrases have a nice ring to them; they suggest weighty thoughts, but they cloud over their subject, surrounding it with a haze of scholarliness while actually saying very little" (pp. 32–33). This tendency to leave behind "the simple and direct" and to take on "airs of profundity, mystery, and powerful impersonal forces is part of a lingering defensiveness about the value of our work" (p. 33). As "the new epistemology" grows ever more abstruse, clinicians lose sight of the experience-based concepts that can serve as blueprints and assist the therapist in formulating therapeutic strategies for a given family.

The Inflated Power of the System

In Nichols' view, there is a direct relationship between the contemporary trend toward abstract theories and the perception that "the family system" is so powerful that a barrage of manipulative techniques is required to defeat this "mechanical beast." Abstract theories seem to go hand in hand with the very idea that the therapist is confronting–and is confronted by–a system that is so powerful that equally "powerful" words are needed to understand and change it. The abstract theory thus becomes a kind of magic, an incantation designed to break the system's power. To Nichols, the truth is that the system is certainly influential, but it is not determinative. Emphasis on the system's enormous power to determine the lives of those who participate in it leads, ironically, to a sense of fatalism that can get in the way of therapy itself. Avoiding blame and faultfinding by emphasizing the systemic nature of family problems is all to the good, but it can also produce a fatalistic view of the family members' capacity to initiate change. They are not held responsible for the family's problems, but neither are they considered capable of making dramatic changes. As Nichols puts it, "avoiding the possibility of self-determination is [also] an invidious myth" (p. 34).

For Nichols, the problem here is that "systems" language easily translates into technological, even mechanical language, so that the interaction of family members comes to be regarded as the mechanical interplay of causal forces: "An act is seen as the causal outcome of a mechanistic interaction of elemental 'systemic forces'" (p. 35). He counters this view of the system as a powerful mechanical beast by reminding us that we, as individuals, "are not just links in a circular chain of events; we are people with names who experience ourselves as centers of initiative. Our most basic impulse is to protect our integrity. What's more, we are hopelessly absorbed with ourselves" (p. 35). Of course, each of us is linked to others: "Much of what we do is with other people in mind, some of what we do is with others, and once in a while for others. But the 'we' who are the authors of the doing are single organisms, with hearts and minds and bodies all encased within our skin. So fundamental is this truth of human experience that we periodically have to be reminded of our intimate connection with others" (p. 35).

As individuals, we can frustrate or undermine the power of the system in various ways, the most obvious of which is that we choose not to give up our own powers of agency and initiative "for the sake of the family." Individuals can refuse to make the sacrifice that the family system seems to require—or demand—by deciding that they will no longer play according to the rules of the system, that they will instead make up their own rules and dare the system to stop them. When they do, they are often surprised at how powerless the system is to constrain or inhibit them. Perhaps one reason that counseling of individuals remains popular (and, as noted, is increasingly being done by family therapists) is that it often empowers individuals to withdraw projections of power onto the system and own these powers themselves. If their counseling of families causes them to inflate the power of the system, family therapists' counseling of individuals may restore the balance, leading them to conclude that the system is not all-powerful, that an individual, with appropriate encouragement and coaching, can neutralize the power of the system.

Nichols concludes that family therapists have taught that our behavior is controlled "in unseen but profound ways by the actions of those around us. Family rules and roles operate as invisible constraints influencing all that we do" (p. 35). He agrees that the very idea that we behave as we do because we are induced to live out defined roles *can* have a liberating effect. If one is playing an assigned role, it is possible to play a new one, or at least play the old role very differently. But systems theory as such can have a debilitating effect as it tends to minimize our inherent powers of self-determination. In the extreme, systems thinking "dismisses selfhood as an illusion. The problem is when roles become reified and rigidified as prescribed determinants of behavior *and* as independent of personal agency on the one hand or wider family relations on the other. Systems thinkers have unfortunately implied that the role plays the person rather than the other way around. Whether they act in concert or separately, it is finally the selves in the system who must act to bring about change" (pp. 35–36). He concludes: "In the process of over-elaborating the metaphor of the system, family therapy has neglected the psychology of persons" (p. 36).

Story and the Possibilities for Change

The core concepts of family therapy are that families have emergent properties that make them different from individual persons; that process, not content, reveals what is most significant about family interactions; and that dyadic and triadic models of behavior are better than monadic ones. However valid these concepts may be in principle, Nichols shows that they are clearly prejudiced against what he calls "the possibility of self-determination."

To explore the implications of his critique of systems theory for a story model designed for ministers to employ in the counselor role, I want to focus especially on the second core concept, that process reveals what is most significant about family interactions more than content does. This concept is especially germane to the view held by Freedman and Combs that a paradigm shift from system to story is currently underway in family therapy. To devalue the stories clients tell as mere "content" is to make a serious strategic mistake, for these stories prefigure the changes that are possible in the life of the one who is telling them. Exclusive focus on process can be self-defeating because, as we have seen, this can easily confirm that the system is a powerful "beast" that no one can control. In contrast, focus on the story that the client tells is inherently more hopeful because stories, by their very nature, envision positive change. We tell stories because we believe that the telling of the story will make a difference. Even when our intention is to reinforce current practice or to lend support to the status quo (as is commonly the case with stories that explain a traditional belief or practice), our intention is to persuade the listener to reconfigure her life in relation to this story, to make the tradition her own. Thus, in the therapeutic context, our task is to listen for the possibilities that are inherent in the story as told and to allow them to guide our interpretations.

Placing primary emphasis on the story, however, does not mean that we must reject the insight of the systems model that families have their own properties and, therefore, are not merely the sum of their individual parts. Nor does it mean that we must reject the insight that the actions of individuals may often be understood more fully by viewing them in terms of interactions between these individuals and others. What it challenges is the tendency of systems theory to inflate the power of the system and thereby deflate the individual's own powers of self-determination. This challenge has its basis in the fact that we, as individuals, are not the mechanical parts of some mechanical beast, but are selves in a story involving other selves, all of whom, as Nichols puts it, are "persons with names who experience themselves as centers of initiative, and whose basic impulse is to protect their own integrity " (p. 27). A therapeutic model based on story assumes that behind every story told is an author who has the power to change the story as it unfolds. This power is based on the simple but vital fact that it is the author's own story. We believe in our power to "authorize" our own life *if* we do *not* believe that the story is already predetermined, that is, that the system itself is determinative and all-controlling (like that of the young Iatmul boy who assumed he was predestined to live his life precisely as his ancestors lived theirs).

Thus, a story model for ministers providing counsel will take the view that we are the authors of our own stories. Therefore, we have considerable power, perhaps more than we realize, to change the story as we go along. Certainly, there are strong forces at work that inhibit these changes. On this point, the story model agrees with the systems model. The crucial difference, however, is the story model's emphasis on the possibilities for self-determination that each individual possesses.

In the stage play and subsequent film version of *The Madness of King George,* there is an oddly poignant scene on a sunny meadow where King George, who has been under psychiatric care for several months, improvises a performance of a scene from Shakespeare's *King Lear*. He plays the role of Lear and assigns his Lord Chancellor the role of Lear's truly faithful daughter, Cordelia. In the middle of the actual scene in *King Lear*, Cordelia kisses her father on the cheek. So, of course, King George instructs his reluctant Lord Chancellor to do the same, much to the latter's initial embarrassment. Later, however, the Lord Chancellor is heard amid the tumult in the House of Commons telling the Prime Minister that, with seemingly small changes in the story—which he details to the obviously impatient Prime Minister—Lear's life would not have ended in tragedy. Therefore, he reasons, the two of them should throw their support behind King George's plan to resume his rule of England in spite of his recent bout with madness.

The final scene of *The Madness of King George* displays King George on the steps of Westminster Abbey admonishing his family to smile and wave to their admiring subjects, thereby serving as a model of the healthy English family, which they decidedly are not. The film's point of view is obviously comedic—King George will never be confused with the tragic King Lear—but the Lord Chancellor nonetheless makes an important therapeutic point: A small change here, a minor alteration there, and the story comes out very differently. He further emphasizes the insight: Are we not each of us free to make these changes, for are we not the authors of the stories we tell? Why, then, should we assume that King George is doomed to live out the remainder of his days in a state of madness? Why not assume that, even with a man as out-of-his-senses as King George, a miracle might occur, and he will again prove himself up to the challenge of being the King of England?

Nichols emphasizes, however, that even though we are the authors of the stories we tell, we are more than authors. We are selves who "experience ourselves as centers of initiative, and whose most basic impulse is to protect our integrity." This means that we are not only *in* the stories we tell, but that we are also the central figure (the main protagonist), the one whom the story is principally about. Because all members of the family tell the story from their own perspectives, family therapists try to hear the family's story from as many members as possible. But alongside these accounts of the family's story are the personal or private stories of each individual, and these are characteristically set aside in the systemic approach to family therapy.

Nichols introduces his criticisms of the systems approach by relating how he discovered in a particular case that knowing something of the personal story of one of the family members would have made a critical difference in the outcome of the therapy. Mrs. Templeton had called to make an appointment for her teenage son, Raymond, who had confided in the school guidance counselor that he wanted to die. When Nichols' secretary asked the whole family to come for the intake interview, Mrs. Templeton was neither surprised nor displeased, for, as she put it, they were a "close-knit family." Present for the first interview were Raymond, shy and awkward; Mrs. Templeton, frightened and eager for help; Mr. Templeton, worried about his son but uneasy about participation; and Nichols, who describes himself as "newly armed with the precepts of structural family therapy" (1987, p. 1). Nichols indicates that the pattern that unfolded was one familiar to all family therapists, one that he had been trained to anticipate and modify. Mother and son were enmeshed (overinvolved, preoccupied with each other), and father was distant. Held a little too close a little too long by his mother, Raymond had been slow to make friends. In school he was always closer to the teachers, and now in his junior year he was beginning to fear that he was doomed to loneliness. His shyness had turned him inward, and the other kids considered him a "momma's boy" and "teacher's pet" (p. 1). When his hopes of a new friendship with a girl were dashed, he felt he could not bear it any longer: "He thought she liked him, but she laughed when he asked her out. From that moment, every trace of hope and confidence in his life was destroyed. Her laughter had crushed his heart" (p. 1).

Nichols' strategy was the customary one of improving the father-son relationship as a wedge to separate the enmeshed mother-son dyad, and then subsequently to bring the husband and wife closer together. Things went well at first: "They were all cooperative and my interventions met with little resistance. They understood and accepted the direction of my endeavors and the crisis passed. I was relieved and pleased" (p. 2). But there was no further progress. Nichols soon began to see that his efforts to reconstruct the family weren't really working. Mrs. Templeton made a real attempt to restrain her involvement with Raymond and to spend more time with her husband. But what could she do when Raymond came home from school moody and needed someone to talk to? For his part, Raymond was happy to spend more time with his dad, especially doing what he considered masculine things, such as making furniture and going bowling. Mr. Templeton tried too. He liked spending time with Raymond, but he was often so tired at the end of the day that he didn't feel like doing anything, and he wasn't much of a talker. Nichols was concerned: "Why couldn't Mr. Templeton be more involved with his son? What were his private thoughts? The truth is, I didn't have the faintest idea" (p. 2).

Only later, several months after he had terminated treatment of the family, when Mr. Templeton came to see him by himself, did Nichols begin to understand "what was going on inside Mr. Templeton's head. Neither my deliberate attention to family structure nor my own reflexive ability to identify with familiar experience prepared me to understand his position" (p. 3). By listening to Mr. Templeton's own story, apart from the family story, Nichols came to a much deeper understanding of Mr. Templeton's difficulty with intimacy. He concluded that as long as his efforts with the Templetons were confined to the structure of their interactions, he overlooked the motivation for their interactional problems. What he did not see and, therefore, did not affect was their individual subjective realities: "Over-emphasizing the family structure paints a passive picture of the self as caught up in a system that it is blind and powerless to resist. In some ways, people are remarkably elastic; in certain key respects, however, we remain consistently who we are despite changes in context. The self is a personality consisting of a pattern of traits that is deeply etched and difficult to modify" (p. 4). These ingrained and habitual ways of functioning emerge from an individual's entire developmental history: "Whether or not a family will master or succumb to problems depends in part on the flexibility of its organization. But this flexibility is also a product of individual personalities, like Mr. Templeton's—a tightly-knit organization of attitudes, habits, and emotions that affect his capacity to cope with life's difficulties" (p. 4).

Thus, it was only when Nichols—quite by chance—heard Mr. Templeton's own personal story, much of it having to do with experiences that predated the family story, that he could understand why Mr. Templeton was unable to participate more effectively in the treatment plan. Mr. Templeton was a person with a name, who experienced himself as a center of initiative, and who therefore was more than a cog in the system. He had powers of self-determination that he could—or could not—exercise in behalf of the therapeutic objectives that the therapist envisioned. Moreover, he had self-limitations that inhibited his full cooperation with these objectives in spite of his willingness, even his determination, to cooperate.

Significantly, Mr. Templeton returned to Nichols for individual counseling, and Nichols did not refuse to see him on this basis. For Nichols, these one-on-one conversations afforded a much deeper understanding of Mr. Templeton than he had gained in the previous sessions with the whole family present. This does not mean that therapy with families is inherently inferior to therapy with individuals. Yet, in discussing his work with the Templeton family, Nichols' concern with his effectiveness as a therapist stands out. In his account of his conversations with Mr. Templeton alone, he comments on the fact that he learned much about Mr. Templeton that he had not previously known. Perhaps what made him almost oblivious to therapeutic results in the latter case is that it focused on Mr. Templeton's personal story. Mr. Templeton talked about himself, and Nichols listened, and both evidently found it meaningful, engaging, and well worth doing again, whatever the "results" might prove to be. We assume that Mr. Templeton got new insights into himself in the course of telling his story and having it listened to by Nichols, and we know from his own account that Nichols gained a great deal from these meetings, as they became an important part of Nichols' own story about how this case influenced him to reconsider his earlier assumptions as a family therapist. Also, Nichols did not seem to feel that his readers would need to know the outcome of Mr. Templeton's therapy in order for the story to be engaging. It was enough for him to claim that "understanding" occurred between the two men, an "understanding" that did not take place in the previous sessions, when Mr. Templeton was viewed solely as a member of the Templeton family.

Why did Mr. Templeton return after the family therapy was terminated? Was it because he wanted to justify himself, to explain (or even rationalize) his inability to cooperate more fully in the therapy? Was it because he felt frustrated that the family therapy centered so much on his son's problems that his own were never dealt with? Was it because he experienced Dr. Nichols as someone who genuinely cared about him as a person in his own right and intuited that Nichols had more to give him in that regard than the family therapy process allowed? Whatever the reasons for his return, this unexpected event drew Nichols' attention to the importance of the personal story that each of us has to tell if only we can find someone who is willing and able to listen.

If I have a quarrel with Nichols' account of his conversation with Mr. Templeton, it concerns his statement that the self "is a personality consisting of a pattern of traits that is deeply etched and difficult to modify," and his use of this understanding of the self's intransigence to explain why the family therapy had not gone as well as it might have. While he also says that "in some ways, people are remarkably elastic," he risks replacing one deterministic structure—the family system—with another—the self system. This is why I would emphasize, along with Freedman and Combs, the possibilities for change that are evident in the personal stories that we tell. Through these stories, we come to know the deeper self of another not in its intransigence, but in its elasticity, in its ability to grow, expand, adapt, and develop in ways that the storyteller could not have imagined prior to the telling.

Basic Postulates of the Story Model

This discussion of Nichols' *The Self in the System* leads to my own proposal of the "basic postulates" of the story model, several of which are implied in the preceding discussion. I have already emphasized the content versus process issue as key to the difference between the two models. Thus, the first postulate of the story model is that *the content of the counselee's story is of critical importance, as the possibilities for change are inherent in the story itself.* This does not mean that the story model takes no interest in process, for, as Nichols rightly points out, "Attending to the process of family conversations has a clarifying effect. Instead of getting lost in the details, we step back and see how they [the family members] work" (p. 27). Such stepping back is also important for the story model. The story model, however, seeks to avoid taking on the "additional baggage" of the process idea, "that there is a superordinate group mechanism that is more significant and more powerful than the individual members of the group" (p. 27). By refusing to take on this additional baggage—this over-belief about the nature of the system—the story approach can instead emphasize the power of the individual members of the group, these individual centers of initiative, to change their lives for the better.

It would be absurd to say that the family is not a real entity, that it does not exist. Clearly, it is not mere fiction, a figment of the imaginations of the individuals who belong to it. But, in another sense, whatever *power* the family—as entity—possesses is the power that its individual members ascribe to it. *They* are the ones who empower the family system. Its "superordinate" powers are bestowed upon it by its members. Therefore, they are the ones who can also disempower it if they choose to do so. By according the family system such superordinate power, the therapist colludes with the family *in its own empowerment of the family.* This leaves the therapist in a rather poor position to help them disempower it so that they can begin to take greater control of their own lives.

Thus, the story model is not opposed to *process* per se, but it does oppose the tendency of the systems model to assert that there is a superordinate group mechanism that is more significant and more powerful than the individual members of the group. To believe that such a "group mechanism" exists is to become caught up in the very pathology from which the members of the family need to extricate themselves, that is, the belief that they are the helpless victims of the mechanizations– the striking power–of the beast called family.

The correlative danger in the story model is that the story *as told* may be accorded the same superordinate power as the system in the systemic model. The word *power* is often associated with stories. We call "powerful" a story that connects at a deep emotional level, or that tells of the triumph of the human spirit over the tragedies of life. But a story can be powerful in a negative sense if it communicates that the characters in the story have no choice but to live out the roles that the story has assigned to them, that they have no power to influence or change the fate it ascribes to them. The use of the genogram to help counselees understand themselves in light of their family history can be an invaluable diagnostic tool, yet it may also have the unintended effect of ascribing great power to the family history and, in the process, of disempowering the individual, sharply curtailing his belief in his own powers of self-determination. Such tools of intergenerational analysis may offer a temporary solace–"Is it any wonder that you are having problems, given *that* history!"–but, in the long run, they may undermine his powers of self-determination.

Therefore, we need to view a story as *powerful* not because it is determinative or fateful, but because it incorporates within itself the possibilities for change. A story is truly powerful to the extent that it is able to envision and inspire change. Thus, if the person receiving counsel recounts the story of her life and concludes, "So that's why I am the way I am," the minister may appropriately respond, "Well, that may be why you are the way you are now. But I heard several things in the story that tell me that you *can* change and that the story can have different endings than your version implies. We are here to discover what these alternative endings are, and how you might go about choosing among them."

A second postulate of the story model is that *every individual is a self and, therefore, has power over the role that he or she plays in the family story.* As Nichols points out, while we all have external realities (roles that we play), we also have interior realities, and these enable us to "individualize" the roles we play: "A woman whose husband and children pressure her into the role of selfless caregiver can either comply or refuse...Systems thinkers have unfortunately implied that the role plays the person rather than the other way around. Whether they act in concert or separately, it is finally the selves in the system who must act to bring about change" (Nichols, 1987, p. 34).

Thus, as with the first postulate, the distinction between content and process is also important here. From a process point of view, each family member's role is a given. One is either parent or child. One is either first, second, third, or so on in the sibling birth order. These roles are unalterable, their factuality cannot be denied. Yet each individual gives the assigned role its own unique content. The role is like an empty vessel that we may fill with whatever we choose. The wife and mother cannot truthfully deny the fact that she is wife and mother, but she can certainly determine how she will play these roles, what content she will give them, how she will "interpret" them in her own individualized manner. Thus, even if the family has the power to ascribe *this* role rather than *that* role, we as individual members of the family have the power to determine how we will choose to play the role. We can decide whether we will allow the others to tell us how we are to play our roles, or whether we will consult our own interior realities—our innermost selves—to play our roles in a manner that is congruent with our sense of selfhood.

If this postulate seems to open wide the door for selfishness and to invite the charge that our story model seems to reduce families to a group of self-centered individuals who care only for themselves, the obvious response is that the dysfunctional family is one in which the roles play the family. It requires courage to bring our interior sense of selfhood—our own individuality—to the roles that we play in the family.

Family members, however, find it easier to cope with other members whose true self shapes their performances—even if this means that they play their roles with a fair amount of eccentricity—than if they allow themselves to be defined by the roles and play them stereotypically. The woman whose husband and children pressure her into the role of selfless caregiver does *them* no favor in complying with their expectations. For her own sake, but also for theirs, she should refuse to play her role as they have defined it for her if this conflicts with her own interior sense of self. Why she may be inclined to play it as defined for her by others may emerge in a private conversation, similar to the one that Nichols had with Mr. Templeton. Yet even without the additional understanding her personal story affords, we may assume that compliance with a particular way of enacting one's role—whatever that role may be—is the seedbed of masochism, and the masochistic role inevitably produces a false self (Wurmser, 1997).

Thus, a second postulate of the story model is that each member of the family is a self, with an interior reality that is inviolable. Each, therefore, has not only the right but also the power to play the ascribed role in a manner that is congruent with this interior reality. The power in this case comes from the interior reality itself. Thus, against the tendency of many social scientists to define the self solely in terms of its social roles, the story model (taking its cues from psychodynamic traditions) sees the self as existing independently of the roles it plays, and as having its own superordinate power. This power, often deeply submerged, unrecognized, and underemphasized, is what the story model seeks to restore. It seeks to resurrect this inner self, to restore its powers of self-determination, not so that we, as individuals, may live in splendid isolation from one another, indulging in callous self-centeredness, but so that we may come to know and appreciate one another for who we really are: the self behind the roles we play.[1]

A third basic postulate of the story model is that *the value of systems language is for exploring the psychodynamics inherent in the story itself.* As we have seen, systems theorists have of late had a very difficult time deciding just what constitutes the "system" to which their therapeutic efforts are addressed. If they are much less likely than their predecessors to be seeing whole families, locating the system becomes a serious theoretical problem having significant practical implications. As noted, Steve de Shazer solves this problem by viewing the therapeutic situation itself as a system. Also, he writes about the "system" or "systems" that inhere in language itself, thus suggesting that the therapist is especially interested in the session's "language system" (de Shazer, 1991, chaps. 2 and 7).

Recognizing these difficulties in *locating* the system—while also appreciating the validity of the systemic insight that dyadic and triadic models of behavior can be more useful than monadic ones—the story model postulates that the system *is in the story itself.* This means that it

---

[1] I use the word *self* throughout the chapter because it relates directly to Nichols' emphasis on "the self in the system." Other pastoral theologians prefer the term *soul.* In *Minding the Soul: Pastoral Counseling as Remembering* (1996), James B. Ashbrook uses the word soul, but emphasizes that it is not a "thing," a specific entity with definite features and fixed boundaries. Instead, soul refers to our subjective experience—"of active, integrating, unitary, coherent consciousness"—and is therefore the expression of "meaning." Because the making of meaning depends on memory (p. 169), Ashbrook contends that "without a story a person has no soul" (p. 153). If the word self invites the misconception that it implies "one's own welfare, interest, or advantage" (the third dictionary meaning of the word), I would emphasize that I am using it here in the sense of the dictionary's first two meanings: (1) the identity, character, or essential qualities of any person; and (2) one's own person as distinct from all others.

attends to the dyadic and triadic relationships that are portrayed in the story the client tells. All stories, however simple or complex, consist of dyadic and triadic relationships. No one in the story acts in total independence or isolation from the other persons in the story. In most stories, a triad becomes the locus of conflict within the story and gives it its narrative energy. Two men love the same woman, or one woman loves two men. Two divorcing parents battle for custody of their child, or, if they are childless, they fight over who gets the house or the car. The therapist is attentive to these dyadic and triadic relationships in the story.

The third postulate ensures that the important insights of the family systems model regarding familial relationships are not lost. The concepts presented in chapter 3 retain their relevance. At the same time, the *second* postulate ensures that the listener will not ignore the fact that the main character in the story has an interior self and that this self is struggling with the question of what to do about her involvement in the dyadic or triadic relationships in her life. The very fact that we *do* have a self-self relationship that exists alongside our self-other relationships accounts for many of the possibilities for change inherent in the stories we tell, for change results when we exercise our own powers of self-determination vis-à-vis the seemingly deterministic powers of the external relationships that compose the "system" of our lives.

Thus, our story model locates the system, with its dyadic and triadic relationships, within the story itself. By locating it there, we take seriously Nichols' complaint that family therapists have moved from saying that the family is *like* a system to saying that it *is* a system. By so relocating it, we restore the system's metaphoric quality. This location also enables us to pay attention to a much broader range of dyadic and triadic relationships portrayed in the stories that individuals tell about themselves. The relationships they portray will, of course, center on the current family situation, but they may also focus on relationships that transcend their current family relationships, whether these have to do with other social contexts (e.g., professional relationships, personal friendships, and the like), with personages from other historical eras (e.g., public figures or authors who have influenced their own self-understanding), or with transcendent realities (e.g., one's relationship to God).

By locating the system in the story itself, we are free to use various other metaphors for the family derived, for example, from visual art, poetry, and music. To be able to exercise such conceptual freedom is itself a means to resist the deterministic, even fatalistic, connotations of systems talk. A commonly held belief among Americans is that "you can't beat the system." This ordinary use of the word *system* applies quite naturally to those social institutions designed to curtail or even to punish individual expression, such as the penal, military, and taxation systems (e.g., the taxation system does not reward individual creativity: "I just made up a bunch of numbers" does not impress the IRS). But when we use the same term for social groups and institutions that are meant to foster the individuality of their members (e.g., the family, the school, the church), we assert the superordinate power of the institution over our own powers of self-determination.

One way to begin to recover our powers of self-determination is to replace the word *system* with other metaphors that more accurately reflect the reality of the social group in question. The family, school, and church are not all-powerful, for individual members of these groups can exercise considerable freedom in resisting others' views of how they are to play or embody their given roles. If a woman whose husband and children pressure her into the role of selfless caregiver can either comply or refuse, so may the pastor in a church, or a teacher or student in a school. (Recall Pattison's decision to quit pretending to be who he was not.) We have far more power to determine how we will fill the roles we play than we commonly realize. One reason that we do not realize this fact is that we choose metaphors that are inherently self-defeating.

As Combs and Freedman show in *Symbol, Story, and Ceremony* (1990), the identification of metaphor possibilities also applies to the stories that clients tell. They note in their chapter "Learning to Think Metaphorically" that a characteristic Eriksonian approach is to "utilize" problems, and thus turn them into a positive strength. Expanding on this idea, Combs and Freedman suggest that "the better you are at finding metaphorical significance in problems, the better you will be able to utilize them" (p. 99).

Combs and Freedman cite the case of a therapist saying to a client, "What would you like to accomplish today?" to which the client replies, "I'm not sure, but I think I have to do something about my feelings toward my husband. He's really a pain in the neck" (pp. 98–99). "Pain in the neck" is a metaphor, and the dictionary actually uses this metaphor to illustrate a type of pain that is more an annoyance than a source of suffering or distress. It also says, however, that the original meaning of pain was "penalty or punishment." One can readily imagine that the client is experiencing her husband's attitudes or actions as an annoyance (how big a one we don't yet know) and that she has been feeling something like, "This is punishment I neither need nor deserve." It might also be noted that the neck is the part of the body that joins the head to the rest of the body, and is also the narrowest part of an object (such as the neck of a bottle). It is the part of the anatomy that is therefore highly vulnerable, something that the infamous Boston Strangler knew only too well. Thus, we can also imagine that the client is experiencing her husband's attitudes or behaviors as directed toward the more vulnerable aspect of herself, where she is least able to defend herself or simply pass something off as unimportant; and that he is most likely aware of what he is doing.

Are we reading too much into the "pain in the neck" metaphor? Are we engaging in the dangerous activity of presuming to read another person's mind? Perhaps so. But by focusing on her seemingly insignificant metaphor, we are beginning to interpret, "to bring out the meaning of" her lived experience. We are interpreting her lived experience insofar as her husband's attitudes and actions are concerned, seeing them as "an annoyance" that is directed to where she feels "most vulnerable," and we are guessing that he is probably aware that—to use another metaphor—he is "getting her goat." The metaphor—pain in the neck—has become the conduit through which we seek to enter empathically into her experience and to draw out its meaning. If we were to say to her, "He annoys you," and were to follow up with, "He seems to know just where you are most vulnerable," we would be offering an interpretation of her metaphorical language.

If this interpretation was then deemed reasonably accurate, she might begin to provide a more self-disclosive account of her perceived vulnerabilities, and this, rather than her husband's attitudes and behavior, may then become the primary focus of the ensuing conversation. What might these vulnerabilities be? At this point, we do not know. What we *do* know, however, is that one's perceived vulnerabilities—and perceived strengths—are matters of the self, and that a significant part of our ministerial calling is to help another "to be that self which one truly is" (a statement by Søren Kierkegaard in *Sickness Unto Death* quoted by Carl Rogers, 1961, p. 166).

The fourth postulate of the story model proposed here is that *the self exists independently of the story.* Some psychotherapists, especially those who are postmodernist in orientation, argue that the self is a construct, created, as it were, in the narrative process itself. Without story, there *is* no self. I simply do not believe this. As the family exists independently of the stories its members tell about it, so the self exists independently of its story. The relationship between self and story is very strong, but self is not entirely subsumed within the story. The ancient Greek term *exphrasis* (from "speaking forth") illumines my point. This term was originally used for poets' descriptions of objects of art–paintings and sculptures–that could not speak for themselves. As James A. W. Heffernan (1993) points out, the poets wanted to tell the image's story. Thus, a unique relationship between word and image was joined, one where the poet sought to tell the story that the visual image would tell about itself if only it could speak. As Heffernan points out, however, this relationship between word and image is not entirely compatible, for the image "resists" the poet's efforts to make a story out of it, and poets have thus complained that the image seems to refuse to reveal her secrets. The use of gender language–*he* for *poet* and *she* for *image*–is deliberate, for, as Heffernan also notes, the image was considered female. She was either condemned to silence or resistant to the demand that she tell her story, that is, witness against herself. The poet, armed with words, took upon himself the task of telling her story for her, thus seeking to break either imposed or self-imposed silence.

This idea of *exphrasis*–of speaking for the other–is applicable to the self and the story. We may view the self as the *image* that exists independently of the story, but which the story attempts to draw out or elucidate. Thus, the self cannot be known unless a story–or stories–are told about it, but the self is not merely the sum of these stories. It is always something more. Anyone who has attempted to write a personal autobiography knows something about the difficulty of putting the self into words.

The story is what the listener or reader is privileged to hear, and it usually suffices for therapeutic purposes. The story, though, is not the self. Indeed, one of the ways we exercise our own powers of self-determination is that we may choose to tell as much, or as little, as we wish to tell about ourselves. About some matters, we may claim the right to remain silent (Goodwin, 1993), thus constructing a protective circle around our inviolate self. In the counseling hour, this is entirely legitimate. We play the counselee role; it does not play us. As for the therapist, her task is not unlike the poet's, to elicit the story of the self, while at the same time acknowledging–even celebrating the fact–that there are features of the self that will remain inaccessible to her, beyond the limits of the story.

In setting forth the basic postulates of the story model of counseling, I am emphasizing that the systems model can be incorporated into the story model. In this way, the important insights of the systems model need not be lost. I have also emphasized, however, that the story model invites much more reflection on the self than the systems model does. I sympathize with Joretta Marshall's critique of Bowen for viewing "self-differentiation" as a good thing and "fusion" as a bad thing, a criticism echoed in McGoldrick and her co-editors' complaint in *Women in Families* that traditional systems theorists either failed to talk about love at all, or talked of it in clinical terms, such as "bonding" or "attachment" (p. 10). In general, the psychological community has traditionally been unnecessarily worried that a strong, loving relationship between two persons (such as those described in Marshall's book) will make the persons unfit for life in the larger society. In this regard, Patricia O. Hudson and William H. O'Hanlon's *Rewriting Love Stories* (1991), which concludes with a chapter on "eliciting love and commitment," is a welcome change from the earlier family therapy literature.

At the same time, relationships are strengthened when the persons within these relationships are more fully themselves, when they do not, for example, allow themselves to be defined by the roles to which they have been assigned or even which they have chosen to play. Thus, I strongly agree with Marshall that the mere fact that the two lesbian women she describes in her book are highly dependent upon each other is not in itself grounds for criticizing their relationship, much less deeming it to be "pathological." At the same time, one would hope that the relationship fosters each woman's self-determination vis-à-vis the roles they assume in this relationship. In this sense, we *can* endorse Bowen's appeal to self-differentiation as a positive goal in any therapeutic process, and we need not view such gains in self-differentiation as being at the expense of relationships. Rather, self-differentiation deepens these relationships as each individual brings a more fully developed self to them.

The Case of the Problematic Dog

How does this story model play itself out in actual practice? How may it assist the minister in interpreting the stories that are told to her in her role as one who provides counsel? Perhaps the best way to answer these questions is to provide an illustration. For this, I will use my conversation with the student who was experiencing resentment of her husband's dog. (In terms of Noyce's conversation schema, I would call this a shared self-disclosure conversation.)

The first postulate says that the *content* of the story she told me is of critical importance, as the possibilities for changes are inherent in the story itself. To see these possibilities is itself an interpretive task. I knew something about the student and her husband outside the story itself, and this would be true for a pastor giving counsel to a parishioner. This pre-knowledge may well have entered into what I found myself "listening for." But, to the best of my knowledge and ability, my stance was that of "not-knowing," for what she was relating this time was news to me. As her story unfolded, I became aware of her frustration, her resentment, and her sense of confinement to her home, all relating to her husband's absence due to his working late and to the presence of his dog in their small apartment. As it continued, I became aware of a deeper level of resentment, bordering on anger, over the fact that her husband was working for a woman in the other woman's home.

Where are the possibilities for change in this story? Here, it is useful to introduce the distinction between first and second order change as presented in *Change: Principles of Problem Formation and Problem Resolution* (1974) by family therapists Paul Watzlawick, John Weakland, and Richard Fisch. In a nutshell, *first-order change* is change where the system is modified to some degree, but remains essentially the same (the room is too cold so the occupant raises the thermostat a few degrees), while *second-order change* is where the system itself is fundamentally changed (one is dreaming of being chased by a bear and, on waking up, discovers that the bear is gone and one is lying, perfectly safe, in bed). The authors refer to second-order change as "change of change itself" (p. 11).

What kind of systemic change is indicated, implied, or desired in the story as told by the woman who resented her husband's dog? Is she on the verge of telling her husband, "Either that mutt goes, or I go?" No, I didn't think so at the time, nor do I think so in retrospect. But is her frustration over being forced to take care of his dog being fueled by a deeper resentment toward her husband over his decision to spend his evenings in another woman's home? This is how I saw it, and, I think, as she heard herself talk, she began to see it this way herself. Interpretation is a collaborative activity. So where does the possibility for "real change" lie? Complaining to her husband about having to take care of his dog when he is not at home? This seemed to me to be first-order change, which would lead, as Watzlawick et al. suggest, to "more of the same." The husband would say that he has to work late in order to support the two of them and that he can't take the dog with him, as this would interfere with his work and his sense of professionalism. What about explaining to him that she understands the necessity of his working late, but she doesn't like the idea of his doing so in another woman's home? This may be a better approach, as it gets to the heart, not just the periphery, of her resentment, but it may evoke the response that there is no reason to mistrust him and that, as far as he is concerned, a client is a client, and gender has nothing to do with it. This too feels like first-order change.

Second-order change would likely begin with recognition that there are ambiguities or gaps in the story. The "not-knowing" or "deconstructive" listener would perceive these gaps and ambiguities: Why is the husband so devoted to his dog that it seems to the listener as though his wife feels that this devotion exceeds his devotion to her? Why does he need to work extra hours to support the two—or three— of them? What fuels her resentment-bordering-on-anger experiential world over her husband's working evenings in another woman's home? Is it fear that the woman might seduce him? That he might seduce her? That he is more concerned for the other woman's welfare than for his wife's? That he is being duplicitous? These are questions that occurred to me. As the "not-knowing" reader, you have probably thought of other, perhaps better ones. The issue is not, however, whether one asks the "right" questions, but whether one recognizes the *fact* that there are ambiguities and gaps in the story, for it is precisely in these ambiguities and gaps that possibilities for real—second-order—change are present.

As the reader may have suspected, the most promising question— and the one that evoked some resistance—was the one about the other woman. The one about his extended working hours evoked the matter-of-fact response that they had agreed she should be a full-time student, which placed the financial burden on his shoulders, while the one about the dog evoked a very touching story about the dog having provided her husband comfort (prior to their marriage) after the death of his father, to whom he had been unusually close. The question about the other woman prompted a response that did not, as I had suspected, have anything to do with her mistrust of her husband (she knew he loved her and wouldn't hurt her in this way) or even the issue of whether he was placing the other woman's welfare ahead of her own (after all, he was working to help her complete her own education). Rather, it had to do with her concern for her husband. She felt that the other woman was using him, exploiting his good-natured willingness to work until he was physically exhausted, and that he was either oblivious to the fact that he was being abused, or that he realized it but was unwilling to do anything about it for fear of losing the income his work for her provided.

This was not, then, the case of a jealous woman that I had assumed it to be, but that of a woman who was frustrated, and perhaps angry, that her husband was being mistreated and either didn't know it or didn't know how to defend himself against it. If there was to be second-order change, it seemed to lie precisely here. It was true that she felt her husband was similarly mistreating her, forcing her by his absence to have to deal with his dog, toward whom she was developing a real dislike. But this was a consequence of the other problem. Judging by the tone of her voice when she talked about the dog vis-à-vis the other woman, it was not as deeply resented. After all, she knew that the dog had been a comfort to her husband after his father's death.

The second postulate of the story model is that every individual is a self and therefore has power over the role that he or she plays in the family story. The ascribed roles in this case were those of wife and student. As her story unfolded, it became increasingly evident to me that these roles were, in fact, playing her more than she was playing them. Playing two roles at once is, of course, a difficult task—it is often referred to as a juggling act—but it is not uncommon. Thus, I found myself feeling some irritation and alliance with her husband when she related, in passing, that he had been complaining that she left dirty dishes piled up in the sink. This was to illustrate her husband's inconsistency, namely, that while he didn't mind having a dog that would spit up food on the carpet, he objected to dirty dishes in the sink. However, when I asked her, "Why does he assume that it is your job to clean up the dishes?" she reminded me that he was working extra hours, and that it was reasonable for him to expect her to do it, but that in her family, they didn't worry about a few dishes in the sink. "But your family would not have tolerated a dog that spit up on the floor?" "That's right. Eventually, the dishes will get washed, but dog spit on the carpet is a lot more permanent." In effect, we had shifted from family *roles* to family *roles* and *rituals,* and were seeing how these had been passed from one generation to the next in the form of expectations. We had opened up a promising line of inquiry, but the apparent incongruence between her "student" and "wife" roles concerned me more, so I asked if her husband's extra hours of working made her feel guilty about being a full-time, unemployed student. She immediately agreed with this interpretation and said that she was "counting the months" until she could graduate and go to work herself. She had even considered getting a part-time job, but her husband had felt that they should not leave the dog alone in the apartment for extended periods of time.

The third postulate says that the value of systems language is for exploring the psychodynamics inherent in the story itself. Another minister in my position might have insisted that the woman and her husband come together for counseling so that the system (or, at least, two-thirds of it) would be immediately present. I do not deny the value of this approach, but my purpose here is to illustrate the story model. I noted in the previous chapter that what immediately came to my mind was the triangle of husband-wife-dog, and that as the story unfolded, it became the husband-wife-other woman triangle. How to "detriangle" the second became more of an issue for me as the conversation developed, though I also began to see that the first triangle would stymie any efforts to think our way through to a second-order change. Whenever our conversation seemed on the verge of allowing me to offer a suggestion along these lines, the issue of the dog would come back into play.

I found myself recalling my response to a colleague who asked me– presumably on the basis that a person in my field would be sensitive to such matters–what he should do about his dog who had become overly dependent. "Shoot him!" I advised. I also recalled the story that circulated around our family when I was growing up about my uncle taking advantage of the fact that my aunt and cousin were visiting relatives for a few days. He dumped the family cat off at the local Humane Society and then, when his wife and son returned home, explained that he had accidentally run over the cat when he was backing the car out of the garage. These recollections indicated to me how frustrating I myself found the first triangulation to be in relation to the second. For our purposes here, however, the important point is that the system was *not* in my office, but was in the story she was telling, and, in this case, there were at least two triadic relationships (as there often are in stories, whether films, plays, novels, or real life), and this fact was symptomatic of the student's own sense of being stymied by the situation.

I was also aware, however, that as omnipotent as I felt these systems and their relationships to be in the story she was telling, an intelligent, caring, and resourceful woman was telling me this story, and that she, with some modest help from me, could "re-author" it. She was not one who would be controlled or undone by these systems. I was convinced that there were elements in her story that challenged the dominant story represented in these triangles. These elements would point the way toward an alternative story, one that broke through the triangles and dismantled their power to control and dominate her life.

This leads to the fourth postulate, that the self exists independently of the story. Put another way, even as the telling of the story places one "outside" it, so the story points to performance outside itself in the real world. I was especially interested in how this woman might express—or perform—her own powers of self-determination vis-à-vis the story itself. Were there any clues to this self-determination in the story, clues that pointed beyond the story itself? In effect, to identify these would also be to identify the possibilities for second-order change that were already embedded in the story.

It did not seem to me that an elaborate strategy for second-order change (a common practice of the Brief Therapy Center where Watzlawick, Weakland, and Fisch were resident therapists) was needed (for an example, see Capps, 1998, pp. 100–105). The problem was serious enough, but I perceived the fundamental strength of their marriage and was also aware that she was, as she put it, "counting the months" (not the years) until the recent arrangement of her husband's extra workload would terminate. So I merely placed the suggestion that the dog had become the "identified patient" or "scapegoat" who was always at hand to enable them to avoid a more significant source of tension (in this case, the tension caused by her husband's working for the other woman). I mentioned that I thought she herself was aware that if she brought up the matter of "the other woman," her husband would make the same—erroneous—assumption that I had made, that she mistrusted him. Aware of this, she was reluctant to say anything to him about it, because she felt he would respond, on the basis of this erroneous assumption, that he was not attracted to the other woman, that he could be trusted, and so forth. So she didn't say anything and instead took out her frustration on the dog, who was, in fact, a real frustration too (he *did* spit up on the carpet, etc., etc.).

I indicated to her that I wasn't sure how she might bring herself to broach the subject that was the most troubling to her in such a way that she could make it clear to her husband—as she had to me—that her concern was not his faithfulness, but his apparent willingness to be used—even abused—owing to his good-naturedness. I admitted that I wasn't sure he *wouldn't* respond defensively to her perspective, but that it was worth a try. I said I thought that whatever his verbal response might be, he would be inwardly flattered—as I would have been—that she was genuinely concerned about him and didn't want him to be taken advantage of. This, after all, was an expression of her love for him.

The metaphorical implications of her reference to the dirty dishes in the sink did not occur to me until after our conversation. Had I thought of them earlier, I might have asked about her family's way of dealing with problems. Did they let them "sit there" for a fair amount of time until someone was forced to do something about it? If so, this might be a clue to how she tended to keep her frustrations to herself until she simply had to do something about them.

The reader is probably curious, as I am, about how this story ended. I suggested at the end of our conversation that she arrange in two or three weeks for another visit if things didn't improve. Was the fact that she did not contact me an indication that things *had* improved? Or was it that our conversation had not been helpful? Perhaps (in retrospect) it was a matter of some embarrassment to her that she had told me—one of her professors—about some of the intimate details of her marriage. Should I have scheduled another conversation with her and not left it to her to contact me if she wanted to talk again? Perhaps. I felt, however, that I had tried my best to be a faithful interpreter of her story and that she knew my invitation to arrange to talk with me again was genuine. This is not, I admit, a very satisfying ending to the story—we (I and the reader) want to know exactly how it all turned out—but this was only one episode in her life, and my role was not to make her dependent on our conversations. Instead, as Becker puts it, it was to help free her from her personal preoccupations so that she could take fuller advantage of the saving graces of the Christian community of which she, her husband—and, I daresay, his dog—are a vital part.

Types of Stories

Before concluding this chapter, I would like to comment briefly on a useful interpretive method or tool that emerges once one adopts the story model presented here. It involves determining what *type* of story the person who is receiving counsel is telling, and using this insight to help him learn to tell a different, less problematic type of story. In *Tales and Transformation: Stories in Families and Family Therapy* (1994), Janine Roberts identifies *types* of stories that a therapist typically encounters in working with a client (pp. 11–21):

1. *Intertwined story.* Here, one story is linked to another, but the client may not be aware that she is connecting them, or, even if aware, may not know the real basis on which she is doing so. For example, a young mother who was unmercifully teased as a child by her older sister

reacts to a similar situation involving her two children by jumping into the middle of their disagreements to protect the youngest child.

2. *Distinct/Separated story.* At the opposite end of the continuum from the intertwined story, these are two stories that are dynamically related, but the person being counseled is unaware of the connection. For example, a man who was ten years old when *his* father abandoned the family finds himself wanting to spend very little time with his own family. His sons are about the same age he was when his own father left. In *Lost Boys: Why Our Sons Turn Violent and How We Can Save Them* (1999), James Garbarino tells about the case of a fifteen-year-old boy who killed a convenience store clerk who dared to oppose him when he demanded all the money in the cash register. The boy's response to the clerk before he shot him—"Don't you ever talk to me like that"—echoed his father's words to him before his father beat him. He was "surprised, even stunned" when the parallel was pointed out to him (pp. 45–46).

3. *Minimal/Interrupted story.* Here, the client does not have much access to stories that bear on her present difficulties. A woman being treated for depression, an only child, had very little to relate about her parents and her childhood. Both parents died when she was in her early twenties. Her therapist encouraged her to find out from living relatives more about her parents and her childhood, as this could have a direct bearing on her present depression. Her aunt informed her how elated her parents had been when she was conceived because they had been trying for years to have a child. As in Freedman and Combs' s example of the woman who focused on her early experience of sitting on her grandmother's lap, this story enabled the depressed woman to begin building an alternative story different from her dominant story.

4. *Silenced/Secret story.* This type has to do with stories, usually family stories, that are hidden and secret. They are powerful precisely because they are not told or acknowledged. Roberts tells the tragic story of her brother, who left an alcohol treatment center when he was in his twenties and disappeared for nine years. The family thought he might be dead. During this period, Roberts (in the course of her own therapy) learned that her parents were having a marital crisis when her brother Mark was born and that her father had moved out and was living with another woman. When he appeared at the hospital to see his new son, he was shamed by the obstetrician into returning to his wife and family. Yet throughout the years, Mark felt like an outsider in the family. When he contacted Janine, she told him the story, and he felt that he finally had an explanation for why he had always felt this way.

5. *Rigid story.* This is a story that is told over and over again in much the same way. Two or more family members tell it exactly the same way, or one family member is the one considered competent to tell it, and the others defer to his interpretation of the event. For example, a father kept telling his son about how no family member came to his own high school graduation to hear him play the trumpet and how he worked like a servant in the family restaurant. Tom, his son, felt that his father's story focused so much on his own childhood deprivations that he, the father, was unable to become involved in his own fathering role. In this case, the therapist suggested that Tom ask his father about times when he *did* feel supported by his family, a suggestion based on the assumption that the father's dominant story, while no doubt true, pushed aside other life experiences that contradicted it.

6. *Evolving story.* This involves recognizing that the story is different at different times of life, that the meaning of the story is always open to reinterpretation. The same story—such as the divorce of the daughter's parents when she was a small child—may be understood very differently as a person goes through life. As we grow and mature, we acquire new experiences and perspectives for viewing the story, or we place it in a new context of meaning. Roberts values the evolving story and sees it as being most different from the rigid story. Whereas rigid stories keep us locked in the past, evolving stories enable us to move into the future. This agrees with Edward P. Wimberly's view (1991, pp. 14–15) that we should allow the story to unfold, for, where God is concerned, we should not assume that we have seen the end of the story. It keeps unfolding, keeps evolving. It is not an aimless story—merely one episode after another—but one that has purpose. Sometimes the plot thickens and gets bent out of shape, and needs to be twisted back to its original design (p. 15). But the important point is that the plot is eschatological, unfolding a chapter at a time.

Roberts' identification of *types* of stories is a valuable resource for interpreting the life stories that persons tell the minister. Identifying the type of story being told helps the minister determine what is missing from the story, or what needs to be changed. These story types grew out of Roberts' experience as a family therapist (and may be viewed as a translation of various systems concepts to the story context), but her own family was an even more pivotal resource. In her acknowledgments, she mentions her daughter Natalya, "who always asked me one more time to tell a story" and "stretched my mind with her requests," helping "me go deeper into memory and imagination" (p. x). Her children Jess and Heather exhibited a "deep capacity to share [their] stories and create new ones together. My three children: Stories have shepherded us through myriad changes in our lives, and as you enter your teenage years I hope they continue to do so" (p. x). Her Uncle Paul's "photographs of historical family events as well as our current gatherings," had proven to be "incredible artifacts that help us remember and stimulate family storytelling" (p. x). And finally, she mentions her husband, David, had committed "so much of his time and energy to research, tell, and connect our family stories, both past and present" (p. xi). Clearly, Roberts drew on her own family background, with its Jewish storytelling culture, as a primary resource in her development of her own story-based therapeutic process.

A full discussion of how Roberts draws on her Jewish storytelling heritage (as well as her training in the systems approach to family therapy) would take us too far afield, requiring us to explore not only biblical narratives but also Hasidic tales, stories of rabbis, the Jewish comedic tradition (see Freud, 1960b), and the like. But Phyllis Trible's *Texts of Terror: Literary-Feminist Readings of Biblical Narratives* (1984), Philip Culbertson's *New Adam: The Future of Male Spirituality* (1992), and Richard Q. Ford's *The Parables of Jesus: Recovering the Art of Listening* (1997) illustrate how deeply these story types are rooted in the dominant history of the Jewish people.

Trible, for example, is especially concerned with the *silenced/secret* story type, or stories about women that are so deeply embedded in the biblical text that special effort is required to bring them out and hold them up to view. Following Trible's lead, Culbertson concerns himself with men's "texts of terror," which tend to be *minimal-interrupted* and *rigid* as far as male relationships are concerned. Ford is concerned with the "gaps" in the stories that Jesus told and emphasizes that these "gaps" require the listener to consider various possibilities and then to make a decision as to the real meaning of the story. While he is therefore more concerned with the interpretive act itself, this approach leads Ford to emphasize the disconnectedness of the stories, as reflected in the *intertwined* and *distinct/separated* story types identified by Roberts.

What we learn from these texts on the Jewish story tradition is that, while the larger history of the Jewish people is an *evolving* one, the individual stories tend to reflect the other story types, and thus create a story atmosphere in which a certain fatalism prevails. Freud called this "the repetition compulsion," or the compulsion to "repeat the past," and used it to interpret the story of Moses (1939, pp. 95–96). In systems terms, this is the concept of homeostasis (while Combs and Freedman's "alternative story" draws on the concept of neostasis).[2]

Concluding Comments

I am well aware that a minister may not have occasion to make full use of the story model presented here in each and every conversation in which she is called on to provide counsel. This model illustrates, however, that what is going on in such conversations *is* interpretation, so that what the minister and the other person are doing is similar to what occurs, for example, in an adult Bible study group. The minister and the other person form an interpretive community as they give their attention to bringing out the meaning of this person's story. As in an adult Bible study group, it is useful–sometimes indispensable–to have interpretive resources available, especially when the story's meaning is inaccessible or when there are competing claims to what the story "really means."

Unless they are full-time pastoral counselors, most ministers devote a relatively small portion of their time to the role of counselor. On the other hand, they ordinarily spend a great deal of their time in the preaching and teaching role and, if they make themselves accessible to their congregants, students, and professional colleagues, they often listen to stories these other persons tell for other reasons than the desire for the minister's counsel. The more the minister can draw on these other experiences to inform his counselor role, the less marginalized– even "specialized"–his counselor role will feel to him. Instead, he will experience it as being all of a piece with the other things that he does. The interpretive resources presented here are intended to demonstrate that there are methods for "bringing out the meaning" of the other person's story that are congruent with the other interpretive roles of the minister.

---

[2] In *African American Pastoral Care* (1991), Edward P. Wimberly discusses stories from the perspective of their emplotment, using both biblical stories and the personal stories told him by his counselees to demonstrate the four stages in "the eschatological plot" of the gospel story: unfolding, linking, thickening, and twisting (pp. 14–16).

5

How to Manage Boundaries

In chapter 3, I quoted J. C. Wynn's observation that the sources of Christian thinking about marriage and family have developed out of the problems and pressures of the ages in which they were written. In recent years, much has been written about the need for ministers to maintain or manage boundaries. As William V. Arnold notes in *Pastoral Responses to Sexual Issues* (1993), there are several types of boundaries to which ministers should be attentive. These include space, time, language, touch, and one's own feelings (pp. 48–53). In this chapter, I will center primarily on boundaries involving time and space, but I will also consider one form of "feeling," that of sexual desire, as this is often a factor in one's failure to manage temporal and spatial boundaries appropriately.

Sexual harassment in the workplace is a boundary issue that may be viewed in spatial terms, as it represents the violation of another person's "space." The movement toward abolition of smoking in public places has been based on a similar argument, namely, that smoking is a violation of other persons' space. We also need to think about boundary issues, however, in temporal terms. This dimension of boundary maintenance has been emphasized, for example, by those who have argued against "workaholism" (a term that Wayne E. Oates was responsible for coining), which is our inability to place appropriate limits on our expenditure of time in work-related activities. This is a boundary issue that has been of particular sensitivity for ministers because their reputation for being workaholics is legendary.

In this chapter, I will take account of both forms of the boundary problem–spatial and temporal–focusing on their relevance to the minister in her role as counselor. Because this issue necessarily raises and impinges on contextual matters, I will consider the minister's counselor role within the context of the congregation. Readers who are located or contemplating location in other forms of ministry–chaplaincy, campus ministry, teaching, social agency, and so on–will need to adapt this congregational discussion to these alternative settings. By and large, the arguments that I will make here apply "across the board," and are therefore relevant to wherever a minister engages in the role of counselor.

Psychodynamic Meanings of "Boundary"

Before moving into this discussion, I want to draw out some of the psychodynamic implications of the meaning of the word *boundary*. The dictionary defines *boundary* as "any line or thing marking a limit." This sounds simple enough until we consider its root word–*bound,* which has four general meanings, including "to move with a leap or series of leaps" (as in Superman's ability to leap over buildings in a single bound); "to be confined by binding" (as in "the thief bound his victim to a chair"); "to be heading somewhere" (as in "bound for home"); and "to be a limit or boundary for" (as in "out of bounds"). A meaning that might be added here is a certain willfulness or even rashness (as in "bound and determined"). The fourth meaning–to be a limit or boundary for–is the one on which the word "boundary" itself is based. It is useful, though, to keep the other four meanings in the back of our minds as we explore the issue of how to manage boundaries, because they point to the ambiguities, even paradoxes, reflected in the word. For example, bound as in "leap" suggests a certain spontaneity of freedom of movement, whereas bound as "binding" implies a situation from which one cannot extricate oneself (as in "a binding contract"). Similarly, the idea that one is heading toward a destination ("homeward bound") stands in rather stark contrast to the idea of limits or boundaries ("this far but no farther").

Erik H. Erikson's discussion of the third stage of the life cycle– initiative versus guilt–illumines the ambiguities involved in the word *bound* in a way that has direct relevance to the minister's own management of boundaries. He describes the child (roughly 4–5 years old) as one whose behavior is dominated by "the intrusive mode." This means that "His learning now is eminently intrusive and vigorous; it leads away from his own limitations and into future possibilities" (1959, p. 76). A variety of intrusive behaviors emerge in this stage, including "the intrusion into other bodies by physical attack; the intrusion into others' ears and minds by aggressive talking; the intrusion into space by vigorous locomotion; the intrusion into the unknown by consuming curiosity" (p. 76). He notes further that this "is also the stage of infantile sexual curiosity, genital excitability, and occasional preoccupation and overconcern with sexual matters" (p. 76).

Erikson emphasizes that intrusion is not in itself an undesirable form of interaction. He warns, however, that it can degenerate into undesirable modes of behavior if not directed toward constructive and ultimately peaceful ends, in which case, it becomes coercive. To be sure, excessive parental restraint on the child's intrusiveness may cause her to become overly unobtrusive, deeply fearful of the dangers that await her when narrowly defined boundaries are trespassed. On the other hand, a lack of constructive ends toward which she is able to direct her energies may lead her to become intrusive in an undisciplined way, her object being merely to boss or coerce other individuals. This distinction between "constructive" and "coercive" intrusion has relevance for ministers. Fear that one will be accused of coercive intrusion may cause a minister to become unobtrusive, leading to missed opportunities for ministry (see Capps, 1979, pp. 61–67).

The variety of intrusive behaviors of children in these formative years also has relevance for ministers. For example, an adult may be a person who is not disposed toward physical attack, aggressive talking, or even vigorous locomotion, and yet be a person whose consuming curiosity impels him into the unknown. As Erikson indicates, one form of such curiosity is sexual, and this, as he also suggests, can become a preoccupation.

As its description indicates, the psychodynamic "crisis" of this developmental stage is initiative versus guilt, and the guilt is a direct consequence of having "transgressed" or "transgressed upon" a boundary. The guilt aroused in this stage is expressed in a deep-seated conviction that not just the behavior involved but the child himself is "bad." The consequences of the guilt aroused may not emerge until much later in life, when "conflicts over initiative may find expression in a self-restriction which keeps an individual from living up to his inner capacities or to the powers of his imagination and feeling" (Erikson, 1959, p. 81). This is the meaning of *bound* as confinement or under an obligation from which one cannot free oneself, and is the precise opposite of *bound* as spontaneity and freedom of movement. Note that this is a self-restriction, one imposed from within oneself. As Erikson notes, this is the stage in which "the great governor of initiative, namely, *conscience,* becomes firmly established" (p. 80). This self-restriction, he suggests, may be more severe than parents or teachers require or demand.

Thus, one psychodynamic outcome of this stage is that an adult may become overly self-restrictive, and thus not feel as though she is living up to her inner capacities or to the powers of her imagination and feeling. Another reaction at this stage, however, occurs when the child perceives that his parents (or other adults) are "getting away with" the "very transgressions which the child can no longer tolerate in himself" (p. 80). Erikson notes that these "transgressions" by adults are usually the natural outcome of the existing inequality between parent and child. For example, the child is not allowed to indulge her curiosity to the same degree that an adult is permitted to do (peep shows are considered adult entertainment), or the child is not allowed to stay up past her bedtime, while adults enjoy considerable latitude in this regard. Often, however, these transgressions by the adult represent "a thoughtless exploitation" of such inequality, with the result that "the child comes to feel that the whole matter is not one of universal goodness but of arbitrary power" (p. 80). Erikson is especially critical of the "moralistic" adult whose vindictiveness provokes a deep suspiciousness in the child. This adult does not live by the same moral code the child is expected to live by. The adult, for example, uses physical attack or abusive language to punish the child for her misbehavior. Thus, a greater transgression is committed in order to enforce the adult's sanctions against a lesser transgression on the part of the child.

If the consequences of the child's suspicions of moralistic adults are not immediately apparent–the child does not have the power to act on them–they may appear in adulthood in the form of a resentment of the fact that other adults are "getting away with" things that this particular adult is not allowed to indulge in. If the minister is placed in the position of being the congregation's "token saint," a resentment of this "double standard" may develop. Under such conditions, the minister may act on this resentment by trying to "get away with" boundary violations of his own.

By introducing these psychodynamic considerations, I am signaling my belief that to understand the boundary violations to which ministers are most subject, interpretations guided by systems considerations should be augmented by psychodynamic ones. This dual emphasis will be evident throughout the chapter. We turn, now, to boundary issues relating primarily to time, or the "temporal dimension."

Boundary Issues Relating to Time

The training of specialized pastoral counselors and the development of pastoral counseling centers from the 1960s to the present have created opportunities for clergy to become full-time counselors. At the same time, it has placed the minister who is located in another context (congregation, hospital, college, seminary, social agency, etc.) in something of a dilemma: If I provide counsel, but not to the extent or depth of specialized pastoral counselors, will I be offering nothing more than a panacea or, even worse, will I be doing actual harm to the other person?

Books written for ministers over the past several decades have reflected the fact that pastoral counseling has become a specialized form of ministry, and a fair number of these texts have presented ministers in other settings with models or approaches to counseling that are quite unrealistic as far as expenditure of time is concerned. Some years ago, a seminary professor who was a trained pastoral counselor presented students a premarital counseling approach involving twelve counseling sessions. He argued that young couples at that time were not well prepared for marriage, and the divorce rate was going up, so the pastor should not bless a marriage until the couple had been thoroughly counseled. He was very critical of the common practice among pastors, one endorsed by Charles William Stewart in *The Minister as Marriage Counselor* (1970), that three sessions should be the norm.[1]

This professor's concern regarding the rising divorce rate was commendable. But was the solution to encourage future ministers to devote twelve sessions to every couple who asked them to perform a wedding? As Edwin H. Friedman has noted, there is a real question as

---

[1] I know a minister, for example, who, in light of the rising divorce rate, announced that he would marry couples only if they agreed to six counseling sessions. When he found that this was an impossible schedule to maintain, the congregation developed laity-led retreats for couples anticipating marriage, and they were required to attend one of these as a prerequisite of marriage in the church.

to how much a couple will be able to "hear" prior to marriage. He likens this to the common lament among clergy "that what they learn in workshops after ordination should have been taught when they were still in school" (1985, p. 94). Friedman contends that it *was* available and taught, but that they were unable to learn it until they had "spent some time in the committed responsibility of their own post" (p. 94). He uses this analogy to argue for an emphasis in premarital counseling on the extended family history rather than a narrow focus on the couple's own relationship. Although this raises the question of whether the couple is any more able to "hear" the implications of these histories than to "hear" their own relational issues, his point about being able to hear *does* raise a serious question about whether the proposed twelve counseling sessions—or even half that number—is itself a boundary problem. Apart from the obvious question of how the minister is expected to find time for this, a series of twelve counseling sessions is very likely to "problematize" the couple's very intention to marry each other, as though their desire to marry warrants a form of coercive intrusion into their lives by the person they have asked to marry them. A more creative response to the rising divorce rate was called for. Merely increasing the number of premarital counseling sessions was not the answer.

Limiting the Number of Sessions

Two books were published in the early 1990s on the subject of "brief" or "short-term" pastoral counseling, both by seminary professors who have specialized training as pastoral counselors. The first, *Short-Term Pastoral Counseling: A Guide* (1990) by Brian H. Childs, is intended for parish pastors, seminarians, and "the advanced student in pastoral counseling or established specialists in pastoral counseling" (p. 10). Although one may ask whether this multiple audience is itself problematic, Childs's assessment of the problems that the parish minister confronts with regard to counseling is noteworthy. He says, "Most pastors do not experience a lack of counseling opportunities; rather two other factors militate against the pastor engaging in pastoral counseling in the parish" (p. 9). The first problem "is the issue of time: there is so little of it to devote to the time-consuming job of responsible pastoral counseling" (p. 9). The second dilemma "is found in the general pastor who often has very little training other than basic pastoral care education and training." This leads to "a lack of confidence in doing good and responsible pastoral counseling in the parish setting" (p. 9). He notes that the seminarian who is interested in better preparation for her future parish work and the ministry of pastoral care and counseling "is probably already aware of the pressures of time and confidence that plague the well-established parish pastor" (p. 10).

As our present concern is "the temporal dimension," I will hold off discussion of the confidence issue, because I consider this to be a "spatial dimension" concern. In addition, Childs is himself particularly interested in the issue of time, as he refers to his book as "an easy-to-follow manual for investigating and performing *time-limited,* problem-solving counseling in the parish setting" (p. 11, my emphasis). In a section of his first chapter on the context of parish counseling, "The Problem of Time," he notes that "good and disciplined counseling takes more time than that used in the direct counseling itself. A pastor also needs to review process notes, get supervision, and plan subsequent meetings with the counselee. All this takes time" (p. 27). He points out, however, that pastors are not unique in their experience of the problem of time, for "psychiatric clinics and counseling agencies around the country are also confronted with time problems" (p. 28).

"Time-limited counseling," which dates back to the 1960s, was developed to address this time problem.[2] It has three basic features: The first is that the counseling is limited to "anywhere from six to twenty or thirty sessions of fifty minutes per session" (p. 28). Later, Childs indicates that time-limited counseling "has been defined as one or two sessions to even twenty or more" (p. 42). The second is that there is no renegotiation for new contracts for additional counseling with the same counselor. The third is that it is task-oriented or problem-centered. It focuses on what Childs calls the "Focal Relational Problem" (FRP), by which he means "the one problem that the counselee has described as recurring so often that emotional and social difficulties arise" (p. 28). It is also called the "Core Conflictual Relationship Theme" (p. 105). This problem usually develops out of "repeated failed or unsatisfying relationships" (p. 28). In the case presented in the book, the FRP

---

[2] In *Change: Principles of Problem Formation and Problem Resolution* (1974), Paul Watzlawick, John Weakland, and Richard Fisch point out that if the original purpose of brief therapy was to address the "problem of time," as Childs puts it, it was soon discovered that brief therapy was not necessarily inferior to long-term counseling. In fact, in many respects, it was far more effective, as it required that better use was made of the available sessions. In addition, brief therapy challenges the assumption that "more is necessarily better than less." As a relative who has a rather jaundiced view of his mother once said to me, "She was too much of a good thing." I will discuss this point in more detail later in the chapter.

concerns a middle-aged man's depression after the last of his daughters has left home.

In his discussion of the problem of time, Childs also offers a theological rationale for "time-limited pastoral counseling." He cites Paul Tillich's view that "a sense of time is part of our existence" and Karl Barth's opinion that the temptation to deny time and "the attempt to rise above temporality," while common to humankind, is irresponsible, as "all human relationships are made manifest by time" (pp. 30–32). Also, "time-limited" counseling takes seriously the view offered by liberation theologies and civil rights leaders that "the realistic end of the present time" can "offer hope that what is *now* does not have to be" (p. 33).

How many sessions does Childs advocate? While he notes that he has no particular theoretical or empirical basis for this, "for the purposes of this work I have selected ten sessions as constituting the duration of time-limited counseling" (p. 43). The contract for ten sessions is made after "an evaluation interview or interviews" (p. 43). This ten-session process is divided into three stages—the opening, middle, and end game. The opening game, comprising the first three or four sessions, is usually one of great energy and excitement. If there is no excitement, this may mean that the FRP has not been sufficiently described and agreed on by both the counselee and the counselor. The middle game, involving the fourth through seventh or eighth sessions, is usually experienced as a waning of excitement, but this stage is where the most important work of the counseling is done. During this stage, the FRP is no longer experienced as something new, "in part because of the redundancy of its interpretation by the counselor" (p. 116). This very redundancy, however, enables the counselee to achieve "mastery over the FRP" and "the ability to look to the future" (p. 116). The end game, the last two or three sessions, involves the counselor's "handing over the counseling responsibility to the counselee" (p. 116). In this stage, the issue of time is faced head on as the counselor reminds the counselee of the number of sessions remaining in the contract.

Like most other authors of books on pastoral counseling, Childs cites the particular problem of "transference and countertransference." These "occur in virtually every counseling relationship," but they are "not well understood by most inexperienced counselors" (p. 108). These issues, he suggests, are best dealt with in the supervision and consultation process that occurs alongside the counseling process itself. Transference is "the projection of feelings, thoughts, and wishes" onto the therapist, while countertransference is the therapist's projection of feelings, thoughts, and wishes onto the counselee. These are not necessarily pathological or maladaptive, but they are often unconscious, which is why a third party–a supervisor or consultant–is needed to point them out to the therapist. If the counselor is able to recognize his own countertransference feelings, thoughts, and wishes, this can be beneficial to the counseling process. If they go unrecognized, they are likely to be harmful to the relationship: "The advice here is: Counselor, know thyself!" (p. 112).

In the case presented in Childs's book, the potential for the occurrence of such projections–both transference and countertransference–was heightened by the fact that the minister (Beth) was a young woman. Since the FRP concerned the depression of a middle-aged man (Edgar) following the departure of his last daughter from home, it was natural that he would relate to the minister as a daughter and that she would reciprocate these feelings by seeking to meet his fatherly desires for the companionship of a daughter. The time limitation placed on the counseling is not of itself a sufficient constraint on these transference and countertransference feelings. As Childs notes, the minister's countertransference "almost got the best of her, and she even had fleeting thoughts of extending the counseling contract. Luckily, because of her supervision and own therapy" (focused on her own "grandiosity and need to be needed") she was able to monitor her feelings "and bring the process to a successful conclusion" (p. 114).

While Childs's discussion of the transference-countertransference issue impinges on issues to be considered in more depth when we take up "the spatial dimension" of boundary concerns, we should note the little but highly significant word *luckily* in the preceding quotation. The transference-countertransference issues here centered around father/daughter psychodynamics, and except for the fact that they manifested themselves in Beth's reluctance to terminate the counseling process, they were relatively inconsequential. It is important, nonetheless, to note Childs's observation that the successful conclusion of this counseling case depended to a degree on luck, namely, the lucky circumstances that the minister was being supervised at the time and that she had been in therapy herself. What about ministers who are not so lucky? If the time constraints of "time-limited" counseling are insufficient in and of themselves to ensure that boundary problems relating to transference-countertransference feelings do not occur, it appears that there is considerable reliance on luck when ministers engage in pastoral counseling of the kind that Childs himself is advocating.

I will return to this point in my discussion of the spatial dimension of boundary issues.

This proposed model for time-limited pastoral counseling raises several boundary issues regarding time. As we have seen, Childs has written this book in large part because he knows that time is a major "problem" for ministers. As he says, "there is so little of it to devote to the time consuming job of responsible pastoral counseling" (p. 9). His time-limited counseling model is intended to address this problem. Then why does he advocate a ten-session model (actually, ten sessions after one or more initial interviews) for ministers? The vast majority of ministers that I know would be surprised to learn that a counseling approach involving ten or twelve sessions is considered time-limited. They would more likely assume that time-limited means a range of one to a maximum of six sessions. (I personally like to think in terms of a "handful" of sessions, as this implies upward of five sessions—four fingers and a thumb—and also has useful metaphorical connotations, such as offering a "helping hand," or a difficult counselee who is "quite a handful."

Why this disparity in most ministers' assumptions vis-à-vis Childs's? I believe the primary reason for this is that he has taken a term and model from psychotherapy (he cites several texts on "brief psychotherapy") and has written a book that makes the model accessible to ministers, but without making any significant modifications to take the very different contexts of psychotherapists and ministers into account. For a psychotherapist, who may be trained to engage in very long-term counseling (for example, a psychoanalytically trained psychotherapist), six to thirty sessions may indeed seem "time-limited." (Freud's estranged colleague, Otto Rank, was "adopted" by American social workers, in part, because he advocated thirty sessions or less; Carl Rogers, who was trained as a social worker, is known to have been influenced by Rank in this connection.) By definition, however, a minister (whether a pastor, educator, chaplain, etc.) has many obligations besides that of counseling. As E. Mansell Pattison points out, the pastor is "the shepherd of the church system" (1977, pp. 43–56). This entails, in his view, seven leadership functions, one of which is the "limit-setting function" (pp. 68–69). Given these other demands on her time, what may appear to a psychotherapist as "time-limited" is "time-extensive" to a minister.

A related criticism is that the proposed model may require the minister to suspend, if not deny, her fundamental assumptions or beliefs about the supportive role—and resources—of the community of which she is part, whether this is a congregation, a college or seminary, or health care facility. My "very brief" counseling of the student with complaints about her husband's dog was justified, in large part, on the grounds that she was part of a supportive seminary community. In this regard, I have to wonder if the minister in the case that Childs presents had already succumbed to "her own grandiosity and need to be needed" by her willingness to adopt a counseling model requiring that she schedule ten sessions with a member of her congregation. Isn't this very willingness itself an indication of her need to be needed, and even of her grandiosity (i.e., that she can provide counseling on a ten-session basis and still do a responsible job with her other tasks and responsibilities)?

We may also wonder why Childs advocates a ten-session counseling program—not one, three, or five—when he acknowledges that he has no theoretical basis "for selecting this number," and also notes that "Research has not shown that ten or fourteen or any other number is better or any more helpful" (p. 43). I believe that the primary reason for this is that he belongs to a school of thought in pastoral counseling that not only emphasizes *the pastoral relationship* as the primary means of change but also derives its understanding of this relationship from psychotherapy. It follows from this view of the pastoral relationship (which I will describe below) that there will need to be a significant number of counseling sessions so that this relationship may not only be established but also achieve its intended purposes. A clear indication that it has been formed and is "working" is that transference and countertransference feelings, thoughts, and wishes have emerged and have been successfully "worked through."

For example, in his chapter on the process of time-limited counseling, the one in which he discusses transference and countertransference issues, Childs notes that the process begins with "joining," which "reinforces the relational aspect of all pastoral counseling. Pastoral counseling is not the relationship between a professional and an objectified part of a person's personality or soul. It is a human relationship based on mutual concern and experience" (p. 100). While the counselee comes to the pastor because she, in the counselee's mind, has special skills and interest in helping people, the counselee "also comes because there is a sense that the pastor is more like than different from him." This perceived similarity, together with their "mutual concern and experience," are the basis for this relationship, which is then furthered and strengthened by the sense that "the pastor as counselor and the counselee are in this thing together" (pp. 100–101). I doubt whether any reader would want to take serious exception to this understanding of the relationship between the minister and the person who has come for counsel. In fact, this describes the relationship that already exists between many pastors and their parishioners. But if so, why does Childs need to make a special point of it?

I believe this is because he is thinking primarily in terms of psychotherapy, where a human relationship based on mutual concern and experience is not assumed to be present prior to the counseling process itself. From a pastor's perspective "a mutual concern and experience" already exists, and minister and parishioner are already aware that they are "more alike than they are different," and that "we are in this thing together." In this sense, there is nothing exceptional about the pastoral relationship as it occurs in the counseling process. This process is simply another manifestation of it. This, in my view, is enough of a relationship for the minister to be able to counsel effectively.

The Relationship: Empathic or Deep?

Childs adds a footnote to this passage, however, directing the reader to "a more detailed discussion of the healing aspects of the pastoral relationship" in John Patton's *Pastoral Counseling: A Ministry of the Church* (1983). He refers to Patton's chapter "What Heals? Relationship in Pastoral Counseling," which begins with the assertion, "If any healing occurs through pastoral counseling, it occurs through relationship" (Patton, 1983, p. 167). Patton notes, "Because pastors must respond to people where they are in the midst of specific human problems, pastoral care and counseling are too easily identified with problem-solving" (p. 167). While "some knowledge of problems is necessary to communicate with persons in need, the pastor's vocation is not to 'cure' these many and varied problems" but "to affirm through relationship that none of the human hurts" that persons experience in life "can separate us from the love of God as revealed in Christ" (p. 167). He continues: "The offering of relationship, however, is not a simple matter. Much of the literature of psychotherapy is a testimony to that fact." His purpose in the chapter is therefore "to examine some of the things that have been learned about the importance of relationship in psychotherapy within the context of the pastoral relationship" (p. 167).

To illustrate this view of the healing relationship, Patton returns to a case he presented in an earlier chapter of a woman, Joanne, who was in pastoral counseling with him on two separate occasions, the first of which continued for more than a year. From the second occasion, whose duration is not indicated, Patton presents a synopsis of a session in which she referred to his caring for her, noting that he was to her a "father, lover, and religious person." These feelings were clearly transference related, though he notes that instead of interpreting the transference or "what was going on in the relationship" more generally, he shared with Joanne his own fantasy at the moment she said this about him of having gone to a wise therapist/friend for supervision, but instead of presenting a case, crying for forty-five minutes. The apparent reason for his tears "was something about the sadness of life, the fact of death, and the inability of caring to take all the hurt away" (p. 32). This account of his fantasy, and Joanne's own caring response, led him to cry openly, eliciting a smile from her: "The session ended with Joanne coming over, hugging me, and hoping I would feel better" (p. 32).

As Patton notes, his emotional response to Joanne's comment that he was a "father, lover, and religious person" had countertransferential features that he chooses not to disclose. On the other hand, by returning to this episode in his discussion of the healing possibilities inherent in the pastoral relationship, he indicates that healing occurs through the transference/countertransference aspect of the counseling process. As he puts it, "However it is expressed, the transference is saying, among other things, what I have been attempting to say in this chapter, namely, that it is the relationship that heals" (p. 184). We should not be surprised, therefore, that the chapter deals extensively with transference and countertransference issues. It focuses to a large extent on "managing the transference" and being aware of one's own "countertransference responses and needs."

Embedded in this chapter, however, is a brief discussion of a case in which Patton departed from his usual practice as a "pastoral counseling specialist." This was a case in which there was no time for the development of a relationship characterized by transference/countertransference dynamics such as occurred in the case of Joanne. Glenda had been referred to him by her physician because he could find no medical reason for the various aches and pains that she was experiencing. When she arrived at the pastoral counseling center, "she had decided that her problem was her seventeen-year-old son who was smoking pot and that I might be able to help her by telling her what to do" (p. 176). He tried to direct the focus to her rather than her son and discovered that at age thirty-five "she still felt compelled to see or call her mother every day. She was very fearful of angering her mother and others and had oriented her life around trying to please" (p. 176). He determined (for undisclosed reasons) that Glenda was not a good candidate for long-term psychotherapy or even weekly counseling interviews. Instead, he gave her a "prescription" of things to do before she came back in two weeks. These included such things as "Talk with your mother no more than three times a week" and "Do something that helps no one but yourself."

When Glenda returned two weeks later, Patton learned, "to my surprise, she had done most of the things in the 'prescription'." The thing she decided to do for herself was to take up swimming lessons. More important, as far as Patton was concerned, his "interest in her life and her problem had helped her get curious about herself, and as a result she brought in some things she wanted to explore" (p. 176). Patton cites this example to illustrate why he is "not willing to limit my ministry to the practice of long-term psychotherapy" (p. 176). He adds that he does not "recommend this particular technique to other pastoral counselors, but with a person like Glenda it was one way of offering myself *in a relationship* when a more traditional psychotherapeutic stance would not have been understood or received" (p. 176, my emphasis).

This illustration is worth examining, as it indicates that healing can occur in what appears to have been a two-session counseling process. Whether or not additional sessions followed once Patton recognized that Glenda was "curious about herself" (he does not say), significant "healing" had already taken place. In addition, he attributes this healing, in part, to the fact that he "offered himself in a relationship," though transference/countertransference dynamics, if present, were not directly involved in the healing that took place.

I find it interesting that Patton does not recommend this particular technique to other pastoral counselors. Is this because it does not afford an opportunity for a "deeper" relationship to occur (such as the one that occurred in the case of Joanne)? In any event, his case of Glenda has particular value for ministers in the congregational setting. This case, in fact, beautifully illustrates how a counselee, judged to be a poor candidate for the kind of in-depth and long-term therapy that a "specialist" in pastoral counseling prefers to do, proved to be a good candidate for the kind of counseling that a minister who does not do counseling full-time *would* be able to do. Transference and countertransference issues have little if any relevance, time is not a problem (Glenda appears for two sessions, two weeks apart), and positive things occurred.

Note that Patton, having been informed that Glenda was suffering from symptoms having no medical basis, focused on her fear of angering her mother and others, not on what she might do about her son's pot smoking. Thus, he chose the problem that would be the focus of their work together. He perceived that she was somatizing her fears, and gave her a "prescription" designed to address this. Having been referred by a physician, Glenda was, in a sense, prepared for a "prescription." Also, the fact that she was willing to go to a pastoral counselor already indicates that she was willing to entertain the possibility that her symptoms were psychological, a willingness not always found among those who somatize their fears and anxieties. A more resistant person would probably have gone to another physician, who would agree with her, she hoped, that her aches and pains had a purely medical basis (on this point, see Cantor, 1996). Her decision to begin swimming lessons also indicated that she could deal constructively with Patton's more general prescription ("Do *something* that helps no one but yourself") in that swimming would address the very fact that she had a tendency to somatize her fears and anxieties.

In my view, therefore, it is the Glenda, not the Joanne, case from which we have most to learn about time-limited counseling as provided by ministers in nonspecialized contexts. The relationship that Patton provided, while not nearly as deep, emotionally, as his relationship with Joanne, was comparable to the relationship that already prevails between most ministers and their parishioners. Although Patton does not explain why he considered Glenda a poor candidate for long-term therapy or even weekly interviews, this is not an issue where a minister and one of his parishioners is concerned. Moreover, the level of expertise required to do what Patton was willing to do for Glenda is well within the reach of the minister who is not a specialist in pastoral counseling.

My point here is not that ministers should ignore the transference and countertransference issues that arise in ministry. In fact, such "projections" and "counterprojections" are, in fact, integral to congregational and other forms of ministry, such as teaching and chaplaincy. Depending on her age and experience, a minister will inevitably be ascribed parental qualities by some, sibling qualities by others, and child qualities by still others. These ascriptions will be reciprocated. In his very valuable discussion of "abstinence" in his chapter on the pastoral relationship, Patton talks about how the counselor's refusal to gratify the transference wishes of the counselee helps the counselee address her real needs (p. 178). Transference/countertransference feelings and ideas are present in the normal, everyday relationship between minister and parishioners, and are therefore likely to be present, to some degree, in any conversation in which the minister offers counsel to a parishioner (or student, patient, etc.). These transference/countertransference dynamics, however, are more likely to become problematic—even if also beneficial in certain respects—when the counseling process is extended beyond a handful of conversations within a relatively brief period of time. If these conversations are truly time-limited, the dynamics are far less likely to become a factor. As Patton's case of Glenda clearly reveals, however, this does not mean that there is "no relationship" between the minister and the other person. What it *does* mean is that this is a relationship that is congruent with the relationship that already exists, and that no special or "deeper" relationship is needed for healing to take place.

The transference/countertransference issue was one that Carl R. Rogers felt he needed to address. This was because questions were being asked in the late 1940s about how client-centered therapy, which typically involved about thirty hours of therapy, differed from psychoanalysis. In *Client-Centered Therapy* (1951) he notes that examination of client-centered therapists' experience and recorded cases indicates "that *strong* attitudes of a transference nature occur in a relatively small minority of cases, but that such attitudes occur in *some* degree in the majority of cases. With many clients the attitudes toward the counselor are muted, and of a reality, rather than a transference, nature" (p. 199). The difference between client-centered therapy and psychoanalysis is in "what happens" to these attitudes: "In psychoanalysis these attitudes appear characteristically to develop into a *relationship* which is central to the therapy" (p. 200). In client-centered therapy, a transference/countertransference relationship would be counterproductive. We saw earlier that Rogers is certainly no opponent of relationship *per se*. After all, he was the therapist who emphasized the importance of empathic understanding as a crucial element in the counseling process. If the question, then, is whether therapy can be carried on without having such a transference *relationship* develop, Rogers' answer is an unequivocal yes. It is not requisite for healing to occur.

The relationship in Patton's case of Glenda is clear proof of this. The relationship that Patton provided Glenda in their first session together was sufficient to enable her to tell her story (about her fears about having her mother and others angry at her) and for him to discern the possibilities for change that were inherent in the story itself. In the case that Childs presents, the relational qualities that he describes—mutual concern, a sense that we are in this together—were already present when the counselee entered the room, in large part because Beth, as Edgar said to her when asking to talk with her personally, had "a wonderful way of preaching" (p. 55). Because her preaching inspired him to ask for her listening ear, I would assume that through the medium of preaching she had already communicated a mutual concern and a sense that we are in this thing—life and its difficulties—together.

I believe, then, that we need to be wary of the view that it is the pastoral relationship itself that heals. In the case presented in Childs's book, it is impossible to determine what it was that enabled Edgar to work his way out of his depression. Of course, the counsel that Beth provided him helped, but so did the fact that Edgar began attending church more regularly (his "payment" to Beth for the attention she was giving him?); the fact that his wife Madge suggested that the two of them take up bowling again; and his anticipation of visiting one of their daughters in sunny (less depressing?) California, where they will see "the kids and the grandbabies and all. I love the California sun" (p. 117). There was even the fact that he and Madge thought "we might volunteer at the food bank" at the church (p. 130), an indication of his desire to make a contribution to the lives of others. We devalue the individual's own resources and the many ways in which God's love manifests itself in human community and the natural world when we give too much credit—or place too much blame—on the pastoral relationship itself.

Briefer Counseling

I mentioned above that two books were published in the early 1990s on the subject of "brief" or "short-term" pastoral counseling. The other book is Howard W. Stone's *Brief Pastoral Counseling: Short-term Approaches and Strategies* (1994). This book is much more realistic than Childs's book as far as time limitations are concerned. Stone wrote this book because, when he surveyed the existing pastoral counseling literature, he found no book that he could use for his introductory course in pastoral counseling "to guide students in ways of helping parishioners in the few sessions they have available" (p. vi). He points out that the majority of the counseling that all ministers (not just students in first parishes) perform is brief. By "brief" he means "less than ten sessions," but he adds the caveat that "most counseling offered by pastors is considerably less than ten sessions—typically one to three" (p. vii). Stone asks: What do people really want from counseling? What hopes do they hold out for its outcome? Do they really want to change? The fact that after the first session most people do not return for any additional sessions indicates that "in addition to relief from their distress or solutions to their problems, *what people also want from counseling is that it be brief*" (p. 2). Is this merely a sign of the times in our "fast is best" society? Is the desire for a "quick fix" part of the counselees' pathology, or the pathology of the culture? Or is it a sign of health, a willingness to tackle a problem head-on and promptly do what is needed to get on with the business of living? Stone acknowledges that it is impossible to say. One or both may be present in any given case. Whatever the motivation, however, "the fact remains that a minister spends on average only two to three hours counseling most parishioners or family units; many counseling encounters are limited to a single session. Even people who have agreed to begin counseling often stop coming after a few sessions" (p. 2).

Stone also discusses the common fallacy that short-term counseling is inherently inferior to long-term counseling, an assumption based on a prevailing cultural value that "more is always better than less" (which is certainly dubious when it comes to food consumption, acquisitiveness, and the like). Because ministers often share this common misconception, they may undervalue the counseling that they normally do. As Stone points out, this assumption has grown up over the years as a consequence of the fact that short-term approaches have been regarded as "the best methods when working with people who are poor, people who are not insight-oriented, undereducated persons, those who cannot delay gratification, and some minority groups" (pp. 2–3). One wonders if Patton's Glenda fell into one or more of these categories. In contrast, long-term counseling is often described as "depth counseling, insight-oriented, dynamic, and intensive–the therapy that gets to the root of the problem and yields enduring benefits" (p. 3). This is the counseling Patton offered Joanne.

While Stone does not disparage long-term counseling, he contends that "most people in counseling do not require long-term methods" and for these persons "short-term methods will be equally as effective" (p. 3). Thus, what seminarians especially need to hear is that the very brief counseling that they will necessarily do–or *should* do–is "equally as effective" as long-term counseling. As Stone indicates, most ministers tend to undervalue or even disvalue their counseling work, referring to it as "band-aid" ministry, a quick panacea with no lasting effects, or merely the occasion for making a referral to someone who is "professionally trained." Because "numerous ministers believe they are offering second class care" (p. 3), they sometimes perform their role as counselor in a halfhearted manner. Stone's book, then, was not written in order "to persuade ministers to practice short-term counseling," as this is what most of them are doing already, but to address "the dissonance that occurs when one believes in the superiority of long-term counseling, but engages primarily in short-term care" (pp. 3–4).

What are Stone's grounds for his claim that short-term counseling is as effective as long-term? He cites the finding of a major review of various existing therapeutic models that successful counseling achieves its major gains early in the counseling process: "A *window of opportunity* seems present early in a helping relationship when people are more open to making changes in their lives. The majority of change, when it occurs, happens in the first few counseling sessions" (p. 7). A second reason is that most people who agree to long-term counseling come for a few sessions and never finish. Stone calls this "perhaps the best kept secret in the counseling profession" (p. 7). This means that whereas individuals engaged in short-term counseling are "more apt to make at least a few changes that can begin resolving their problems before they drop out," persons in "long-term therapy who drop out usually do so while they are still in the process of uncovering the roots of their problems and have not yet begun to make positive changes" (p. 7).

I would add to Stone's argument a point made by Paul Watzlawick, an advocate of brief therapy, for whom five sessions ("a handful") is the norm, in a workshop discussion of this very issue. When it was suggested that his clients might feel rejected or abandoned after such a brief period of therapy, he pointed out that he has been living in Palo Alto, California, for more than three decades and "my name is in the phone book. If they need me later on, they can contact me." He then went on to tell about a client whom he has seen off and on for twenty years, but never for more than a handful of sessions at a time. Thus, in contrast to the client who drops out of long-term therapy and then feels embarrassed or ashamed to ask the same therapist for "reinstatement," Watzlawick's client feels he can always call on him when the need arises. Watzlawick's self-portrayal–"My name is in the phone book"–is very comparable to the minister (as pastor, teacher, campus chaplain, etc.). Parishioners, too, are known to ask their ministers for help again and again over the course of the minister's tenure in a given location.

Because my concern in this chapter is with managing boundary issues, I will not discuss Stone's model for short-term pastoral counseling in any real detail. I do, however, want to take special note of his point that if the minister begins with the assumption that the counseling will be limited to one to three sessions, the counseling should be structured around this expectation rather than around "some ideal that presumes an unlimited number of sessions" (p. 8). He suggests that "each session should be regarded as potentially the last one," and, therefore, at each meeting, "every effort should be made to provide counselees with what they require in order to resolve their distress," with "what they need to carry on" (p. 8). He also emphasizes in his discussion of the time factor that the minister should inform the counseled person (or persons) of the amount of time she has to devote to this session. For example, if she does not have more than thirty minutes to give, it is best to indicate this at the beginning of the session. I would add to this that even if she does not have anything scheduled subsequent to the counseling, she should indicate at the beginning the time frame for the session so that the other person knows at the outset the minister's expectations in this regard. This can often be done informally, "Well, let's see what we can accomplish this hour," or, "I'm free to talk until 11 o'clock. This should give us plenty of time for you to tell me what's been bothering you." Stone mentions that the minister should be conscientious about keeping the promises she has made (for example, being available at the agreed-upon time and giving the amount of time that was originally promised). Of course, illnesses and emergencies may result in the need to reschedule an appointment. What he is cautioning against here is a cavalier attitude toward the counseling role that leads one to appear late for appointments, to try to sandwich appointments between other commitments, and so forth.

The basic approach that Stone takes is a "problem-resolving" one, which he illustrates with the case of Pastor Christine Lin and Roger Pendley. Pastor Lin had gone to the Pendley home to work out the last few details of a summer education program with Gloria Pendley, the church school superintendent and the daughter-in-law of Roger, a retired 71-year-old machinist who had left his home in New York nine months earlier to come to live in Texas with his son and his family. When Pastor Lin asked Glenda how Roger was doing, she rolled her eyes and, with a clear note of exasperation, said, "Why don't you ask *him*?" To avoid intruding on the family (itself a boundary issue), Roger spent most of each day in his room on the lower level of the house. When Pastor Lin knocked on his door and he invited her in, he reminisced about New York, commented on his lack of productivity and his difficulty in reading or watching TV because of cataracts in both eyes. He admitted that when he did join the family, he gave too much advice to his son and daughter-in-law about raising their two high school–age daughters.

Stone asks: What should Pastor Lin do? She *could* decide not to act, assuming that Roger would adapt to his new life over time. She *could* use crisis intervention methods (for more on this method, see Switzer, 1974; Stone, 1976; and my interpretation of the case of Job and his counselors in Capps, 1990), but this would have been more appropriate when Roger first arrived at his son's home. As he is no longer in a crisis state, these methods are less appropriate now. She *could* make additional pastoral visits to his home so that "an informal sort of counseling might occur" (p. 16). She *could* recommend family counseling to the three generations of Pendleys on the grounds that Roger's problem is everyone's problem. Or she *could* recommend extended pastoral psychotherapy, such as that provided in a pastoral counseling center.

The approach she decided on was to ask the family to meet with her as a group. In the two sessions they met together, various ways in which Roger could contribute to their life together were mentioned. The most promising ones were that he would tend the neglected flower and vegetable garden that Gloria had started several years ago and that he would be included in family discussions and given a voice in decisions that affected them all. After these two meetings with the family, Pastor Lin met with Roger alone once more and found him to be more relaxed and at home in his new environment. He even appeared to be hearing and seeing better. (If Pastor Lin had been thinking metaphorically, it might have occurred to her that her interventions in Roger's behalf occurred nine months after his arrival in the Pendley home; thus, her role was one of pastoral midwifery.)

Although this illustration *could* be viewed as evidence of the superiority of family over individual counseling, this is not Stone's point. Rather, his point is that in the brief counseling that ministers will inevitably do, it is important to focus on a problem, to define it as clearly and concretely as possible, to establish limited goals, and to develop a plan designed to meet these goals. In Roger Pendley's case, the definition of the problem would be that he was depressed, he had been passive about finding things to do or in making new friends, and he had become a pain in the neck to most if not all members of the family. (Depressed men is what Childs's and Stone's cases have in common.)

Had Pastor Lin chosen to counsel Roger on an individual basis (as Pastor Beth did in Childs's case of Edgar), she might have focused on ways to get Roger out of the house. The same "passion for gardening" that had been revitalized in his cultivation of Gloria's garden might also have been employed in caring for the church grounds. Capacities developed through his occupation as a machinist might also have been utilized. Thus, brainstorming similar to what occurred in the family sessions could also have borne fruit in a conversation with Roger alone. In having the family meet together, though, Pastor Lin was also able to elicit from the others an awareness that even if Roger did not contribute financially to the family (union officials had absconded with most of the company's pension funds), he had a right to participate in discussions that directly affected him. By including him in these discussions, it could be anticipated that he would feel less need to advise his son and daughter-in-law on how to raise their daughters.

Stone also addresses the relationship issue, which he describes as an empathetic one. He suggests that the "crucial first step" in counseling, doubly important in brief pastoral counseling, is "to establish a solid base of rapport and acceptance with the troubled individual" (p. 21). This involves "physically attending to the other person by listening carefully, temporarily suspending judgment, and offering appropriate warmth and respect" (p. 21). If there is already a good relationship, as was the case with Pastor Lin and the Pendley family, it is a matter of strengthening the already existing relationship. This strengthening is not so much to make the relationship deeper (as long-term therapy would conceive it) as to enable the minister to motivate the other person (or persons) to help them cooperate with the changes they themselves desire.

Many other issues could be considered on the subject of time. For example, William Arnold notes that a parishioner who discovers that her minister gives time "in proportion to the drama of the story" may use this knowledge for control. The offer to meet outside regular hours may give rise to the perception that intimacy, not the desire to be available, is the intended message (Arnold, 1993, pp. 50–51). Enough has been said, however, to alert future ministers to the time problem and to the sorts of boundary issues it raises for the minister as counselor.

Boundary Issues Relating to Space

I now wish to turn to "the spatial dimension" of boundary issues. Here, I want to take particular note of Erik Erikson's views on the intrusive mode and the distinction between constructive and coercive intrusion. (Our earlier discussion of the issue of confrontation in chapter 2 assumes this distinction.) The primary issue that will concern us here is that of sexual misconduct. But before we launch into this subject, I want to comment on William Arnold's brief discussion of the "boundaries of space" in his consideration of pastoral conduct in counseling (Arnold, 1993, pp. 49–50).

Arnold notes that "space has to do with place, and the place at which people meet communicates a great deal about the nature of the relationship that they share" (p. 49). An office, for example, communicates formality and focus: "Work is being done there, and the place of work and the kind of work are known publicly. People who are there have come for a purpose, and the purposes are at least generally defined. Those purposes, defined by the space in which they are accomplished, provide definition and boundaries" (p. 49). Thus, when people come to the pastor's office, "the place itself sets certain expectations and guidelines for behavior and subject matter. Those limits provide a sense of safety," and this safety "provides freedom to explore sensitive matters with little fear of harm" (p. 49). Of course, these expectations and guidelines *can* be violated, and this is what sexual harassment and misconduct in the workplace is all about.

A person's home defines a different set of boundaries. While it is "less in the public eye," it is "a reminder of the relationships that exist within its walls and the expectations and commitments that those relationships represent" (p. 49). Thus, "the home may very well be a safe place," (p. 49) though here as well these expectations and commitments are subject to violation. The suggestion of an "out-of-the-way" place, such as an intimate restaurant in the evening, "communicates its own set of expectations and freedom" (p. 49). Arnold warns, therefore, that a "clergyperson needs to be very sensitive to the messages being conveyed by such a choice of place," and adds that the basic point here "is that a wise pastor uses place judiciously. A place is more than just a geographical area. It is a reminder of relationships, of role definitions, of personal and professional promises made. The place at which a pastor chooses to meet communicates intentions to the other person and can set limits, encourage openness, arouse feelings, or threaten to invade" (p. 50). The same point applies to the arrangement of furniture and seating patterns, as these "signal levels of distance, safety, or inappropriate closeness" (p. 50).

I would also emphasize that the temporal and spatial dimensions may interact in complex ways. As Arnold's illustration of an out-of-the-way meeting place indicates, there may also be a time factor involved, for such a meeting may have very different connotations depending on whether it takes place during the day or in the evening. Similarly, a counseling session in the minister's office in the evening or on a weekend may convey greater informality than, say, a conversation during the week over lunch at a local restaurant. A minister friend of mine does virtually all his counseling at a fast-food restaurant, usually during the daytime hours. This location has the advantage of informality–which is congruent with the general ethos of the congregation–and protection against any possible allegation of overt sexual misconduct. It also communicates his desire to meet his parishioners in the very places that they themselves frequent. The inexpensive fare does not place a financial burden either on him or on the parishioner in the event–which commonly happens–that one offers to pay for the other's food.

I have often suggested in my introductory course in pastoral care and counseling that premarital counseling be done in a local restaurant over dinner. There are several advantages to this that outweigh the obvious objection that the couple will not be able to discuss intimate issues, especially of a sexual nature, in a public place. In fact, this handicap is relatively easy to solve by choosing a restaurant that has private booths and that has sufficient background noise to preclude being overheard by persons in the next booth. The advantages are that, inasmuch as the couple does not ordinarily request counseling (this is almost invariably the minister's expectation that the couple has to meet in order to gain what they *have* requested, the wedding ceremony itself), the minister is able to "buy" their cooperation by insisting on paying the bill for the first two meetings, in which the "real" counseling occurs. Since the third session is devoted to the wedding arrangements, the minister may graciously accept the couple's offer to pay the bill. Equally important, the conversations occur over meals, and this in itself has significant symbolic value. In addition, the bathroom breaks that each of them takes afford the opportunity to ask the other if they are talking about her or his central concerns, and then seemingly offhandedly to say as the other person returns, "While you were gone, Dave and I have been talking a bit about…" The pastor's own departure–whether absolutely necessary or not–affords the two of them the opportunity to talk over how the conversation seems to be going and to suggest a different direction, new topic, or so forth, on her return.

As I have written elsewhere about my belief that premarital counseling should focus on a central issue in the couple's history together that they have either worked through or that is currently troubling them (Capps, 1981, chap. 3), I will not take time to discuss the actual content of the conversation. My concern here is simply to make the case for using some imagination in deciding on the location in which one provides counsel. As Jay S. Efran, Michael D. Lukens, and Robert J. Lukens write in *Language, Structure and Change* (1990), "There is nothing sacred about an office. Sometimes there are other locations that provide more suitable environments for moving an inquiry forward. We have no hesitation about leaving the office when necessary" (p. 129). They indicate, for example, that they have taken a number of phobic clients to a nearby amusement park: "It is a phobic's nightmare. There are giant Ferris wheels, sky rides, roller coasters and 'free-fall' machines–and it's all safety-checked and well-insured" (p. 129). Here, there are opportunities for phobic clients to test and challenge themselves, to conduct mini-experiments in reactivity and survival methods, and they can confront their belief systems and study the strategies by which they were formed and sustained: "We think of it as an elaborate outdoor laboratory facility with sophisticated equipment. Best of all, it has been made available to us at low cost–the price of admission" (p. 129). If psychotherapists are able to leave their sacred offices, then surely ministers–who serve a Lord who was itinerant–can do the same.

The Misuse of Pastoral Power

The issue of sexual misconduct is certainly the most publicized boundary issue affecting ministers today. In an article I wrote several years ago (1993b), in which I focused on Karen Lebacqz and Ronald Barton's *Sex in the Parish* (1991), I noted that had a book with this title been published when I was a seminarian in the early 1960s, one would have assumed that it was intended for youth workers concerned about how to control their adolescent charges at summer camp or weekend retreats. If, however, it had been published in the late 1960s or early 1970s, one would have assumed from the title that it was written for pastors and adult lay leaders who were troubled by the fact that "sensitivity groups" sponsored by congregations were having unintended destructive effects on some marriages. (I alluded earlier to a minister's lament that his church's sensitivity group had become the springboard for spouse-swapping among some of the participants.) That we now, however, assume that a book entitled *Sex in the Parish* is about pastor-parishioner relationships tells us how far we have come in being able to talk publicly about the fact that significant numbers of pastors are betraying the sacred trust of their profession by entering into morally indefensible relationships with one or more of their parishioners. Lebacqz and Barton begin their book with this declaration: "This is a book about sex. Specifically, it is about sex in the parish–about pastors and parishioners, about how pastors handle their sexuality in general, and about what they do in particular when they find themselves sexually attracted to a parishioner. Above all, it is about whether sexual intimacy between pastor and parishioner is wrong, and if so, what makes it wrong" (p. 7).

Their basic argument is that, while most pastors have given serious thought to the importance of maintaining appropriate professional boundaries with their parishioners, they lack an ethical framework to support or challenge their intuitions about the matter. A common response of pastors when the subject is raised is that they let conscience be the guide. Another is simply that they know what's right and what's wrong. But these authors are not persuaded that conscience is always a reliable guide in matters involving boundaries and limits, nor do they agree that it is sufficient to say that we know what is right and wrong. Not only the individuals involved but also the church as an institution needs an ethical rationale for the judgments it makes about sexual relationships between pastors and parishioners, and it is this ethical rationale that Lebacqz and Barton offer.

They focus on the issue of *pastoral power,* noting that while pastors may not feel powerful, they do in fact have power. Moreover, the power that they have is rather unique to their profession. Pastors have the *power of freedom,* that is, the power that comes with not being under continual supervision or surveillance of others, and they have the *power of access and accessibility,* that is, the privileged access to the personal lives of parishioners that comes with being in a profession long associated with hospitality and care. These may not seem or feel like powers, but they decidedly are. I would add a third power that is implied in the second, the *power of knowledge.* Pastors often know a great deal about the families in their congregations and the individual members of these families, the sorts of things that it takes a counselor or therapist several weeks to learn about their counselees. Pastors may not consciously exploit this knowledge but sometimes may do so unconsciously. If, for example, a pastor is aware that the husband of a parishioner is inferior in intellectual and social skills, he may unconsciously "one-up" her husband by meeting her needs for someone who is intelligent and understanding to talk to.

For Lebacqz and Barton, the ethical issue is the misuse of these pastoral powers. To frame the issue, they turn to medical ethics, because a central feature in pastoral ethics, as in medical ethics, is the issue of consent. In the medical context, issues concerning consent involve whether the patient is fully informed, understands the information given, is legally competent to give consent, and is truly free to consent. Exceptions to informed consent usually cited are emergency, incompetence, waiver, and therapeutic privilege. Among these, the most problematic is therapeutic privilege, for, as Gerald Dworkin argues in *The Theory and Practice of Autonomy* (1988), therapeutic privilege tends to be paternalistic and a clear infringement on the autonomy of the patient (e.g., "In my judgment, the patient is better off not knowing"). A similarly paternalistic argument is frequently resorted to by professional therapists who claim that they engaged in sexual acts with a client "for the client's own good."

For Lebacqz and Barton, the crucial issue is the parishioner's *freedom* to consent to sexual intimacy with the pastor, and here they argue that such freedom should be assumed to be limited or nonexistent where there is an *inequality of power between the two parties.* Since pastors have the power as professionals, and parishioners as parishioners do not, we must assume that, in the vast majority of cases, parishioners are not in a position to consent freely in situations involving sexual behavior. The authors emphasize that the issue is not the *perceived* power of the pastor, but the *actual* power. Perceived power is deceptive, as pastors often do not perceive themselves to have power. Many identify, emotionally, with the powerless. Nor is the issue whether the *parishioner* has greater power *outside this relationship.* The parishioner may be more powerful in other contexts: financially better off, from a "better" family, a "higher" social class, and so forth. These, however, are irrelevant to the power differential in the pastor-parishioner relationship itself. In this relationship, the pastor, being the professional, has the power, as the power differential favors the professional. Also irrelevant is the parishioner's powers of seduction. In a relationship in which one is the professional and the other is not, the *sole* issue is whether the nonprofessional is in a position to consent freely. Even when parishioners "make the first move," it does not mean that they are therefore consenting freely. Exploitation is still involved.

Are there situations where a parishioner might consent freely? Lebacqz and Barton do not want to rule out this possibility categorically. An unmarried parishioner *may* be in a position to consent freely to dating and eventually marrying her single pastor (the same holds true for an unmarried single man and a single woman pastor), but the authors set forth some rather strict guidelines for this, including the securing of another pastor for the parishioner, informing a church leader or pastoral relations committee of the dating relationship, and facilitating an ongoing relationship of the pastor with professional colleagues for honest feedback regarding the performance of the pastor's professional duties. Yet in a review of the Lebacqz and Barton book in *The Christian*

Century (April 1, 1992), Pamela Cooper-White, who works with survivors of clergy sexual abuse, challenges the authors on this point, arguing that the harm to both parties is substantial when the relationship does not eventuate in marriage, and that the potential for divisiveness in the parish community is also great. Cooper-White therefore argues that there should be no exceptions to the rule that pastors avoid a dating relationship with a parishioner.

Since many of us who entered the ministry years ago recall the efforts of older parishioners to arrange for their daughters or nieces to meet eligible young male pastors, the fact that Cooper-White would so vigorously challenge Lebacqz and Barton's view that a relationship between a single pastor and single parishioner might be acceptable according to their own ethical framework indicates that we confront a radically different situation from the one that prevailed some thirty years ago. My guess is that what has changed are assumptions about pastors and premarital sex. The assumption that because a pastor was involved, the relationship would remain "platonic" until marriage was implied in the more traditional practice of encouraging dating between single pastors and single parishioners. If the relationship between a male minister and the daughter or niece of an elder ended unhappily, it would be painful for all concerned and potentially divisive in the congregation, enough so that the pastor might be asked to leave. But the shame and guilt that sexual intimacy would add to the already difficult situation would not have been a factor. (The famous story of John Wesley and Sophy Hopkey during his ministry in Savannah, Georgia, is a case in point.) In any event, the assumption that the relationship would remain "platonic" prior to marriage no longer seems a safe assumption, and the fact that it is not lends support for Cooper-White's criticism of Lebacqz and Barton's attempt to argue for possible exceptional cases in which a dating relationship between a single pastor and single member of the congregation need not be proscribed.

The Church as Total Institution

While Lebacqz and Barton are very concerned about the potential divisiveness that sexual misconduct can create in the congregation, they do not in fact place their ethical analysis of the problem within a larger analysis of the congregation as a social entity. However, their use of a *medical* ethics model as the basis for pastoral ethics is revealing in a way they may not have intended, for the congregation has some strong affinities to what sociologist Erving Goffman has called total institutions

(1961). Examples of the total institution are prisons and detention centers, as well as medical facilities, such as residential mental hospitals, rehabilitation centers, and nursing homes. These are precisely the institutions in which freedom of consent is notably problematic. Yet what especially interests me here is the fact of their *totality*, that is, that these are total institutions in the sense that one does not have a life outside them. As Goffman points out:

> Every institution captures something of the time and interest of its members and provides something of a world for them; in brief, every institution has encompassing tendencies. When we review the different institutions in our Western society, we find some that are encompassing to a degree discontinuously greater than the ones next in line. Their encompassing or total character is symbolized by the barrier to social intercourse with the outside and to departure that is often built right into the physical plant, such as locked doors, high walls, barbed wire, cliffs, water, forest, or moors. These establishments I am calling total institutions. (p. 4)

Goffman identifies five types of total institutions: (1) those established to care for persons judged to be incapable of taking care of themselves who are harmless (e.g., homes for the elderly, the blind, the orphaned); (2) those established to care for persons felt to be incapable of looking after themselves who are an unintended threat to the community (e.g., sanatoria, mental hospitals, leprosaria); (3) those organized to protect the community against what are felt to be intentional dangers to it (e.g., jails and penitentiaries); (4) those established for people who are pursuing some worthwhile task (e.g., army barracks, boarding schools, work camps); and (5) those designed to be retreats from the world (e.g., abbeys, monasteries, convents). In *Asylums* and other writings, Goffman gives considerable attention to the strict regulations and sanctions against fraternization between the staff members and the patients, inmates, and residents in total institutions, as such fraternization is considered to subvert the fundamental purposes and goals of the institution, which are considered therapeutic and/or punitive. (I cited a case of just such violations in my discussion of confrontation in chapter 1.) While we may certainly question how well these institutions realize these fundamental purposes and goals, and may even question the validity of these purposes and goals, it isn't difficult to recognize and appreciate the fact that unsanctioned fraternization between staff and patient or inmate—especially when this involves sexual acts—subverts these purposes and goals.

I suggest that the church tends to function like a "total institution" *for the pastor.* This is reflected in the fact that pastors often complain that they have no life *outside* the church, that the church consumes their every waking hour and frequently interrupts their sleeping hours as well. Pastors complain that they have no time for their families. Their families complain that they are often coopted by the church, that they too are not allowed to have a private life outside the church. Pastors and their families struggle against this situation, and some pastors and their families have devised methods and strategies for insulating their family life from their church life. Yet, by and large, the church functions as a total institution for the pastor. In that sense, the pastor's personal situation is akin to that of the *patient* in a long-term care hospital or the *inmate* in a prison, in spite of the fact that she "works for" the church and is therefore, in terms of social organizational structure, comparable instead to the hospital or prison staff.

Conversely, parishioners' relationship to the church is rather akin to that of the hospital or prison staff in the sense that they can come and go. Staff persons may take some of their meals in the institution and may even occasionally sleep there (when they are "on call"), but they do not live there. Parishioners often describe "overinvolvement" in the church as occurring when they find they are sacrificing their family life or professional careers for the church, and pastors try to be sensitive to this problem, actually encouraging a parishioner in this situation to decrease commitment to the church so as not to jeopardize family life or professional careers. It is unthinkable that such conversations could occur between a member of a hospital or prison staff and a patient or inmate. For the patient or inmate, there is no choice but to be "overinvolved" in the hospital or prison, as they have no life outside the institution. Even opportunities to go "off campus" or "on parole" are carefully supervised and monitored.

Thus, because the pastor experiences the parish as a total institution while the parishioner does not, the "power differential" between them may appear to have been overcome, if not reversed. For in the church, it is the pastor—the professional—for whom the institution is total or virtually so, and who therefore feels as the patient or inmate does— that is, as virtually powerless. Pastors feel themselves to be more the patient than the doctor, more the prisoner than the guard. Biblical statements about the church being a community based on power reversals (the weak being the strong, the powerful being brought down) and about Christ not counting equality with God a thing to be grasped but instead humbling himself, taking the form of a servant, provide legitimation for this apparent power reversal, as do theologies that emphasize the priesthood of all believers and the ministry of the laity. It is not all that difficult to see why the appearance of the elimination of the power differential between pastor and parishioner might be perceived to be the reality of the situation, and why pastors, for whom the church has become a total institution, might begin to act out the role of patient or inmate, viewing themselves as powerless to resist a parishioner's sexual advances (or even misrepresenting the parishioner as the one who made the first sexual overture).

I suggest, therefore, that we should situate Lebacqz and Barton's ethical model within an analysis of the congregation as a social institution, and that pastors should bring to conscious awareness what they know intuitively, that, for them, the church is very much like a total institution. In total institutions, there is a strong taboo against fraternization between the staff and the hospitalized or incarcerated. Both can be hurt badly by such boundary violations.

A Lutheran bishop said in an interview that if a pastor is found to be guilty of an illicit sexual relationship with a parishioner, this usually results in the pastor's being advised to leave the ministry and find another career (Miller, 1993, p. 31). This means that the pastor takes leave of the parish, which has been a total institution for the pastor and the pastor's family, and enters a career in which there is less inherent confusion over the matter of power than is present in ministry, where the professional who has actual power (akin to staff) feels as though he or she is the powerless one (akin to patient and inmate). This suggests that, for some, ministry becomes a nonviable profession because they cannot handle the power ambiguities that are inherent in the profession.

It may also be noted that while there are many pastors who are on power trips and who demonstrate their power through sexual exploits and exploitation, the ones who are most likely to become involved in an affair are those who are trying to reduce the power differential between the pastor and the parishioner. As Marilyn Peterson points out (1992), affairs between pastors and parishioners often begin when the pastor expresses concern for the situation of the parishioner (for example, a troubled marriage, a demoralizing family problem). This is then followed by the pastor's being queried or volunteering similar information about his marriage and family situation. With these mutually shared self-disclosures, a bond between them is formed, leading, in some cases, to a sexual liaison. Thus, pastors who make a conscious effort to reduce the power differential between themselves and a parishioner—by taking personal interest in the other and by engaging in mutual self-disclosures—are the most likely to become involved in an affair with a parishioner. These are pastors who do not insist on standing on a pastoral pedestal but who, on the contrary, make an effort to *reduce* the power differential: "Just call me Bob, none of that Reverend stuff."

What needs to be recognized (and seldom is), however, is that such efforts to reduce the power differential actually increase it. Why? Because power in ministry is precisely the power of freedom, of access and accessibility, and of knowledge. Thus, as the parishioner shares intimate facts about herself, making her personal life accessible to the minister, the power differential is actually increased, not decreased, appearances to the contrary notwithstanding. This is because the sources of his power—accessibility and knowledge—are increased by her self-disclosures. And, if the pastor proceeds to share intimate facts about himself, this does nothing to counteract the increase in the power differential, for, through these self-disclosures, his access and accessibility to the parishioner are greater than ever. The more successful the pastor becomes in appearing to reduce the power differential, the greater the power differential becomes. This is what we might call the *paradox of pastoral power:* The more you succeed in reducing the power differential between you and the parishioner, the greater it becomes. Then, of course, Lebacqz and Barton's ethical maxim applies: Where there is a power differential between two adults, we must assume that the one who has less power is not free to consent, appearances notwithstanding.

The pastoral care field itself must bear some of the responsibility for failing to couple its encouragement of a more "personal" pastoral style with cautions and warnings that this more personal style will increase, not decrease, the power differential between pastor and parishioner. Also, those who have advocated the empowerment of the laity and who have attempted to minimize or erase the distinction between pastoral and lay ministry must also bear some responsibility, for these initiatives have contributed to the illusion that the power differential between pastor and parishioner can be minimized, if not eliminated altogether. Peterson's point that affairs often begin between pastors and parishioners when the minister is called on to give counsel to a parishioner who is experiencing a crisis and who is likely, therefore, to be especially vulnerable, is a very important one. While the minister's own self-disclosures–his own troubled marriage or family difficulties–may be intended to demonstrate that he understands what the other person is going through, these very disclosures may evoke an alliance based on a shared sense of victimization (of being misunderstood or unappreciated by their respective spouses).

In my introductory course on pastoral care and counseling, I mention that the percentage of ministers who will engage in sexual misconduct in their professional lives has been estimated to be as high as 20 percent, while for psychotherapists the figure is 5 percent, one-fourth that of ministers (Lebacqz and Barton's figures are 13 percent and 4 percent respectively). Students are always surprised to learn that ministers are three to four times more likely to engage in sexual misconduct than are therapists. One does not need to hold a negative view of psychotherapists as "secular" or "valueless" for this to be a surprising statistic. What accounts for it? There are at least two explanations. One is the minister's power of freedom, or power that comes with not being under continual supervision or surveillance by others. The spatial environment of psychotherapy is more severely restricted than a minister's (for example, psychotherapists are less likely to visit a client at home), and they usually work in a setting with several other colleagues. The temporal dimension also differs, as the psychotherapist's daily schedule is usually less flexible; they have been "scheduled in" by the receptionist or by the simple fact that they see clients at a preestablished time week after week.

The second is the fact that therapists have been taught to recognize the transference/countertransference dynamics discussed earlier in this chapter. Thus, where a minister may take at face value a parishioner's indication that she has "fallen in love" with him, this statement would prompt a psychotherapist to wonder whom he might be "representative of" or a "stand-in" for. Conversely, where a minister might take his own sense of being "in love" with a parishioner at face value, the psychotherapist would wonder why he has these feelings toward this woman–"Whom does she represent for me?" "Who has evoked similar feelings in the past?" "What fantasies about myself are operating here?" Such "wonderings" are not a denial that such feelings are truly felt, but they enable one to gain some objectivity on what is occurring and to respond and act more rationally, more calmly, less gullibly, less like a smitten schoolboy or adolescent Romeo.

An African American male student who was tall, attractive, and impeccably dressed and who had been in ministry before coming to seminary, was about to graduate and return to be the minister of a church. He came to speak to me about his fears that he would return to his "old ways" when he got back into a congregational setting. He had a history of "womanizing" in his earlier years in ministry. He wanted advice from me for how to handle situations where women would "offer themselves to me." What he wanted was something that would "fortify" him in these moments so that he would "resist the temptation" placed before him. I asked him if he might think of Joseph and Potiphar's wife at that moment. He replied, "I could try that, but the image of David lusting after Bathsheba would probably come to mind instead. You've got to realize, Professor Capps, that there are some very beautiful women in the churches I serve." I indicated that I wouldn't doubt that for a moment. Realizing that my appeal to a biblical story didn't seem to fire his imagination—or fired it in an unintended way—I told him a little about how transference and countertransference works, and he seemed interested. I felt, though, that I needed something more concrete—an illustration—to bring these concepts home to him. So I told him that if he were working as a psychotherapist in a clinic of some sort, and if any one of these beautiful women "offered herself" to him, he would have to say to himself, "Aw, shucks, if she were three offices down and talking with that fat, bald-headed, unkempt colleague of mine, she'd have done the same thing." If after saying this to himself, he could honestly say, "Hey, I'm still flattered that she offered herself to me," then he should go ahead and reciprocate her feelings. He laughed and said, "Now *that's* a parable I'll be sure to remember!" I cautioned, "Remembering is one thing; believing is another."

Before we leave our discussion of Goffman's theory of the total institution and its implications for the sexual misconduct of pastors, one further point is worth making. This is that his theory of the total institution may also help to explain why pastors are more likely to have affairs with members of their own congregations than with individuals who have no association with the church. If, as I have argued, the parish functions as a total institution for the pastor, it is not surprising that the pastor would not go outside the church to find someone with whom to have an affair. In a very real sense, the church *is* the pastor's world, and parishioners are, in that sense, the only ones who are truly available to the pastor. Furthermore, those who are the most vulnerable to being perceived as uniquely available are not necessarily those who are unattached, but those who express sympathy for the pastor's plight (which is the fact that he or she *is* confined to the world of the church). Thus,

Goffman's concept of the total institution may help to explain why a pastor would carry on an affair with a parishioner rather than someone who has no connection with the church, doing so in spite of the fact that an affair with a parishioner will have even greater repercussions in terms of personal and congregational hurt and pain.

What Goffman's theory does not enable us to address, however, is the congregational system's complicity in the boundary violations known as sexual misconduct. For this, Rene Girard's theory of scapegoating is especially helpful.

Scapegoating Theory

Girard (1977) argues that human societies are fueled by mimetic desire, that is, the fact that when one person or group desires something, another person or group will find themselves desiring it too, mainly because the first person or group desired it. At first, the rivalry centers on the desired object as both try to acquire the object or goal in question. In time, however, they focus their attention on each other, on the rivalry itself, as it carries greater fascination for them than competing for the desired object. As the rivalry itself becomes the focus of attention, and the two persons or groups square off against each other, the conflict intensifies, becoming increasingly personal and increasingly hostile. As the conflict continues, the possibility of an outbreak of violence becomes greater and greater. To prohibit the outbreak of violence, which would have negative consequences for all members of the society, not just those who are locked in conflict, a scapegoat is identified, one who will be blamed for the conflict and who will be sacrificed so that the threatened violence is averted, at least for now.

In *Job: The Victim of His People* (1987; see also 1986, chap. 10), Girard suggests that Job was the designated scapegoat and that it was his three counselors' task to communicate this fact to him. They were acting on behalf of the rest of the community, which desired that violence be avoided at all costs. This would be achieved by making Job the scapegoat, blaming him for the rising threat of violence, and thereby defusing the situation. As Girard puts it: "The friends regard the sacrifice of Job as socially therapeutic. It is not so much a question of curing certain individuals as of watching over the well-being of the entire community" (p. 79). Their task, then, "is to persuade Job to recognize in public that he is guilty. It does not matter of what he is guilty, provided that he confesses it in front of everyone. In the last analysis, the unfortunate man is asked to confess that he has been struck by an infallible god rather than by fallible men. He is asked to confirm the sacred union of the unanimous lynching" (p. 117). But, says Girard, Job refused to play the role of the scapegoat. Instead, he protested his innocence, and eventually the counselors gave up. The effort to defuse the situation by making Job the scapegoat failed. For the scapegoating process to work, the scapegoat must go along with it, accepting the idea that there is no other alternative available to the community. When Job refuses to go along, a more compliant or defenseless scapegoat had to be found.

Girard notes, however, that, in some societies, the designated scapegoat is given ample time and opportunity to commit the wrongs for which he will then be punished. For example, he will be given free access to women in the village and receive every encouragement to have sexual relations with them. Then, when the time comes for him to be sacrificed, his guilt is well-established, and he cannot, as in the case of Job, plead his innocence. If he is not guilty of creating the original situation of rising potential for violence, he *is* guilty of something, and this is really all that matters. He is punished, and the situation is defused.

Girard's analysis of the scapegoating mechanism may help to explain why some pastors become sexually involved with parishioners. His theory would suggest that such affairs between pastor and parishioner are most likely to occur in congregations where there are two rival factions who have long since ceased competing for the object of their desire (for example, a congregational mission or goal) and have been fighting each other for the sake of the rivalry itself. Alarmed that the fight might destroy the congregation, but powerless to do anything about the combatants themselves, the noncombatants cast about for a scapegoat, for someone to blame for the escalating strife. The pastor makes a perfect scapegoat. Like Job, the pastor is important enough to the community that his sacrifice will be considered socially therapeutic, and yet, like the orphan (a common scapegoat), he is marginal enough to the community—not having deep family roots in the congregation—that few, at least among the congregation's powerful constituencies, will mourn his loss. "Friends of the pastor"—persons who have been close to the pastor for one reason or another—will be designated, or will designate themselves, as the ones to break the news to the pastor that he must go "for the sake of the church." More likely than not, he will protest his innocence, claiming that he is not at fault. As Girard points out, however, the main thing is not the truth of the charges against him but that the community satisfies itself that the guilty one has been identified and gotten rid of.

I suggest that some pastors accommodate the scapegoating process by giving the congregation good cause for getting rid of them. These pastors are akin to those designated scapegoats who, wittingly or unwittingly, play the role assigned to them, and commit wrongs for which they are justifiably punished (expelled from the community). Having an affair with a *married* woman *in the church* is a wrongdoing that, when discovered, demands such punishment. It also allows the congregation to avoid any serious soul-searching on its own behalf, especially by way of identifying and challenging its underlying mimetic structure. Nor is it punished for *its* sins, as the scapegoating mechanism has successfully diverted attention away from the congregation and has focused the spotlight, instead, on the designated sinner. Even the issue of "splitting the church" and the blame for this is successfully displaced from the mimetic structure (that is, the original rivalry that had already factionalized the church) to the pastor's sexual affair, thus confusing cause and effect.[3]

This systemic analysis is not intended to make the pastor the "victim" when the real victims are the parishioners (usually women) who have become involved with pastors (usually men) without freedom to consent. Nor is it an attempt to exonerate pastors who become sexually involved with parishioners. As the story of Job demonstrates, it *is* possible to refuse to participate in the scapegoating mechanism. Although no pastor is perfect, one can refuse to oblige those who have something to gain from the designated scapegoat's failure to withstand temptation. If one is truly innocent, the burden of proof is placed on one's accusers. In Job's case, the counselors were eventually forced to withdraw their claims against him. This does not mean, however, that he was spared a painful, humiliating ordeal, one that nearly destroyed both him and his family. For ministers who have been falsely accused of sexual misconduct, the ordeal is often worse than if they were actually guilty, for there is no emotional catharsis that may result from a confession followed by expressions of forgiveness.

Girard's analysis is especially threatening when applied to congregations because it challenges the very idea that what is going on has anything remotely to do with God. The whole thing—beginning with the mimesis of desire and concluding with the expulsion of the scapegoat—

---

[3]Candace R. Benyei (1998) has argued that some ministers are predisposed to accept the scapegoat role because they assumed a similar role in their families of origin, either as the "identified patient" or as the child, often the firstborn male, who is drawn into a "symbolic incest" relationship with his mother (pp. 88–89). A case in point is Saint Augustine's relationship with his mother, Monica (see Capps and Dittes, 1990; also Dixon, 1999).

is nothing more than an exercise in human fallibility. It is in the interests of the rival factions, however, that the process be understood by the others—the community at large—as a process ordained by God, as having a sacred purpose. Congregations and their pastors are, however, highly disposed to interpret events as having a divine purpose, however difficult this may be to discern at any given moment. They are not very good at debunking the idea that God is behind the whole process. Thus, if a pastor were to say publicly (as some have) that the process has nothing to do with God but only to do with human sinfulness, this very claim would be considered further evidence that this pastor is unfit for ministry.

Systemic Factors beyond the Congregation

So far, I have been focusing on congregational dynamics in order to argue that systemic forces contribute to the boundary violations referred to as clergy sexual misconduct. However, other systemic forces at the higher judicatory level may also be a contributing factor. Anson Shupe (1995) explores these issues in his book *In the Name of All That's Holy: A Theory of Clergy Malfeasance.* By clergy malfeasance, he means "the exploitation and abuse of a religious group's believers by the elites of that religion in whom the former trust" (p. 15). The types of malfeasance that most interest him are instances where clergy have misused funds or engaged in acts of sexual exploitation. He does not discuss what may predispose individual clergy to exploit and abuse the trust vested in them. Instead, his interest is "structural" issues, or the institutional aspects of clergy malfeasance.

He focuses on power and specifically on the fact that power is unequally distributed in every organization. This power inequality is complicated in the case of religious organizations because they are "trusted hierarchies" in which "those occupying lower statuses...trust and believe in the good intentions, nonselfish motives, benevolence, and spiritual insights/wisdom of those in the upper echelons (and often are encouraged or admonished to do so" (p. 29). Thus, paradoxically, religious organizations, as trusted hierarchies, offer special opportunity structures for exploitation and abuse. Rather than attributing clergy malfeasance to the fact that there are a few bad apples in every bushel, Shupe argues that "the nature of trusted hierarchies systematically provides opportunities and rationales for such deviance and, indeed, makes deviance likely to occur" (p. 30).

He distinguishes two types of religious organizations, *hierarchical* (with episcopal and presbyterian subtypes) and *congregational.* Hierarchical organizations have relatively more levels of accountability than congregational organizations. He uses this distinction to explore the issue of the repeat offender, and argues that hierarchical groups promote more long-term recidivism of clergy malfeasance than do congregational groups, but they ultimately do better in discouraging normalization of clergy malfeasance. In other words, the offender is able to get away with it longer in a hierarchical group, but the hierarchical group is less disposed to view these activities as acceptable behavior. For example, the Roman Catholic Church (hierarchical) has systematically protected its malfeasant priests but has not accepted their actions as normal or acceptable. In contrast, Shupe says, the elite in Pentecostal groups, new religious movements, and televangelism (congregational) are more vulnerable to sudden disclosures leading to mass defections, but are more successful in persuading their members or supporters that what the world calls "deviant behavior" is a higher form of spirituality.

In discussing the fact that religious elites try to "neutralize" victims' complaints, Shupe contends that hierarchical groups provide greater opportunities for neutralization of clergy malfeasance than do congregational groups, but they ultimately are more likely to develop policies addressing clergy malfeasance. In other words, there are more ways in which cover-ups may be employed in hierarchical groups, but in the end hierarchical groups are more likely to develop policies for controlling clergy malfeasance. Methods of neutralization (or cover-up) include bureaucratic inertia, sentimentality, "reassurance and reconciliation," bargaining and intimidation.

In discussing the fact that organizational polity is an important factor in whether victims will succeed in having their grievances redressed, he suggests that victims in hierarchical groups tend to experience more ambivalence and reluctance to blow the whistle about their abuse than those in congregational groups, but that victims in hierarchical groups are more likely to become empowered to focus their grievances on group-specific reforms than are victims in congregational groups. His point here is that hierarchical groups are less permeable to grievances. A victim has to confront various levels of authority, and each of these levels is strongly motivated to neutralize the complaint (to do "damage control") so that the complaint does not reach the next organizational level. On the other hand, hierarchical organizations provide paradoxical advantages, first to elites, but ultimately to their victims, as victims eventually obtain a structural focus for redress that aids their mobilization of grievances.

Shupe distinguishes between "primary victimization," or the immediate realization one has been exploited or abused, and "secondary victimization," the long-term consequences of primary victimization. Common to the former are feelings of ambivalence, fear, guilt, and shame, while typical of the latter is the suppression (or repression) of emotional pain. Victim mobilization, a third response, involves redressing injuries and wrongs and is more common among hierarchical than congregational groups. One reason for this is that hierarchical group members are more likely to believe that the group to which they belong is their only choice, so they choose redress rather than defection. The *episcopal* type of hierarchical organization is more likely to retreat to formal guidelines or procedure, protocol, and legality, whereas in *presbyterian* hierarchical organizations the initial neutralization attempts by elites are more likely to inspire efforts to redress, and such grassroots redress activities become institutionalized.

By viewing clergy malfeasance as deviant behavior made possible by the very fact that religious institutions are trusted hierarchies, Shupe shows that the "a few bad apples in every bushel" explanation is itself a rationalization in behalf of the institution and its trusted image. His theory also explains why *clergy* malfeasance is more scandalous than similar malfeasance in other institutions (as religious organizations are trusted hierarchies), and why religious institutions are so slow to hear and redress grievances (as preservation of their trusted hierarchy status encourages denial and efforts to suppress the charges). This leads to still another paradox that Shupe does not explicitly identify, namely, the fact that when the elite close ranks behind the clergy offender in order to maintain membership trust, it thereby damages trust by seeming to condone behavior that it would otherwise denounce. Moreover, the unscrupulous offender may thereby play the institutional elite and his victims off one another. Normalization of his conduct is officially rejected, but recidivism—repeat offenses—is subtly encouraged.

Prevention: The Issue of Sexual Desire

Shupe's analysis extends the systemic approach to the problem of clergy sexual misconduct beyond the congregation to include the larger structures of the church (the hierarchy). As indicated, however, he does not discuss what may predispose individual clergy to exploit and abuse the trust vested in them, nor does he consider ways in which individual clergy may avoid these boundary violations. In fact, while several books have been written about the problem itself (perhaps the best known of which is Marie M. Fortune's *Is Nothing Sacred? When Sex Invades the Pastoral Relationship* [1989], which, as the book cover states, is "the story of a pastor, the women he sexually abused, and the congregation he nearly destroyed"), there has not been nearly as much attention given to the issue of prevention. Because, as we have seen, the congregation and the church hierarchy give ambiguous signals at best, the primary burden for *avoidance* of sexual misconduct rests with the individual clergyperson. I have intimated in my illustration of a particular African American male student that there are psychodynamic issues involved here that a purely systemic approach to the problem fails to address.

In his article "Training for Prevention of Sexual Misconduct by Clergy" (1995), Donald C. Houts notes that the movement for a thoroughgoing education of clergy on sexual misconduct issues is now picking up momentum. In 1990 he began conducting workshops focusing on issues of sexual abuse, including power, inappropriate touch, forms of harassment, times of personal vulnerability, need for a support network, and so forth (p. 370). He reports the results of a survey of nearly 400 clergy who participated in workshops on clergy misconduct. It revealed that 19 percent reported feeling themselves to be "at risk" in one or more areas of "sexual vulnerability," and that these "at-risk" clergy were equally distributed by age group. However, 36 percent of this "at-risk" group were in the smallest churches (fifty members or less). After the workshops, 76 percent of the "at-risk" participants reported changes they had made in their counseling practices as a result of the training. Among those who did not make such changes, but who found confirmation from the workshops for what they were already doing, the most frequently mentioned preventative measures were "establishing professional limits, taking care of one's marriage, increasing self-awareness, and appropriate use of touch" (p. 371).

I want to focus on the issue of "increasing self-awareness" as this enables us to consider the psychodynamic dimension of a minister's boundary violations, and to give particular attention to the problem of desire. In his discussion of boundary issues and themes, William Arnold devotes the first part of his book to "the pastor's responsibility for self-awareness," the first chapter of which is titled, "Caring for Others Means Owning Up to Who We Are." Because "owning up" has an unnecessarily moralistic connotation, I would prefer to say, simply, that caring for others means "owning" who we are, and that this entails being aware of all aspects of oneself to the extent possible. One such aspect is desire, the fact that we are "desiring" creatures by nature. In fact, as

I pointed out in my book *Agents of Hope,* the ability to hope or be hopeful presupposes that we are desiring creatures, for hopes are "fueled by desire" (1995, pp. 58–60).

While much of the current discussion of sexual misconduct among clergy centers on the issue of power, little attention has been given to the role of desire in sexual misconduct. As we have seen, a systemic analysis, especially one that takes larger institutional structures into account, lends itself to a power analysis of ministers' boundary violations. This type of analysis takes us a very long way toward understanding the phenomenon of clergy sexual misconduct. It fails, however, to take adequate account of the deeper psychodynamic issues involved when there is sexual misconduct involving a clergyperson and parishioner (or, in an educational context, teacher and student).

At first glance, introducing the matter of desire into the discussion may appear to obfuscate the moral issues involved and weaken the ethical arguments against clergy sexual misconduct, especially those that emphasize–as I have done–the principle of the inequality of power between the professional and the nonprofessional in the counseling relationship. Instead, the ethical argument is actually strengthened by taking the role of sexual desire seriously. The power analyses currently in place emphasize the fear of exposure and punishment by higher judicatories as the best deterrents to ministers' sexual misconduct (see Fortune and Poling, 1994, which refers to four offenders by name). Perhaps because of the ambiguous ways in which higher judicatories handle such cases (as Shupe's analysis shows), Fortune has crusaded for exposure of those who have been accused and convicted of sexual misconduct. By taking sexual desire more seriously, however, additional remedies besides fear of exposure and punishment present themselves.

To set the context for a discussion of sexual desire, we may consider a case of sexual misconduct presented by Larry Kent Graham in his book *Care of Persons, Care of Worlds: A Psychosystems Approach to Pastoral Care and Counseling* (1992). This case concerns a small, activist Mennonite congregation that Graham served as a consultant after the pastor's resignation over allegations of sexual misconduct. The controversy had begun when a female member confided to a study group that a year earlier the pastor had made sexual advances to her when they were alone in a house while working on a church-sponsored project. Her disclosure brought to light that the pastor had initiated "intimate sexual caressing" with several women in the context of pastoral counseling. In private conversations with members of the congregation, he acknowledged similar behavior with twelve women over the years. Although he made general apologies and requests for forgiveness, those who spoke with him in private felt he was neither genuinely remorseful nor repentant, for he justified his actions on the grounds that what took place was "a higher form of spiritual love and those who do not understand it are not as spiritually advanced" (p. 228).

In his "psychosystemic analysis" of this case, Graham asserts that "the core issue is a power struggle between contextual creativity and contextual organization." By contextual creativity, he means "the pervasive capacity for change which is built into reality, however limited it may be in particular cases" (p. 231). By contextual organization, he means "the identifiable continuity of the system as a whole, and of each subsystem or entity comprising the system" (p. 231). This continuity reflects the organizational pressures toward homeostasis, or the tendency of the system to continue to replicate itself. Graham identifies several dynamics within this contextual power struggle, including the fact that "strong-willed and strong-minded individuals dominated what was supposed to be a communal process," with the congregation polarizing into three groups: those who were "projectively bonded" with the victims and social justice; those who were projectively bonded with the minister and wanted him to be accountable on the one hand and not victimized on the other; and those who were projectively bonded with the congregation itself and did not want this situation to divide it or diminish its ministry. The struggle and tensions between these three groups were exacerbated by the minister's claim that he was the victim of the anger of the women who began to speak out against him: "Some members of the church identified his pain as the pain of abuse, while others identified it as the pain of accountability. The need to clarify power accountabilities was paramount at this time. Because of intractable power arrangements, fueled by sexism, it was impossible to do so" (p. 233).

Graham notes that when the matter was just coming to light, the congregation experienced great difficulty in knowing how to name the problem: "Early on, there was a wide range of opinion: some saw this as sexual indiscretion or inappropriate touching, others as abuse of power, others as sexual abuse, others as seduction on the part of the women, and so on." However, "To its credit, the congregation came to identify the events as an abuse of the role and power of the pastoral office by the pastor's inducting parishioners into a sexualized relationship in the name of the ministry" (p. 233). In his role as consultant, Graham did not disclose his own view until the second feedback session:

At that time, I shared my conviction that the main ethical issue here was that the minister violated the integrity of the pastoral office and abused the unequal power differential between the professional minister and vulnerable parishioners by inappropriately sexualizing the pastoral relationship without the presence of genuine mutual consent. In my view, which is heavily influenced by Marie Fortune, it was the minister's role to keep such events from occurring, and that he must accept the full responsibility for his behaviors and for setting the subsequent dynamics into motion (pp. 257–58).

The ethical principle that where a power differential is present, the one whose power is limited or nonexistent does not have the freedom to consent, provides a sound basis on which to begin the process of establishing responsibility and accountability in cases of sexual misconduct involving pastors and parishioners. In this particular case, it led to clarification of the issue—how to name what had been going on—which had been the focus of so much dispute, anger, and recrimination among the congregation's members. On the other hand, this articulation of a clearly stated ethical norm tended to silence those individuals in the congregation who saw the matter as adultery and/or affairs between consenting adults, as sexual indiscretion or inappropriate touching, or even as seduction on the part of the women. Reaching clarity about the ethical issue of the abuse of power did allow the congregation to reach closure on the matter and get on with its life. Nevertheless, still further analysis of the many factors at work in this case suggests that more than abusing power was at stake. Acknowledging these factors—especially desire—may alert us to ways in which clergy sexual misconduct may be prevented.

In *The Age of Desire: Reflections of a Radical Psychoanalyst* (1981), Joel Kovel discusses how, in its original form (that is, the experience of infants), desire "consists of striving toward an object that cannot yet be named" (p. 70). The infant experiences a sense of lack but does not yet know what it is that she longs for. In time, she identifies the "other"—usually mother—as the "object" of her desire. Thus, at first, desire is an undifferentiated emotion that then becomes focused on a particular object selected or chosen from the vast array of objects that make up one's world. This focusing of desire goes hand in hand with the infant's development of increasing visual acuity, the ability of the eyes to identify discrete objects in the external world.

Kovel further suggests that desire involves the naming of objects from the standpoint of self-appropriation. Mother is "*my* mother." Thus, "Without desire, the world consists only of things, inert masses. Desire makes of inert things 'things-for-us,' that is, objects. Desire is therefore a constitution of both self and object" (p. 81). This means that desire is more than a subjective or intrapsychic process, for if the desire is to come to fruition, the external world must be altered. If the object of the infant's desire is "*my* mother," then mother must acknowledge the infant as "*my* child." In fact, ideally, it was mother's desire to have this child that originally constituted the infant as "*my* child." The process thus involves mutual self-appropriations of objects in cases where two living beings desire each other.

Kovel also discusses the situation in which desire is not reciprocated. He suggests that in such instances desire typically takes the form of hate as the unwanted or rejected one attempts to destroy the other to avenge this injury to self (p. 104). In this and various other ways, desire can become pathological, symptomatic of unmet expectations from the external world of objects. A more mature way of responding to desire's frustration, however, is to recognize that the world comprises other objects that are capable of inspiring self-appropriations. Much of what occurs in psychoanalysis is the reeducation of desire, or training in the art of recognizing the value and worth of objects that one did not originally desire. In essence, this is the psychoanalytic theory of sublimation. It is an alternative to either the hopeless enterprise of destroying the original object (desire transformed into hatred) or the repression of desire altogether.

In his discussion of desire, James R. Kincaid (1992) claims that the Victorians, whom we usually accuse of being sexually repressed, were actually more enlightened than we are about desire. They understood that desire often affords greater pleasure when it remains in the state of longing—free-floating—and does not attempt to fulfill itself by realizing an instrumental objective. The Victorians were capable of admiring from afar. The pleasure here derives largely from the fact that if desire remains in limbo, so to speak, it remains free from the power relations that often lead to the distortion and misdirection of desire (p. 31).

Even in this thumbnail sketch of desire, its relevance to cases of sexual misconduct similar to the one discussed by Graham should be apparent. The minister in Graham's case would have saved himself and others (including his own family) great grief had he undergone training in the reeducation of his sexual desire. One of the redirections that Freud himself advocated was an appreciation for art and its objects of value and beauty. In the context of art, one may "own" one's sexual desires in a way that does not result in the transformation of unreciprocated desire into hatred. Developing an interest in the visual arts, poetry, music, and architecture are among the ways in which pastors may redirect their sexual desires.

The minister in Graham's case might also have developed a tolerance for the *non*fulfillment of sexual desire, for holding desire in limbo. *Limbo* was originally a religious term. In contrast to purgatory, it was the place "for human beings not weighed down by any personal sin but only by original sin" (for example, children who died without benefit of baptism or righteous souls who predated Christ). For these, limbo was conceived as the bosom of Abraham, a place, like a mother's womb, of calm and tranquil peace (Le Goff, 1984, pp. 158, 220–21). Limbo is much preferable to purgatory.

Moreover, in Graham's case, the implied threat of the transformation of desire into hatred was the basis for the minister's ability to enforce a woman's silence. If pastoral powers of freedom, access and accessibility, and knowledge provide the necessary conditions for sexual abuse, the threat of the transformation of desire into hatred enables the sexual abuse to persist. In effect, the pastor now has or claims the power to destroy.

In some cases of clergy sexual misconduct the minister's desire is reciprocated by the woman involved. This does not affect in any way the ethical argument that, where there is a power differential involved, there is no freedom of consent, and, therefore, the pastor's behavior is wrong. Still, it is important that women, no less than men, be allowed to "own" (but not act out) their sexual desires. They should not be required to disown these desires as the price to be paid for speaking out against and making disclosures of, pastoral abuses of power.

The deficiencies in the discourse of desire that prevailed in the Mennonite congregation cited by Graham were an indirect contributing factor. These deficiencies were evident in the minister's claim that he was offering the women a higher spiritual love, implying that sexual desire in its natural form is not good enough. They were also evident in one of the women's statements that her experience of being counseled by the pastor "clearly included gratification of sexual appetite which I knew then and now was appropriate only to your wife and required an agreement to secrecy" (p. 227). The language of "gratification" may be accurate in this instance, for it captures the power aspect involved; but it conveys that sexual desire, even in the husband-wife relationship, is appetitive, and says nothing about desire as a mutual self-appropriation between two living—and loving—beings. Thus, the Christian community itself bears a certain responsibility for such cases of sexual misconduct because it has failed to develop a discourse of desire that is truly worthy of itself.

A related issue is what William Arnold calls "boundaries of language." He notes, for example, how a minister's use of the word *love* may be misunderstood by a parishioner: "We may assure a person of our love and care only to discover later that our words were heard as a proposal of a more intimate relationship" (p. 51). A married seminary student reported to me that he got himself into a great deal of difficulty when he assured a troubled married parishioner that she could count on his love during her struggles. He recalls also having assured her of the church's love for her. Her husband, however, who had been listening in on the other phone line, assumed when he heard this that they were having an affair.

Another minister of my acquaintance frequently concluded a telephone conversation with an expression of his love for the parishioner, whoever she or he might be. To him, this was no different from, say, the coach of a basketball team pointing to his team after a hard-fought victory and telling the reporter, "I love these guys!" Since this minister regularly made such statements publicly and to women and men alike, his regular parishioners knew that he meant this in a pastoral sense. But a divorced woman who attended irregularly and suffered, he later learned, from borderline personality disorder, took similar statements of his in conversations over the phone very differently and began circulating stories that the two of them were sexually involved. The very fact that the church uses a "spiritualized" form of love discourse means that ministers need to be especially careful about how their language is being construed by others. The centuries-old discussion in the church about how Song of Solomon is to be construed—is it romantic or spiritualized love?—should serve as a cautionary note to ministers concerning their use of language that could be misunderstood or exploited.

There is another aspect to this issue, however, that Arnold does not address. This is the fact that, when ministers provide counsel, boundary violations involving language are likely to precede those involving touch. As the Victorians also understood, sexual desire can be aroused by language. Victorian novels are replete with episodes in which the woman prohibits the man from making an indiscreet or rash statement,

"Stop, don't say it," or "I know what you are thinking, but it must not be said." Freud's response to those who doubted that "mere talk can possibly cure anybody" countered that words are inherently powerful. "By words one of us can give to another the greatest happiness or bring about utter despair...Words call forth emotions and are universally the means by which we influence our fellow-creatures" (1952, pp. 21–22). There is an irony, perhaps, in the fact that we refer to the power of language when we discuss preaching (which we all know can be as enervating as it is empowering) while we rarely discuss the power of language in the context where the minister provides counsel. The language of sexual desire itself is one of empowerment and disempowerment, depending on the circumstances in which it is used.

The examples I have just cited are instances in which the minister's use of "love language" was misinterpreted. They were not, technically speaking, boundary violations. Real boundary violations occur when the minister says things that *do* cross the boundary, that *are* meant to be taken as expressions of personal attraction or even of sexual desire. It is one thing for a male minister to say that he admires a woman's courage in the way she is coping with her husband's infidelity and quite another to say that he finds her attractive or that the perfume she is wearing reminds him of a woman with whom he was once in love. Similarly, it is one thing for a female minister to say to a man that she admires the inner strength he has shown in coping with the loss of his wife and quite another to say that if he ever feels the need for companionship, to be sure to call her.

By limiting the number of meetings and keeping them problem or issue focused, the opportunity for such boundary transgressions is significantly lessened. But what if one nonetheless occurs? If the thing that ought not to have been said *has* been said, what then? Because it has not "owned up" to the desire issue itself, pastoral counseling literature has not addressed the problem of what a minister who has crossed this boundary should do. While there are no easy answers, it is important for him to recognize that the language of desire can unleash forces over which he will not be able to exercise control. In the words of the title of this chapter, he may find them "unmanageable." While I cannot offer a "prescription" that will apply to all instances in which rash or indiscreet language has occurred, this thought may be helpful: Since what has occurred is a boundary violation, it is usually possible to retrace one's steps by means of an honest admission, such as, "What I said was out of line, and I apologize." The force of this simple admission of guilt should not be rationalized or papered over by adding, "Being a minister (or teacher) I get carried away by the sound of my own voice" or some such comment. To do so both trivializes the offense and takes advantage of the inequality of power that exists between pastor and parishioner by claiming the right to rationalize one's own behavior, thereby "forgiving oneself," when it is the sole prerogative of the other person to forgive or not to forgive.

By offering this suggestion, my intention is not to minimize the fact that sexual misconduct has occurred or the possibly irrevocable damage done to the pastor-parishioner (or teacher-student) relationship. Nor is this suggestion intended to encourage repeat offenders. There are, however, ministers who on a single occasion have gone over the line and know that they have done so, yet are perplexed as to how to deal with this. In my view, there is no substitute for—or alternative to—an honest, unadorned confession that one has transgressed the boundary accompanied by assurance that it will not occur again.

What about inappropriate touch? Arnold says that it is the "rare professional person who is not sensitized today to the ways in which touch can be misused and misunderstood" (p. 51). Noting that the "pastoral hug" can be reported later as inappropriately familiar, he laments that "we need to be extra sensitive to matters of touching, but we live in a world in which touch is too often considered invasive instead of supportive" (p. 51). While recognizing that touch is "a reminder of what a powerful and healing force it can be when offered with care," he emphasizes the importance of being "careful about when we touch and how or where" we touch another: "A pat on the hand may be preferable to a hug until we know the person better and have more comprehension of her or his response to these exchanges that take place through touch. Remember that interpretations of touch vary not only with personal preference but with cultural norms as well" (p. 52).

I would add to these cautionary notes that, as we have seen in our discussion of the "paradox of pastoral power," the tendency these days of pastors to be more relational and less patriarchal in demeanor means that their power in relationships is greater, not less, than that of their more formal predecessors. A minister's touch is therefore an expression of the inequality of power that exists between the minister and the other person. Thus, the seemingly innocuous pat on the hand is itself an expression of power. It may, indeed, be empowering. The other person may feel, much as in the case of Jesus' use of touch to heal persons, that the minister's power has "flowed," as it were, from pastor to parishioner.

However, it may also be experienced as condescending, not unlike patting a child on the head.

Of course, in a situation of deep grief (loss of a loved one) or great elation (an engagement to marry or admission to Harvard Law School), a pastoral hug may be precisely the right response, and the likelihood of its being misinterpreted is minimal. Otherwise, except for a friendly handshake before or after the conversation, my own preference is that the minister providing counsel not engage in physical touching unless it is requested. A woman student who had been through a great deal of personal turmoil once took me somewhat by surprise when she said, before she left my office, "I need a big hug." At that moment, the handshake I was about to offer *did* seem rather paltry. The hug we shared was hardly different, however, from situations in which my wife, a preschool teacher, will say to a child who is having a particularly bad day, "Do you need a hug?" and the child, with an affirmative nod, rushes headlong into her arms.

What I believe we ministers *could* do much more of, however, is to make use of "embodied language." I have written on this subject already in *The Poet's Gift: Toward the Renewal of Pastoral Care* (1993a, chap. 2, "Pastoral Conversation as Embodied Language") and will not repeat that discussion here. However, the minister cited in chapter 2 (the case of Mrs. O.), who parroted her statements and then added, "Is that it?" virtually redeemed himself when he prayed for her and spoke of relying on God's "guiding hand to steady our walk in life." After crying softly for a few moments, Mrs. O. replied, "There is a steadying hand. I'll be all right." This use of embodied language—ascribing physicality to God—was at least as empowering as the minister's physical touch would have been, without any risk of its being misunderstood.

Concluding Comments

Much has been written in the course of the past several decades about the management skills of the minister. Theologians have tended to look askance at the church management literature, while many pastors have found it helpful. I have deliberately used the word *manage* and not *maintenance* in this chapter on boundary issues because *manage* implies a more active, intentional surveillance over boundary matters. The word *manage* has several meanings, but perhaps the most important is "to have charge of." The word *management* means, in one of its senses, "careful, tactful treatment." The elements of agency and art implied here are missing from the word *maintenance,* which means "to keep up" or "continue with," or "provide support for." If it is true, as many have argued, that there is a power inequality between the minister and the person receiving the minister's counsel, it follows that it is the minister's responsibility to manage the boundaries when giving counsel to another person. Responsible management of these boundaries often gives the other person insights into how to be a better manager of the boundary transgressions that have created the difficulties or problems prompting the counseling session, such as the problem that his children are "out of control," or that she has piled up so much credit-card debt that she doesn't know how she could possibly repay it on her present salary, and so forth. Some of the more lasting lessons from being counseled are indirect, and especially important in this regard is the way the minister manages the process itself.

Even if the minister has been asked to provide counsel (premarital counseling being the exception that proves the rule), counseling is inherently intrusive. In counseling, the privacy of the other is compromised. This very fact makes it incumbent on the minister to be zealous in the management of boundaries so that intrusion into the life of the other is constructive, not coercive. The inequality of power that exists between minister and parishioner (or teacher and student, etc.) cannot be overcome through declarations of equality, however sincerely spoken or deeply felt. This means that the minister is always in a position to be coercive, and such coerciveness need not be openly aggressive. It may masquerade, for example, under the guise of concern for the other. At the same time, when used strategically and responsibly, the minister's power can be a constructive force in the life of the counseled person (or persons). This may also, within limits, be true of desire that is effectively and thoroughly sublimated. By emphasizing both a limited number of meetings and that the pastoral relationship is essentially the same as when the minister is engaged in other roles, the sublimation of sexual desire in this context is also not fundamentally different from what occurs in the normal course of pastoral relationships, where "admiration from afar" may also occur. The two individuals' being in closer physical proximity and enjoying a greater degree of privacy—for the purpose of carrying on an uninterrupted conversation—does nothing to alter this "from afarness."

A Final Word

When our Midwest and West Coast relatives come to the East Coast, one of the things they want to do is visit the historical district in Philadelphia. When my wife's mother came to visit, we felt it would be best, given her difficulty in walking significant distances, to take the tour bus instead of going by foot. When the tour bus paused so that we could observe an old historic tavern, the guide informed us that the first floor had been a tavern and the second floor had been where the men, many of them sailors, would bunk for the night. Because there was considerable liquor on the first floor, the bartender had very firm instructions from the tavern owner to lock up all the liquor at night so that the men would not have access to it. To ensure that the bartenders were complying with the proprietor's instructions, they were obliged to keep a ledger in which they noted each sale. The tour guide told us that since liquor was sold by pints and quarts, this was the origin of the phrase, "Mind your p's and q's."

As the bus continued on its way to another historical landmark, I said to my wife, "That can't be right. I'll bet you that 'Mind your p's and q's' had its origins in the schoolroom, where children were being

241

taught penmanship, and were being warned not to mistakenly reverse the two letters." My wife replied, "Well, if you want to get technical about it, my high school typing teacher said it originated when secretaries were told that they had to be especially careful to press down hard on the p and the q, because these two letters are on the outside of the typewriter keyboard and you use your little finger to strike it." I protested, "But the typewriter wasn't invented until the late nineteenth century, and kids were being taught their letters centuries earlier." She paused a moment to think about that and answered, "Well, if you're right–but I'm not saying you necessarily are–the really interesting thing is that someone made a connection between what children learned in the classroom and how to maintain some accountability and order in the tavern."

This friendly argument–to which my wife's mother was utterly oblivious as she took in the historical landmarks–has direct relevance to what I have tried to accomplish in this book. As I stated in the introduction, I view this as a guidebook for seminarians in how to "make their way about" in their role of providing counsel. I acknowledged, though, that a guidebook can only familiarize a person with the broad and general features of a place where one has not visited before. It is like taking the tour bus. The real question–which only the reader can answer–is whether and how what has been presented here can be connected or related to the world outside the classroom. Minding one's letters in the schoolroom is one thing; minding the liquor supply in an unruly and volatile tavern is quite another. It should go without saying that I assume the reader will want to adapt, modify, and expand on what I have presented here. Many excellent books in pastoral counseling–on specific age groups, persons with special needs, and so forth–can assist the reader in this regard.

Another tour guide story: This time, my wife and I had agreed to meet our son and his wife in Charleston, South Carolina, a city the two of us had not visited before. Like Independence Hall and the Liberty Bell in Philadelphia, Fort Sumter–the site where the Civil War began– is a must-see. As the ferry approached the fort, which is situated on a small island, and especially as its occupants began to disembark and step onto the grounds of the fort, I felt a certain tension in the air. I do not think I was imagining it. After all, here were Southerners and Northerners walking side by side on the very site that symbolized, as no other site could, the deep split in the nation's psyche that has not completely healed nearly a century and a half later. The tour guide who met our group—a young African American man wearing the benign uniform of the U.S. Forestry Service—was a very welcome sight. Who was better positioned to reduce the anxiety we were all experiencing? And reduce it he did. He first asked those who were from north of the Mason-Dixon line to raise their hands. Many hands shot up. Then he asked those from south of the Mason-Dixon line to raise their hands. At least as many—perhaps more—hands shot up. Then he asked if there was anyone from New Jersey. My wife and I raised our hands—no one else did—drawing the curious (or was it the sympathetic?) looks of everyone else. Then the tour guide took off his broad-brimmed hat and declared to the two of us, "Welcome to the United States!"

The whole crowd burst out laughing, and whatever tension remained in the air was magically released. My son said to me, "It took guts for you and Mom to raise your hands." I replied, "Well, anything we could do to help." As the guide signaled to us that we were free to move about, I overheard a young woman (who had identified herself as a visitor from Germany) asking her American host, "What was that about New Jersey? It *is* a part of the U.S., isn't it?" Her host whispered, "It's sort of an inside joke among Americans. I'll explain it to you later."

Of course, I would hasten to add that most of the fourteen million people who live in the state of New Jersey are remarkably nondefensive about this fact, as few of us really believe that we belong in this state. When a television commercial extolling the natural beauty and recreational opportunities afforded by the state concludes with the governor intoning the slogan, "New Jersey and You—Perfect Together," most of us take personal offense at the very suggestion of a perfect fit between us and the state where we happen to reside.

But back to the tour guide. He must have been aware that there is a certain tension in the air when persons from the South and North set foot on this historic site. This was reflected in part by the fact that he invited Northerners and Southerners to identify themselves. It was especially reflected, however, in his New Jersey gambit. On the issue of New Jersey, Southerners and Northerners were solidly united.

Now, we *could* interpret this story in the light of Rene Girard's scapegoat theory (as presented in chapter 5), that where two rival factions who must, nonetheless, coexist, are on the verge of a violent conflict, they find a scapegoat to defuse the situation. By this means, the violent conflict is averted. Perhaps, during the first several decades following the Civil War, Girard's theory would have applied. On this occasion, though, violence was not the issue. Rather, it was tension or, as I would now like to say, it was *anxiety*. Not, of course, the kind of anxiety that a tornado or hurricane warning elicits, but a lower grade anxiety having roots in our national history, in events that occurred nearly a century and a half ago.

I discussed anxiety in the first chapter of this book, and will not rehash what was said there. I would, however, like to draw attention, once more, to the concluding chapter of Erik H. Erikson's *Childhood and Society* (1963), and specifically to his view that anxieties, which are "diffuse states of tension" that "magnify and even cause the illusion of an outer danger, without pointing to appropriate avenues of defense or mastery," may be combated by "a judicious frame of mind." Judiciousness, he says, is "in its widest sense," a "frame of mind that is tolerant of differences, cautious and methodical in evaluation, just in judgment, circumspect in action, and–in spite of all this apparent relativism–capable of faith and indignation" (p. 416).

Its opposite is prejudice, "an outlook characterized by prejudged values and dogmatic divisions; here everything seems to be clearly delineated and compartmentalized, and this by 'nature,' where it must stay forever the way it always has been" (p. 416). This prejudicial frame of mind has "the advantage of permitting the projection of everything that feels alien within one's own heart onto some vague enemy outside" (p. 416). The person of judicious mind forfeits the advantages of projection, thus opening herself to the possibility that she will have "an over-concern with the evil" in herself, that is, become prejudiced against herself. But a judicious frame of mind comes into play here as well, as it enables one to "cope judiciously with the anxiety aroused by a renunciation of prejudice" (p. 417).

If there is a single statement that sums up what I have attempted to communicate here about the minister's role in providing counsel, this would be it: *To provide counsel, one needs a judicious frame of mind.* This is not moral weakness or mere relativism–as those of a more dogmatic mind-set would allege–but a special kind of strength, one that we as ministers need to exhibit in offering counsel to others, and, by our example, to encourage in those whom we seek to help in this way.

I suggest that the judicious frame of mind is especially reflected in two qualities. The first quality is treating others with kindness. The dictionary makes an important distinction between *kind, benign,* and *benevolent. Kind* implies the possession of sympathetic or generous qualities. *Benign* suggests a kindly nature and is applied especially to a gracious superior. *Benevolent* implies a charitable or altruistic inclination to do good. I use the word *kind* here, not *benign* or *benevolent,* as *benign* suggests an inequality in status between the one who counsels and the one who receives counsel; while *benevolent,* building on this inequality, adds the disposition to act charitably or altruistically. Kindness does not have these additional features, though, of course, it is susceptible to these further elaborations. In the context that concerns us here—that of providing counsel—these elaborations, however well-intentioned, are likely to be detrimental. A basic kindness is sufficient. The injunction in Ephesians 4:32 to be kind to one another assumes an equality among persons, a reciprocal kindness, not one where one person gives and the other person receives charity.

In *God Bless You, Mr. Rosewater* (1965, pp. 92–93), Kurt Vonnegut's "hero," Eliot Rosewater, has agreed to baptize Mary Moody's twins because no one else would do it. When challenged about his qualifications to perform this religious act, he totally agrees with his questioner. After all, he had already told Mary herself

> "that I wasn't a religious person by any stretch of the imagination. I told her nothing I did would count in Heaven, but she insisted just the same." "Then," asked his questioner, "What will you say? What will you do?"

> "Oh, I don't know." Eliot's sorrow and exhaustion dropped away for a moment as he became enchanted by the problem. A little smile played over his lips. "Go over to her shack, I guess. Sprinkle some water on the babies, say, 'Hello, babies. Welcome to earth. It's hot in the summer and cold in the winter. It's round and wet and crowded. At the outside, babies, you've got about a hundred years here. There's only one rule that I know of, babies: 'God damn it, you've got to be kind.'"

Admittedly, this is not a very elegant way of putting it, especially in what is supposed to be a religious act. Nonetheless, Eliot exhibits a judicious frame of mind in this improvised baptismal service. Put another way, there is great wisdom in the saying that "It doesn't hurt to be kind." The best statement that I have read on kindness, however, occurs in Kelly Cannon's *Henry James and Masculinity: The Man at the Margins* (1994). Cannon suggests that James, the novelist, was aware that "To be genuinely kind necessitates an appreciation of the complex life within every person" (p. 157). Possessing this appreciation, kind persons do not "impose their way of life on others." We have all experienced

a so-called act of kindness by someone who did not at first take the trouble
to learn enough about us, our thoughts, feelings, tastes, values, interests,
and so forth. The act may have made the other person feel good about
himself–as benign or benevolent–but our response was one of resentment
that we were placed in the position of having to express gratitude for
a gift, gesture, offer, or suggestion that took little if any note of who we
were. Parents who claim to treat each child equally by giving each one
the very same Christmas gift are in fact treating them differentially, as
the gift that makes one child feel his wants are known and perceived
by his parents can cause another child to feel precisely the opposite.
In the role of one who offers counsel, "an appreciation of the complex
life within each person," even if it cannot be fully known, is a precondition
of being "genuinely kind."

The second quality of a judicious mind follows from this. It is the
ability to value the other person's unique individuality. In his *The Will
to Believe and Other Essays in Popular Philosophy* (1956), William James
has an essay on "The Importance of Individuals." Here, he quotes an
"unlearned carpenter of my acquaintance" who once said in James's
hearing: "There is very little difference between one person and another;
but what little there is, *is very important"* (p. 256). James builds his essay
on this astute observation and makes the case that what truly interests
us about another person is what "we do not take for granted." Elaborating
on this point, James writes:

> We are not a bit elated that our friend should have two hands
> and the power of speech, and should practice the matter-of-
> course human virtues; and quite as little are we vexed that our
> dog goes on all fours and fails to understand our conversation.
> Expecting no more from the latter companion, and no less from
> the former, we get what we expect and are satisfied. We never
> think of communing with the dog by discourse of philosophy,
> or with the friend by head-scratching or the throwing of crusts
> to be snapped at. But if either dog or friend falls above or below
> the expected standard, they arouse the most lively emotion. On
> our brother's vices or genius we never weary of descanting; to
> his bipedism or his hairless skin we do not consecrate a thought.
> *What* he says may transport us; that he is able to speak at all
> leaves us stone cold. The reason of all this is that his virtues
> and vices and utterances might, compatibly with the current
> rage of variation in our tribe, be just the opposites of what they

are, while his zoologically human attributes cannot possibly go astray. There is thus a zone of insecurity in human affairs in which all the dramatic interest lies; the rest belongs to the dead machinery of the stage. This is the formative zone, the part not yet ingrained into the race's average, not yet a typical, hereditary, and constant factor of the social community in which it occurs. It is like the soft layer beneath the bark of the tree in which all the year's growth is going on. (pp. 257–58)

James calls this "the zone of the individual differences" which, when they gain the common consent of others, "is the zone of formative processes, the dynamic belt of quivering uncertainty, the line where past and future meet" (p. 259).

Another more prosaic formulation of the unlearned carpenter's point is the distinction formulated by the anthropologist Clyde Kluckhohn and psychologist Henry Murray several decades ago that every person is (a) like all other persons (universal characteristics); (b) like some other persons (group characteristics); and (c) like no other persons (idiosyncratic characteristics). Building on these distinctions, Gordon W. Allport, a psychologist and ethicist, notes that psychologists often want to use universal and group norms only: "We want to know whether Bill, relative to others, is high or low in intelligence, in dominance, in affiliativeness. But although Bill can be compared profitably on many dimensions with the average human being or with his cultural group, still he himself weaves all these attributes into a unique idiomatic system. His personality does not contain three systems, but only one. Whatever individuality is, it is not the residual ragbag left over after general dimensions have been exhausted. The *organization* of Bill's life is first, last, and all the time, the primary fact of his human nature" (Allport, 1968, pp. 87–88).

When the minister provides counsel, she should not focus on how Bill or Emily do or do not fit universal or group norms, but on the "organization" woven from the universal, group, and idiosyncratic characteristics that make Bill or Emily the unique persons they are. When we mourn the loss of a loved one, we mourn the passing of a person who was *sui generis,* one of a kind. It is perfectly true—not just hyperbole or exaggeration—when the mourners say to one another, "We will not see the likes of him—or her—again."

Milton Erickson has been quoted as saying that he didn't really have a therapeutic theory or method because for each individual who came to him for help, he had to formulate a new theory or method. This may be a slight exaggeration, but it makes the important point that, as James's unlearned carpenter put it, "There is very little difference between one person and another; but what little there is, *is very important*" (James, 1956, p. 256).

If the ability to value the unique individuality of the person receiving counsel is important, no less important is the minister's ability to value her own unique individuality in her role as counselor. As members of a common profession, we ministers share a great deal in common with other ministers. Much can be taken for granted when one is known, or declares oneself, to be a minister. But the minister's individuality–that which cannot be taken for granted–is the very factor that a guidebook such as this can emphasize the importance of–as I am doing now–but is unable to say anything specific or concrete about. If, however, the individuality–the "not taken for grantedness"–of the person receiving the minister's counsel is where "the dramatic interest lies," this is also the locus of the minister's unique capacity, in Michael Nichols' words, to generate and communicate a "devoted alertness to another's well-being" (Nichols, 1995, p. 247).

This book has necessarily been written for seminarians in general, but nothing that I have said here should be taken to mean or imply that your own individuality is to be suspended or denied as you assume the role of one who counsels. As the unlearned carpenter put it, what makes you different from all the others who have assumed or will assume this role *is very important.* Be genuinely kind by appreciating the complex life within the other, value the other's unique individuality, and use who you are for the other's well-being. If you do this, the rest, as they say, is a piece of cake.

References

Ackerman, Nathan W. (1958). *The Psychodynamics of Family Life: Diagnosis and Treatment of Family Relationships.* New York, Basic Books.

Allport, Gordon W. (1968). *The Person in Psychology: Selected Essays.* Boston: Beacon Press.

Arnold, William V. (1982). *Introduction to Pastoral Care.* Philadelphia: Westminster Press.

—— (1993). *Pastoral Responses to Sexual Issues.* Louisville: Westminster/John Knox Press.

Ashbrook, James B. (1984). *The Human Mind and the Mind of God: Theological Promise in Brain Research.* Lanham, Md.: University Press of America.

—— (1996). *Minding the Soul: Pastoral Counseling as Remembering.* Minneapolis: Fortress Press.

Bakan, David (1967). *On Method: Toward a Reconstruction of Psychological Investigation.* San Francisco: Jossey-Bass.

Becker, Russell J. (1963). *Family Pastoral Care.* Philadelphia: Fortress Press.

Belenky, Mary Field, Blythe McVicker Clinchy, Nancy Rule Goldberger, and Jill Mattuck Tarule (1986). *Women's Ways of Knowing: The Development of Self, Voice, and Mind.* New York: Basic Books.

Benyei, Candace R. (1998). *Understanding Clergy Misconduct in Religious Systems: Scapegoating, Family Secrets, and the Abuse of Power.* New York: Haworth Pastoral Press.

Billman, Kathleen D., and Daniel L. Migliore (1999). *Rachel's Cry: Prayer of Lament and Rebirth of Hope.* Cleveland: United Church Press.

Bohler, Carolyn Stahl (1996). Female Friendly Pastoral Care. In *Through the Eyes of Women: Insight for Pastoral Care,* edited by Jeanne Stevenson Moessner. Minneapolis: Fortress Press, pp. 27–49.

Browning, Don (1976). *The Moral Context of Pastoral Care.* Philadelphia: The Westminster Press.

Cannon, Kelly (1964). *Henry James and Masculinity: The Man at the Margins.* New York: St. Martin's Press.

Cantor, Carla (1996). *Phantom Illness: Recognizing, Understanding, and Overcoming Hypochondria.* Boston: Hougton Mifflin Company.

Capps, Donald (1979). *Pastoral Care: A Thematic Approach.* Philadelphia: Westminster Press.

—— (1980). *Pastoral Counseling and Preaching: A Quest for an Integrated Ministry.* Philadelphia: Westminster Press.

—— (1981). *Biblical Approaches to Pastoral Counseling.* Philadelphia: Westminster Press.

—— (1990). *Reframing A New Method in Pastoral Care.* Minneapolis: Fortress Press.

—— (1993a). *The Poet's Gift: Toward the Renewal of Pastoral Care.* Louisville: Westminster/John Knox Press.

—— (1993b). Sex in the Parish: Social-Scientific Explanations for Why It Occurs. *The Journal of Pastoral Care* 47: 350–61.

—— (1995). *Agents of Hope: A Pastoral Psychology.* Minneapolis: Fortress Press.

—— (1998). *Living Stories: Pastoral Counseling in Congregational Context.* Minneapolis: Fortress Press.

—— (1999). *Social Phobia: Alleviating Anxiety in an Age of Self-promotion.* St. Louis: Chalice Press.

Capps, Donald, and James E. Dittes (1990). *The Hunger of the Heart: Reflections on the Confessions of Augustine.* SSSR Monograph Series, no. 8. West Lafayette, Ind.: Society for the Scientific Study of Religion.

Capps, Donald, and Gene Fowler (2001). *The Pastoral Care Case: Learning About Care in Congregations.* St. Louis: Chalice Press.

Carkhuff, Robert R. (1969). *Helping and Human Relations: A Primer for Lay and Professional Helpers.* New York: Holt, Rinehart and Winston.

Childs, Brian H. (1990). *Short-term Pastoral Counseling: A Guide.* Nashville: Abingdon Press.

Claridge, Gordon (1985). *Origins of Mental Illness: Temperament, Deviance, and Disorder.* Cambridge, Mass.: ISHK Publishers.

Clinebell, Howard J. (1966). *Basic Types of Pastoral Counseling: New Resources for Ministering to the Troubled.* Nashville: Abingdon Press.

—— (1984). *Basic Types of Pastoral Care and Counseling.* Nashville: Abingdon Press.

Combs, Gene, and Jill Freedman (1990). *Symbol, Story, and Ceremony: Using Metaphor in Individual and Family Therapy.* New York: W. W. Norton.

Cook, Philip W. (1997). *Abused Men: The Hidden Side of Domestic Violence.* Westport, Conn.: Praeger.

Cooper-White, Pamela (1992). Review of *Sex in the Parish* by Karen Lebacqz and Ronald G. Barton. *The Christian Century,* April 1.

Cryer, Newman S., Jr., and John M. Vayhinger, eds. (1962). *Casebook in Pastoral Counseling.* Nashville: Abingdon Press.

Culbertson, Philip (1992). *New Adam: The Future of Male Spirituality.* Minneapolis: Fortress Press.

de Shazer, Steve (1991). *Putting Difference to Work.* New York: W. W. Norton.

—— (1994). *Words Were Originally Magic.* New York: W. W. Norton.

Dittes, James E. (1967). *The Church in the Way.* New York: Charles Scribner's Sons.

—— (1999a). *Pastoral Counseling: The Basics.* Louisville: Westminster John Knox Press.

—— (1999b). *Re-Calling Ministry,* edited by Donald Capps. St. Louis: Chalice Press.

Dixon, Sandra Lee (1999). *Augustine: The Scattered and Gathered Self.* St. Louis: Chalice Press.

Doehring, Carrie (1995). *Taking Care: Monitoring Power Dynamics and Relational Boundaries in Pastoral Care and Counseling.* Nashville: Abingdon Press.

Duneier, Mitchell (1992). *Slim's Table: Race, Respectability, and Masculinity.* Chicago: University of Chicago Press.

Dworkin, Gerald (1988). *The Theory and Practice of Autonomy.* New York: Cambridge University Press.

Efran, Jay S., Michael D. Lukens, and Robert J. Lukens (1990). *Language, Structure, and Change: Frameworks of Meaning in Psychotherapy.* New York: W. W. Norton.

Elkins, James (1999). *Why Are Our Pictures Puzzles? On the Modern Origins of Pictorial Complexity.* New York: Routledge.

Erickson, Milton H. (1982). *My Voice Will Go with You: The Teaching Tales of Milton H. Erickson,* edited by Sidney Rosen. New York: W. W. Norton.

Erikson, Erik H. (1958). *Young Man Luther: A Study in Psychoanalysis and History.* New York: W. W. Norton.

—— (1959). *Identity and the Life Cycle: Selected Papers.* New York: International Universities Press.

—— (1963). *Childhood and Society.* 2d ed. New York: W. W. Norton.

—— (1964). *Insight and Responsibility: Lectures on the Ethical Implications of Psychoanalytic Insight.* New York: W. W. Norton.

—— (1975). *Life History and the Historical Moment.* New York: W. W. Norton.

Fenichel, Otto (1953). The Psychology of Boredom. In *The Collected Papers of Otto Fenichel.* First series. New York: W. W. Norton, pp. 292–302.

Ford, Richard Q. (1997). *The Parables of Jesus: Recovering the Art of Listening.* Minneapolis: Fortress Press.

Fortune, Marie M. (1992). *Is Nothing Sacred?: When Sex Invades the Pastoral Relationship.* San Francisco: Harper San Francisco.

Fortune, Marie M., and James N. Poling (1994). *Sexual Abuse by Clergy: A Crisis for the Church.* Decatur, Ga.: Journal of Pastoral Care Publications.

Freedman, Jill, and Gene Combs (1996). *Narrative Therapy: The Social Construction of Preferred Realities.* New York: W. W. Norton.

Freud, Sigmund (1939). *Moses and Monotheism.* Translated by Katherine Jones. New York: Vintage Books.

—— (1952). *A General Introduction to Psychoanalysis.* New York: Washington Square Press.

—— (1959). *Inhibitions, Symptoms and Anxiety.* Translated by Alix Strachey. New York: W. W. Norton.

—— (1960a). *Group Psychology and the Analysis of the Ego.* Translated by James Strachey. New York: Bantam Books.

—— (1960b). *Jokes and Their Relation to the Unconscious.* Edited and translated by James Strachey. New York: W. W. Norton.

Friedman, Edwin H. (1985). *Generation to Generation: Family Process in Church and Synagogue.* New York: Guilford Press.

Friedman, Lawrence J. (1999). *Identity's Architect: A Biography of Erik H. Erikson.* New York: W. W. Norton.

Frost, Robert (1975). *The Poetry of Robert Frost: The Collected Poems, Complete and Unabridged.* Edited by Edward Connery Lathem. New York: Holt, Rinehart, and Winston.

Garbarino, James (1999). *Lost Boys: Why Our Sons Turn Violent and How We Can Save Them.* New York: Free Press.

Gerkin, Charles V. (1997). *An Introduction to Pastoral Care.* Nashville: Abingdon Press.

Gilmore, Mikal (1994). *Shot in the Heart.* New York: Doubleday.

Girard, Rene (1986). *The Scapegoat.* Translated by Yvonne Freccero. Baltimore: Johns Hopkins University Press.

—— (1987). *Job: The Victim of His People.* Translated by Yvonne Freccero. Stanford, Calif.: Stanford University Press.

Goffman, Erving (1961). *Asylums: Essays on the Social Situation of Mental Patients and Other Inmates.* New York: Doubleday & Company.

Goodwin, Antoinette (1993). The Right to Remain Silent. *Pastoral Psychology* 41: 359–76.

Graham, Larry Kent (1992). *Care of Persons, Care of Worlds: A Psychosystems Approach to Pastoral Care and Counseling.* Nashville: Abingdon Press.

Grotjahn, Martin (1960). *Psychoanalysis and the Family Neurosis.* New York: W. W. Norton.

Haley, Jay (1987). *Problem-Solving Therapy.* 2d ed. San Francisco: Jossey-Bass Publishers.

Heffernan, James A. W. (1993). *Museum of Words: The Poetics of Ekphrasis from Homer to Ashbery.* Chicago: University of Chicago Press.

Hess, Carol Lakey (1996). Education as an Art of Getting Dirty with Dignity. In *The Arts of Ministry: Feminist-Womanist Approaches,* edited by Christie Cozad Neuger. Louisville: Westminster John Knox Press, pp. 60–87.

Hess, Robert D., and Gerald Handel (1959). *Family Worlds: A Psychosocial Approach to Family Life.* Chicago: University of Chicago Press.

Hiltner, Seward (1949). *Pastoral Counseling.* New York: Abingdon Press.

Houts, Donald C. (1995). Training for Prevention of Sexual Misconduct by Clergy. In *Breach of Trust: Sexual Exploitation by Health Care Professionals and Clergy,* edited by John C. Gonsiorek. Thousand Oaks, Calif.: Sage Publications, pp. 368–75.

Hudson, Patricia O'Hanlon, and William Hudson O'Hanlon (1991). *Rewriting Love Stories: Brief Marital Therapy.* New York: W. W. Norton.

James, William (1950). *The Principles of Psychology.* Vol. 1. New York: Dover Publications.

—— (1956). *The Will to Believe and Other Essays in Popular Philosophy.* New York: Dover Publications.

—— (1992). The Psychology of Belief. In William James, *Writings 1878–1899,* edited by Gerald E. Myers. New York: The Library of America, pp. 1021–56.

Justes, Emma J. (1985). Women. In Robert J. Wicks, Richard D. Parson, and Donald E. Capps, eds., *Clinical Handbook of Pastoral Counseling.* Mahwah, N. J.: Paulist Press, pp. 279–99.

Kincaid, James R. (1992). *Child-Loving: The Erotic Child and Victorian Culture.* New York: Routledge.

Kohut, Heinz (1984). *How Does Analysis Cure?* Chicago: University of Chicago Press.

Kovel, Joel (1981). *The Age of Desire: Case Histories of a Radical Psychoanalysis.* New York: Pantheon Books.

Kris, Ernst (1952). *Psychoanalytic Explorations in Art.* New York: Schocken Books.

Kuhn, Thomas S. (1970). *The Structure of Scientific Revolutions.* 2d ed. Chicago: University of Chicago Press.

Lankton, Stephen R., and Carol H. Lankton (1983). *The Answer Within: A Clinical Framework of Ericksonian Hypnotherapy.* New York: Brunner/Mazel.

—— (1986). *Enchantment and Intervention in Family Therapy: Training in Ericksonian Approaches.* New York: Brunner/Mazel.

Lebacqz, Karen, and Ronald G. Barton (1991). *Sex in the Parish.* Louisville: Westminster/John Knox Press.

Lee, Li-Young (1990). *The City in Which I Love You.* Brockport, N.Y.: BOA Editions.

Le Goff, Jacques (1984). *The Birth of Purgatory.* Translated by Arthur Goldhammer. Chicago: University of Chicago Press.

Levertov, Denise (1978). *Life in the Forest.* New York: New Direction Books.

McGoldrick, Monica (1989). Sisters. In *Women in Families: A Framework for Family Therapy,* edited by Monica McGoldrick, Carol M. Anderson, and Froma Walsh. New York: W. W. Norton, pp. 244–66.

—— (1995). *You Can Go Home Again: Reconnecting with Your Family.* New York: W. W. Norton.

McGoldrick, Monica, Carol M. Anderson, and Froma Walsh, eds. (1989). *Women in Families: A Framework for Family Therapy.* New York: W. W. Norton.

McGoldrick, Monica, Randy Gerson, and Sylvia Shellenberger (1999). *Genograms: Assessment and Intervention.* 2d ed. New York: W. W. Norton.

Marshall, Joretta L. (1997). *Counseling Lesbian Partners.* Louisville: Westminster John Knox Press.

Martz, Louis L. (1954). *The Poetry of Meditation: A Study in English Religious Literature of the Seventeenth Century.* New Haven, Conn.: Yale University Press.

May, Rollo (1939). *The Art of Counseling: How to Gain and Give Mental Health.* Nashville: Cokesbury Press.

Miller, David L. (1993). Perpetrators Seldom Returned to Pulpit. *The Lutheran* (June).

Napier, Augustus Y., and Carl A. Whitaker (1978). *The Family Crucible.* New York: Harper & Row.

Nichols, Michael P. (1987). *The Self in the System: Expanding the Limits of Family Therapy.* New York: Brunner/Mazel.

—— (1995). *The Lost Art of Listening.* New York: Guilford Press.

Niebuhr, H. Richard (1951). *Christ and Culture.* New York: Harper & Row.

Noyce, Gaylord (1981). *The Art of Pastoral Conversation.* Atlanta: John Knox Press.

—— (1989). *The Minister as Moral Counselor.* Nashville: Abingdon Press.

O'Hanlon, Bill, and James Wilk (1987). *Shifting Contexts: The Generation of Effective Psychotherapy.* New York: Guilford Press.

Pattison, E. Mansell (1977). *Pastor and Parish—A Systems Approach.* Philadelphia: Fortress Press.

Patton, John (1983). *Pastoral Counseling: A Ministry of the Church.* Nashville: Abingdon Press.

Peterson, Marilyn (1992). *At Personal Risk: Boundary Violations in Professional-Client Relationships.* New York: W. W. Norton.

Poling, James N. (1991). *The Abuse of Power: A Theological Problem.* Nashville: Abingdon Press.

Pruyser, Paul W. (1976). *The Minister as Diagnostician: Personal Problems in Pastoral Perspective.* Philadelphia: Westminster Press.

Roberts, Janine (1994). *Tales and Transformations: Stories in Families and Family Therapy.* New York: W. W. Norton.

Rogers, Carl R. (1951). *Client-Centered Therapy: Its Current Practice, Implications, and Theory.* Boston: Houghton Mifflin Company.

—— (1961). *On Becoming a Person: A Therapist's View of Psychotherapy.* Boston: Houghton Mifflin Company.

Satir, Virginia (1964). *Conjoint Family Therapy.* Palo Alto, Calif.: Science and Behavior Books.

—— (1972). *Peoplemaking.* Palo Alto, Calif.: Science and Behavior Books.

Scot, Barbara J. (1995). *Prairie Reunion.* New York: Farrar, Straus, and Giroux.

Shupe, Anson (1995). *In the Name of All That's Holy: A Theory of Clergy Malfeasance.* Westport, Conn.: Praeger Books.

Spacks, Patricia Meyer (1986). *Gossip.* Chicago: University of Chicago Press.

Srole, Leo, and Associates (1962). *Mental Health in the Metropolis: The Midtown Manhattan Study.* New York: McGraw-Hill.

Stahmann, Robert F., and William J. Hiebert (1997). *Premarital and Remarital Counseling: The Professional's Handbook.* San Francisco: Jossey-Bass Publishers.

Stewart, Charles William (1970). *The Minister as Marriage Counselor.* Rev. ed. Nashville: Abingdon Press.

Stone, Howard W. (1976). *Crisis Counseling.* Philadelphia: Fortress Press.

—— (1994). *Brief Pastoral Counseling: Short-term Approaches and Strategies.* Minneapolis: Fortress Press.

Switzer, David K. (1974). *The Minister as Crisis Counselor.* Nashville: Abingdon Press.

—— (1979). *Pastor, Preacher, Person: Developing a Pastoral Ministry in Depth.* Nashville: Abingdon Press.

Taylor, Charles W. (1991). *The Skilled Pastor: Counseling as the Practice of Theology.* Minneapolis: Fortress Press.

Trible, Phyllis (1984). *Texts of Terror: Literary-Feminist Readings of Biblical Narratives.* Philadelphia: Fortress Press.

Underwood, Ralph L. (1985). *Empathy and Confrontation in Pastoral Care.* Philadelphia: Fortress Press.

Vonnegut, Kurt (1965). *God Bless You, Mr. Rosewater.* New York: Laurel Books.

Watson, John B. (1970). *Behaviorism.* New York: W. W. Norton.

Watzlawick, Paul, Janet Helmick Beavin, and Don D. Jackson (1967). *Pragmatics of Human Communication: A Study of Interactional Patterns, Pathologies, and Paradoxes.* New York: W. W. Norton.

Watzlawick, Paul, John Weakland, and Richard Fisch (1974). *Change: Principles of Problem Formation and Problem Resolution.* New York: W. W. Norton.

White, Michael, and David Epston (1990). *Narrative Means to Therapeutic Ends.* New York: W. W. Norton.

Wimberly, Edward P. (1991). *African American Pastoral Care.* Nashville: Abingdon Press.

Wittgenstein, Ludwig (1958). *Philosophical Investigations.* 3d ed. Translated by G. E. M. Anscombe. New York: Macmillan.

Wurmser, Leon (1997). The Shame About Existing: A Comment About the Analysis of "Moral" Masochism. In *The Widening Scope of Shame,* edited by Melvin R. Lansky and Andrew P. Morrison. Hillsdale, N.J.: The Analytic Press, pp. 367–82.

Wynn, John Charles (1957). *Pastoral Ministry to Families.* Philadelphia: Westminster Press.

—— (1982). *Family Therapy in Pastoral Ministry.* San Francisco: Harper & Row.

Index

Ackerman, Nathan W., as psycho-dynamic family theorist, 108
advising responses. *See* conversation, types of responses in
affirmation. *See* listening, attitudes that contribute to
Allport, Gordon W., on individuality, 247
Anderson, Phoebe, founder of Couples Christian Concern Groups, 141
anomaly, in paradigm shifts, 154–55
anxiety, as inhibiting listening, 14–20; and judiciousness, 244; and loss of immediacy, 47–48; as paralyzing, 20; and prejudice, 244
appreciation. *See* listening, attitudes that contribute to
Arnold, William, 1; on boundaries of language, 235; on boundaries of space, 211–12; on boundaries relating to touch, 237–38; on implied messages, 210; on types of boundaries, 189
attention, and boredom, 48. *See also* listening, attitudes that contribute to
attitudes, in listening, 23–28
Augustine, Saint, 225

Barth, Karl, on time, 196
Barton, Ronald. *See* Lebacqz, Karen
Bateson, Gregory, interest in metaphor, 150; interest in stories, 149–50; as systems theorist, 149
Becker, Russell J., on counseling and congregational resources, 110, 151, 184; on "crisis of intimacy," 141–42; and family counseling, 107–13; and family scapegoat, 108; and systemic thinking, 108
Belenky, Mary Field, and women's ways of thinking, 93

Benyei, Candace R., on ministers as scapegoats, 225
Bohler, Carolyn Stahl, on listening, 52
boredom, as threat to listening, 48–50; and William James's views on belief and attention, 48
boundary, psychodynamic meanings of, 190–93; transgression of, 191–92
boundary issues, interaction of time and space dimensions, 211–12; language related, 235–37; management of, 239–40; and sexual misconduct of minister, 213–29; and space-time distinction, 189–190; space related, 210–38; time related, 193–210; touch related, 237–38
Bowen, Murray, scale of self-differentiation of, 137–38, 147; self-differentiation, concept of, 136–38, 156, 178; as transgenerational theorist, 137; on triangulation, 159
brief counseling, argument for, 205–7; case of, 201–4

Cannon, Kelly, 247
Capps, Donald, on constructive versus coercive intrusion, 19; on diagnosis, 99; on embodied language, 238; on hope, 97; on issue-focused premarital counseling, 212–13; on pastoral care cases, 9; on poetry and concreteness, 36; on problem-solving counseling, 3, 89; story model of, 170–78; on types of pastoral counseling, 3
Carkhuff, Robert R., on conditions that facilitate a helping relationship, 28
Chance, Erika, and mother as regulator, 108–9

255

Lightning Source UK Ltd.
Milton Keynes UK
UKHW011530150921
390625UK00001B/214